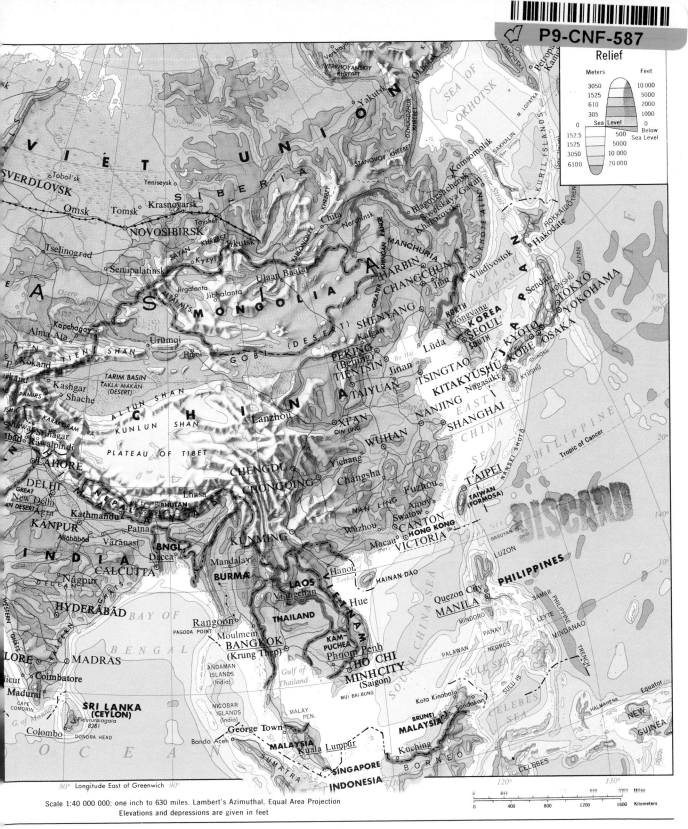

Relief

Meters		Feet
3050		10 000
1525		5000
610		2000
305		1000
0	Sea Level	0
		Below
152.5		500 Sea Level
1525		5000
3050		10 000
6100		20 000

Scale 1:40 000 000; one inch to 630 miles. Lambert's Azimuthal, Equal Area Projection
Elevations and depressions are given in feet

0   400   800   1200   1600   Kilometers
0 ... 500 ... 1000 Miles

Worldmaster World Atlas, © Copyright 1989 by Rand McNally & Company,
R.L. 88-S-147

New International Atlas, © Copyright 1989 by Rand McNally & Company,
R.L. 88-S-147

Enchantment of the World

BHUTAN

By Leila Merrell Foster

Consultant for Bhutan: James F. Fisher, Ph.D., Chair, Asian Studies Committee, Carleton College, Northfield, Minnesota

Consultant for Reading: Robert L. Hillerich, Ph.D., Bowling Green State University, Bowling Green, Ohio

 CHILDRENS PRESS®
CHICAGO

Girls in brightly colored blouses on their way to market.

Library of Congress Cataloging-in-Publication Data

Foster, Leila Merrell.
  Bhutan / by Leila Merrell Foster.
    p.   cm. — (Enchantment of the world)
  Includes index.
  Summary: An introduction to this small, strategically important Himalayan kingdom.
  ISBN 0-516-02709-3
  1. Bhutan—Juvenile literature. [1. Bhutan.] I. Title. II. Series.
DS491.4.F67   1989   88-37375
954.9'8—dc19   CIP
                                                      AC

Picture Acknowledgments
© **Marie Brown:** 4, 6, 10 (2 photos), 14, 16 (top), 23, 50 (left), 53 (2 photos), 58, 61, 62, 66 (top left), 71, 72, 77 (left), 80 (left), 81, 82 (2 photos), 84 (right), 86, 89 (2 photos), 91 (bottom right), 95 (right), 96 (2 photos), 97 (right), 99, 101 (bottom right), 104, 106 (2 photos), 107, 108, 119
Shostal Associates, Inc.: 98, 102; © Giorgio Ricatto: 5, 22, 48, 51, 64 (bottom left), 91 (top and bottom left), 101 (top), 103 (right); © Hubertus Kanus: 49, 54, 97 (left), 109; © Kenneth Arnold and Jacqueline Niedt Proctor: cover, 65; © Silvio Fiore: 78 (2 photos), 92
© **Leila M. Foster:** 8, 15, 16 (bottom), 18 (3 photos), 57, 64 (top and bottom right), 66 (top right, bottom left and right), 74 (2 photos), 80 (right), 84 (left), 88, 93 (2 photos), 94, 95 (left), 100 (2 photos), 101 (bottom left), 103 (left), 105 (2 photos), 112
© **Thomas R. Ostrom:** 9, 21 (left)
Permanent Mission of the Kingdom of Bhutan to the United Nations: 21 (right), 24, 32, 35
Historical Pictures Service, Chicago: 26, 27, 29
AP/Wide World Photos, Inc.: 36, 40, 45 (2 photos)
© **Photri, Inc.:** 50 (right)
© **Leila M. Foster:** 74 (2 photos)
Root Resources: © Kenneth W. Fink: 77 (right)
Len W. Meents: Maps on 104, 108
Courtesy Flag Research Center, Winchester, Massachusetts 01890: Flag on back cover
Cover: Typical farmhouse in Bhutan

1989 Childrens Press $405

The Temple Monastery in Thimphu shows a subtle use of color, typical of Bhutanese architecture.

TABLE OF CONTENTS

Chapter 1   *The Kingdom of the Thunder Dragon* (An Introduction) 7

Chapter 2   *The Land Where the Continents Crunched* (Geological History and Geography) 11

Chapter 3   *The Hidden Holy Land* (Pre-history to 1907) 19

Chapter 4   *The Dragon Kings* (1907 to the Present) 31

Chapter 5   *Development of an Underdeveloped Country* (Industry, Economy, Transportation, and Communication) 47

Chapter 6   *Gross National Happiness* (Religion, Government, Education, Health, and Conservation) 63

Chapter 7   *Life of the Dragon People* (The People, Culture, and Sports) 79

Chapter 8   *Maps of the Universe* (Towns and the Future) 99

Mini-Facts at a Glance 113

Index 120

Laya is in a valley in the northern mountains.

Chapter 1

THE KINGDOM OF THE THUNDER DRAGON

Bhutan is a small country of great beauty and strategic importance situated between India and China in Asia. It covers an area of about 18,000 square miles (about 47,000 square kilometers) — larger than the nation of Switzerland, but smaller than the state of West Virginia. Bhutan begins in the south in a sand-and-gravel plain and humid semitropical forests next to India and climbs north up to the highest mountain range in the world on the border with China.

Bhutan is a term that the people of India used to describe the whole of the region around the Himalayan mountains, including Tibet. Now Tibet is a territory occupied by the Chinese (and called the Tibetan Autonomous Region of the Peoples Republic of China, by the Chinese). It adjoins Bhutan in the north. When the Bhutanese talk with each other about their country, they call it *Druk-yal,* which means "Land of the Thunder Dragon." It seems that many centuries ago dragons were thought to produce the sound of thunder. When some monks of a Buddhist order were consecrating their first temple in Tibet, the thunder was loud. Thus dragons came to be associated with this sect that helped to unify Bhutan back in the seventeenth century.

Today, dragons are featured on the flag and the seal of the

The seal of Bhutan

nation. The violent storms originating in the Himalayas still provide plenty of thunder for the country.

The territory that was to become Bhutan began to form fifty million years ago when the area of India—then separate from Asia—drifted against and then pushed under the continent with China. The Himalayan mountains were pushed up where the continents collided. There is very little flat land in Bhutan. Many of the crops are grown on terraces built on the sides of the hills.

Bhutan is known as "The Hidden Holy Land" also. For many centuries the country was ruled by the Buddhist clergy. It developed its own culture in isolation from outsiders. Trade with India was limited because goods had to be carried on narrow mud mule tracks across mountains and plank bridges over mountain streams. The mountain routes to Tibet were not easy either, though over the centuries fighting and troubles in Tibet would bring refugees down into Bhutan. The Bhutanese often gave refuge, but they repelled invaders.

In some areas, horses and mules provide better and safer transportation than cars or trucks.

This isolation of the country from main trade routes provided protection during the days that people could barricade themselves inside forts strategically placed on mountain passes and on rivers. However, today with mechanized armies that can drop paratroops into isolated spots, dragging up ladders into forts is no longer an adequate defense of a population. Bhutan has ended its isolation and has joined the United Nations. As an underpopulated country rich in hydroelectric power, timber, and other resources, it needs protection from overpopulated neighbors wanting to expand. Highways are being built as an aid to defense. Development and conservation of resources is receiving attention and outside help.

The Buddhist king, who rules the country, has changed laws and is providing education for the Bhutanese so that they may make the transition from a medieval society to a modern nation as painlessly as possible. Care is being taken to preserve the cultural heritage of the Bhutanese, who are proud of the independence of their Kingdom of the Thunder Dragon.

Wherever it is possible, the Bhutanese engage in farming.
Even so, the country still must import some foodstuffs.

Chapter 2

THE LAND WHERE THE CONTINENTS CRUNCHED

Why should there be so little flat land in Bhutan? Geologists are in general agreement that at one time India was not attached to Asia. It was on a continental plate that was situated below the equator. This plate drifted north and, fifty million years ago, collided with Asia. When the continents crunched, they were struck together. The Himalayas, the highest mountains in the world, were formed. India is still moving against the rest of Asia. The northern part of India still is slowly being forced under the rest of Asia and pushing China eastward toward the Pacific Coast. This theory is called the continental drift or plate tectonics. It accounts for why Bhutan rises from the Indian plain to the heights of the Himalayas.

MYSTERIES GEOLOGISTS ARE SOLVING

How do geologists know what went on fifty million years ago and how the continents are moving now? They are like detectives, and they have not yet solved some of the mysteries. The geologists still do not know why there is a high plateau farther to the north in Tibet. International teams of scientists are just beginning to study this region that has been so long unexplored. Here are some of the tools these scientists use. Some rocks contain good geological clocks, because their minerals contain radioactive elements that disintegrate at an established rate telling geologists when they were formed. A blue-gray granite rock found in the area shows that this stone is of a recent geological age—only fifty to one hundred millions years ago.

Then there are the different kinds of rocks. Some rocks are formed as they are laid down as layers of sediment on the floor of some sea. In fact, the geologists believe that from about 225 million years ago to sometime before 30 million years ago, there was an immense sea, which they have named Tethys, to the south of the Asian plate. The sedimentary rocks that were formed in this sea provide clues for the geologists. Animals and even trunks of big tropical trees that grow only at sea level became trapped in the layers of sandy sediments. They tell the geologists that once the land had forests with rivers that deposited the sand, together with some tree trunks in layers at the bottom of the sea. The sediment became sandstone that was later lifted to some of the highest elevations in the world. Also the sandstone records the magnetic field of the earth when the rocks were formed. Some of the minerals in the rocks are like little compasses that become fixed at the time the stone forms. The dip of these compasses is a measure of the latitude at which the rock formed. The geologists tell us that 100 million years ago the Asian plate was near the equator.

The scientists know that the continental crust on top of the denser rocks below is unusually thick in this region. They discovered this fact by setting off explosives and measuring how the pressure waves traveled through the rocks. Where the crust is thick, the surface will have a high altitude. Also, by studying the formations where there have been earthquakes, the geologists can detect the direction of movement in which India is still pushing against Asia.

Scientists studying an area in Tibet have discovered rocks that were on the bottom of the ocean below 16,000 feet (4,877 meters) of water 100 million years ago. Now the rocks are 13,000 feet (3,962 meters) above sea level. Our scientist-detectives have reconstructed what happened to make this change. Around 80 million years ago India was 4,000 miles (6,437 kilometers) south of Asia. It moved fast by geological standards—at the rate of 30 feet (9 meters) a century. Then 50 million years ago when India crunched into Asia, it slowed to about 15 feet (4.5 meters) a century. The Tethys Sea, which once is estimated to have been 2,000- to 3,000-miles (3,219- to 4,828-kilometers) wide, was pushed out of existence. The Himalayas and the Tibetan plateaus were formed. The crunch still produces earthquakes in China. The Indian continental plate continues to slide under Asia. Part of its upper crust has been shaved off and piled up to form the high chain of the Himalayas. If this movement of India continues, in 10 million years some of the towns in Bhutan may be at the top of a new Himalayan chain of peaks.

THREE ZONES OF LAND AND CLIMATE

The geography of present-day Bhutan gives the country an unusual variety of land and climate. There are three major zones. The northern part of the country, along the Himalayas, contains

Majestic snow-covered peaks in the north

snow-covered peaks of more than 24,000 feet (7,315 meters). Five mountain passes into Tibet can be used only by pack animals and porters—not by automobiles. The lower slopes are covered with birch trees and rhododendrons. Some of the high valleys here are located at the height of 12,000 to 18,000 feet (3,657 to 5,486 meters). Pastures in this area are used in the summer months for the grazing of cattle and yaks. This territory tends to be dry.

The cultivated Paro valley in the southwest

The middle temperate zone covers from 5,000 to 15,000 feet (1,524 to 4,573 meters). From 10,000 to 15,000 feet (3,048 to 4,573 meters) there are cold winters and cool summers and from 5,000 to 10,000 feet (1,524 to 3,048 meters), cool winters and hot summers. The annual rainfall is between 40 to 60 inches (102 to 152 centimeters). Some of the broad river valleys in this zone are well populated and cultivated. The hills are covered with forests.

The third zone, the Duars plain adjoining India, is a little above sea level. It contains land that is subtropical with high humidity. The heavy rainfall here is estimated to be as much as 80 to 200 inches (203 to 508 centimeters) a year. The northern part of this region has dense vegetation and is home to elephants, rhinoceroses, and other wild animals. The southern part is grassland and a bamboo jungle. Some of the grassland is being cleared for the cultivation of rice.

Dividing the country almost in half between east and west is the Black Mountain range that marks the watershed between two of the rivers. Bhutan has four main rivers. These flow from the

Above: The Paro Chu river
Below: A family walking along a paved road near Punakha

higher land in a generally southerly direction. They cut through gorges and narrow valleys. None of them is navigable, but they are potential sources of hydroelectric power.

DIFFICULT TRANSPORTATION AND COMMUNICATION

Bhutan has different kinds of great scenic beauty. However, transportation and communication have been difficult here. The first paved road was completed in 1962. Then for the first time it was possible to drive from the Indian border to the capital in seven hours. Before that it took at least a week over difficult trails through territory where blood-sucking leeches made travel uncomfortable. Now there is an airstrip in one of the broader valleys for small planes. A flight from Calcutta in India to Paro, Bhutan, takes ninety minutes.

Communication before the days of radio and teletype was slow. Messengers had to be sent across the mountains to get a message from the eastern to the western part of the country. Often people in one village would not be able to communicate with the neighboring village in another valley because their spoken languages would be different. The difficult travel may account for the fact that there are many languages in this small country. The official language is Dzongkha, similar to Tibetan especially in the scripts that have been derived from the same source. It is the language used for official business. Dzongkha and now English for technical purposes are taught in school.

The geography of this country encourages isolation and a small population. It rewards the person who is strong and self-sufficient, for the weak will not long survive the rigors of this climate and land.

Above: The watchtower of the Paro National Museum
Below: A prayer wheel (right) and paintings (left) —
some of the historical objects that are being
preserved in the National Museum.

Chapter 3

THE HIDDEN HOLY LAND

Telling the story of Bhutan is a problem because so many important records have been destroyed by fire and earthquake. As recently as 1828, a good manuscript giving the story of this country was destroyed in a fire at the location where it was printed. In 1832 there was another fire at the capital of the country. More manuscripts were destroyed. Finally, a bad earthquake in 1896 and more fires the same year destroyed most of the remaining records.

What is left to help reconstruct the history are a few manuscripts that have been discovered in another part of Bhutan, some accounts by outsiders of events in this land, some artifacts that need to be interpreted, and stories and memories the people have repeated and handed on to their children. All of this material is being preserved and studied. Written materials are being discovered and analyzed. A museum in Paro preserves objects that will help to disclose the history of the country. Students are being trained to gather "oral history" by talking to people and collecting information about their stories, customs, and traditions.

PRE-HISTORY AND MYTHS

That Bhutan was inhabited early, probably around 2000 B.C., is deduced from stone axes and tools that have been found in the country. These stone implements have been highly polished, developed for a number of purposes, and made out of various kinds of stone. These tools together with megaliths, or stone pillars, that might have been used in rituals or as boundary markers, imply a fairly advanced Stone Age culture. However, in order to know more about this very early history of the region, archaeological surveys and research must be completed.

Myths and legends supply the speculation that in the seventh century B.C., an Indian prince, Sangladip, from the part of India that is now Assam, extended his rule into Bhutan. It is said that this Indian influence lasted until A.D. 650 when the political influence was lost and many small units were ruled by local kings. Since not much is known of this period and given the difficult transportation and communication problems of the country, it is likely that local rule has always been strong.

PADMA SAMBHAVA—BUDDHIST MISSIONARY

In the eighth century A.D., a religious teacher appeared who still is of great importance to the Bhutanese. Padma Sambhava was a Buddhist monk from India, who brought his faith to both Bhutan and Tibet. (The founder of Buddhism was an Indian prince, Siddhartha Gautama, who lived in the fifth century B.C.) Padma Sambhava converted several rulers of parts of Bhutan to Buddhism from the Bon religion, which was a belief system that all objects have consciousness or personality and that these spirits

Above: Guru Padma Sambhava
Right: The Taktsang Monastery

must be appeased or outwitted. The Buddhism taught by Padma
Sambhava was able to incorporate some of the elements of Bon.
His form of religion emphasized meditation and rituals.

Padma Sambhava also is called the *Guru Rimpoche*, which is
sometimes translated "Precious Teacher." He is known as the
Second Buddha. According to one story, he flew to Bhutan on the
back of a tiger. Meditating in a cave on a cliff, he conquered
demon spirits that were preventing the spread of Buddhism. The
monastery built on this spot, perched high on a 3,000-foot (914-
meter) cliff, is known as the Taktsang Monastery, or Tiger's Nest.
A number of other temples have been built on spots that are
associated with him, and he is honored in almost all the temples
in the country. His teachings were known as *termas*, or treasures,
and were hidden to be discovered later when they were needed.
Thus Bhutan also came to be known as "The Land of the Hidden
Treasures" or "The Hidden Holy Land."

*Lamas from
the Drukpa sect*

DRUKPAS, OR RED HATS

As Buddhism became established in the areas of Bhutan and Tibet, different denominations or schools were established that sometimes fought over matters of doctrine or practice. Some of the teachers, called *lamas*, were forced out of Tibet into Bhutan or came in missionary efforts. In the twelfth century one such lama, Gyalwa Llhanangpa, founded a sect that applied the *dzong* system of Tibet to Bhutan. The dzongs are buildings serving as fortresses, temples, and monasteries from which the surrounding territory was governed. Another lama, Phajo-Drukgom-Shigpo, came from Tibet and brought the *Drukpa*, or Red Hat, sect. The royal family and most of the aristocrats claim descent from this man, and the Drukpa sect became the dominant religious group in Bhutan.

In the fifteenth century, Bhutan was home to a master engineer, famed for iron chain suspension bridges. Thangthong Gyalpo built his bridges over the mountain streams of the Himalayas and

Rope bridges are common throughout Bhutan.

also in central Asia. His most famous bridge was over the Kyichu River, south of Lhasa in Tibet. The iron he used was mined in Bhutan near his monastery. The iron chains had bamboo crosspieces on which to walk. These bridges have been washed away by the floods from the melting snow. One of his big chains is kept in a monastery as a venerated relic. Thangthong Gyalpo is considered a saint who created his bridges with supernatural help.

NGAWANG NAMGYAL—UNIFIER

Although before the seventeenth century Bhutan was an independent political unit, it had no central authority. The separate towns and valleys had their own local rulers, religious sects, and languages—often unintelligible to their neighbors. The person who is credited with unifying the country under one government and one religion is Ngawang Namgyal.

Ngawang Namgyal came to Bhutan in 1616, when he fled from the persecution of his Drukpa sect by the *Gelugpas*, or Yellow Hats. He received support from the families who already backed the Drukpas. He began building dzongs in the important valleys. He conquered other groups in Bhutan and united the country against a Tibetan king. He repelled an invasion by the Mongol leader, Gushi Khan, and by the fifth Dalai Lama of Tibet.

Assuming the title of *shabdrung* (or ruler) rimpoche, he became a theocratic ruler—a person combining spiritual and temporal power. He appointed a *je khempo*, or head abbot, to manage the

23

A statue of
Ngawang Namgyal

religious institutions and gave civil authority to a *druk desi*, a prime minister. He divided the country into administrative units and appointed governors of the regions, called *penlops* and chiefs of districts, called *dzongpons*. The governors and district chiefs together with other officials could be called to a central council known as the *lenchen*. He devised the first system of laws.

When Ngawang Namgyal died in 1651, his death was kept secret for over fifty years. Why? The problem lay in finding his successor. The Buddhists believe in reincarnation—the rebirth in a baby of the spirit of someone who has died. The process of finding that baby was complicated. Often the child was expected to identify objects belonging to the person who died. The child might not be located for several years, and it was usually some time before the person selected reached the age of eighteen and could govern. During the time the new shabdrung was a minor, the prime minister assumed power. When the heir apparent reached the age of eighteen, the prime minister often did not want to give up power. The office of shabdrung gradually lost importance. The prime minister also lost power to the regional governors. While the identity of Bhutan was recognized and the country could be mobilized when needed, the strong central authority achieved by Shabdrung Ngawang Namgyal was lost.

DOOPGEIN SKEPTOON—FORT BUILDER

In the latter part of the seventeenth century, a monk named Doopgein Skeptoon came to power with great support from the people. He is credited with building forts, providing a code of law, which included provisions for the protection of peasants, and keeping the regional governors under control. Three years after his death, the child in which his spirit was reincarnated was identified. When the child grew up, he attended only to religious matters, so the power to govern was even more in the hands of the prime minister.

The position of prime minister was an elective office. The religious authority was centered in an office that depended on the appearance of reincarnated spirits. The instability that this system caused whenever someone in one of these offices had to be replaced resulted in factions fighting each other even to the extent of civil war. In 1768, another strong ruler became the prime minister and put down the power of the clergy. His name was Sonam Lhendup, popularly known as Shidar.

SHIDAR AND THE BRITISH PROBLEM

Shidar also tackled the problems of foreign relations by seeking allies in Tibet and Nepal. Cooch Behar, an independent state established in 1510 on the borders of Bhutan, had caused Bhutan trouble for several hundred years. Cooch Behar made war on Bhutan and forced payment of tribute. Not long thereafter, Bhutan

London headquarters of the East India Company in the 1700s

stopped the payment and made raids into Cooch Behar. It even manufactured coins for use in Cooch Behar to disrupt the economy there. In 1772, Bhutan captured the *raja*, or ruler, of that territory. Cooch Behar appealed to the British by asking for help from the East India Company—a commercial organization through which the British exercised influence. Britain was interested in extending its political influence to keep the Russians out of the area.

In response to a payment by Cooch Behar of a sum of money to cover the cost of troops sent in to fight the Bhutanese, the British supplied a small force that drove the Bhutanese from the territory and went on to capture three forts. Bhutan appealed to its allies and neighbors in Tibet and Nepal, who intervened to support a treaty of peace that was signed in 1774 on behalf of the East India Company by Warren Hastings. The Bhutanese had to send back the captive king of Cooch Behar and his brother and to give the British access to Bhutan to cut timber.

Warren Hastings

This treaty opened the door for British trade missions that also served an intelligence gathering purpose. These missions in which Warren Hastings and George Bogle represented the East India Company opened the possibility of trade and commerce between the territory of present-day India and the northern countries of Bhutan and Tibet. The Bhutanese obtained the exclusive rights to trade in specific items. The independent status of Bhutan was protected by the need to obtain passports to enter the country.

In 1783, Hastings sent in another mission composed of Captain Samuel Turner of the Bengal army together with Lieutenant Samuel Davis, a surveyor, and Robert Saunders, a surgeon. Davis left a diary and drawings of his trip to Bhutan, which provide a picture of the country seen through the eyes of an Englishman at that point of history. Turner was impressed with the knowledge of the Bhutanese about diseases in their country and their practice of medicine. The prime minister gave the surgeon more than seventy specimens of local medicines. After this mission, there was a lull of about forty years in the relations between Bhutan and the East India Company.

THE DUARS—BORDER DISPUTES

Frequent border disputes continued. In 1826 another British mission was sent to Bhutan to try to get a settlement. The Bhutanese were taking over a narrow strip of land that was very fertile just at the base of the lower ranges of hills next to Assam and Bengal in India. This territory was called the Duars, meaning passes from the hills. About 4,400 square miles (11,400 square kilometers) were involved in this strip of about 220 miles (354 kilometers) in length. Lawlessness existed in this area. A number of attempts at settlement of the frequent conflicts always seemed to fail.

Finally in 1841 the British annexed the Assam Duars in return for an annual compensation of ten thousand rupees. This move helped the British secure the frontiers. It also gained an area that was well suited for tea plantations. However, the Bengal Duars were still a trouble spot.

The British were engaged in fighting on other frontiers and in 1857 put down a revolt in India against their rule. The Bhutanese, in sympathy with the Indians, stepped up their raids and kidnapped British subjects and allies. Treaty efforts failed. In 1864 the British annexed the Bengal Duars, and the Anglo-Bhutanese War broke out.

The prime minister of Bhutan threatened to send against the British the divine force of twelve gods who, he said, were very ferocious ghosts. The threat was followed by Bhutanese forces that attacked and cut off the water supply in places. In the following year, the British counterattacked and won back positions from which they had retreated. Moreover the British threatened to carry on battles farther inside Bhutan.

British officers and their families were brutally attacked by mutineers during Bhutan's civil wars.

TREATY OF SINCHULA

After peace negotiations, the Treaty of Sinchula was agreed to on November 11, 1865. This treaty gave the British the entire territory of the Duars in exchange for an annual payment of fifty thousand rupees by the British. This agreement continued after the British pulled out of India and the independent country of India took over and signed a treaty in 1949. Also in the 1865 treaty were provisions for open and duty-free trade. The British were designated as judge of any border disputes between Bhutan and two of the neighboring territories—Sikkim and Cooch Behar.

While the Bhutanese were fighting the British, national unity was possible. With peace, internal quarrels broke out. In 1869, 1877, 1880, and 1885, there were serious civil wars. During these conflicts, a strong leader emerged, Ugyen Wangchuck. He was the governor of Tongsa, a territory in the middle of Bhutan. His only real rival, the governor of Paro, favored closer ties with Tibet. Wangchuck believed that the best interests of Bhutan lay in good relations with the British. When the British sent a mission to Tibet in 1904, Wangchuck provided assistance. He even went to Lhasa in Tibet with the mission to assist in communications with the Tibetan officials. The Paro governor offered no help. The British expressed their appreciation of Ugyen Wangchuck by awarding to him the title of knight commander of the Indian Empire.

UGYEN WANGCHUCK—FIRST KING

An important year for Bhutan is 1907. Ugyen Wangchuck, the Tongsa governor, consolidated his power within the nation. In 1901 the prime minister died, and in 1903 the shabdrung died. Both offices were held briefly and for the first time in Bhutanese history by one person. This man was interested in the spiritual affairs of the country and left all civil matters to Ugyen Wangchuck. With this power problem, the Bhutanese civil governors and the principal lamas unanimously elected Ugyen Wangchuck to be their hereditary monarch. To have a king whose family members would succeed him in office was something new for the Bhutanese. The British political agent, John Claude White, said at the installation ceremony on December 17, 1907:

> I am convinced that you have taken a wise step in thus consolidating the administration of the State. Sir Ugyen has been my friend for many years, and you could not have made a better choice. His integrity, uprightness, and firmness of character commend him to every one, and his accession to the Maharajaship is not only a gain to Bhutan, but is of great advantage to the British Government, who will henceforth have a settled government, with a man of strong character as its head, to negotiate with.

Chapter 4

THE DRAGON KINGS

The installation of Ugyen Wangchuck as the first *druk gyalpo*, the hereditary monarch or king, marked a turning point in Bhutanese history. The problem of who would succeed to this office on the death of the occupant appears to have been settled, since it has been tested now three times with a son being installed on the death of the father: Jigme Wangchuck (August 1926), Jigme Dorji Wangchuck (March 1952), and Jigme Singye Wangchuck (July 1972).

The current monarch was enthroned two years after the death of his father. He was eighteen years old and the youngest of the twenty-nine monarchs then alive in the world.

UGYEN WANGCHUCK: FOUNDER

This dynasty has been concerned from the beginning in bringing modern advantages to Bhutan without jeopardizing the nation's ancient culture. The British agent, John Claude White,

Ugyen Wangchuck

reported that Ugyen Wangchuck, at the beginning of his reign sought the best methods for development of the country:

> I remained behind, at the urgent request of the new Maharaja and his Council, to discuss with them many projects and schemes for the welfare and improvement of the country. These covered a large area—Schools and education, population, trade, the construction of roads, the mineral resources of the country and the best way for utilizing them, the desirability of encouraging tea cultivation on the wastelands at the foot of the hills, which are excellent for the purpose and equal to the best tea land in the Duars.

The big problem in this development effort was lack of funds. Revenue might be obtained through sale of timber, permissions for mining, and grants of tea land. Bhutan entered into negotiations with India about these matters.

The Treaty of Punakha was signed on January 8, 1910 by Ugyen Wangchuck and other Bhutanese officials and C.A. Bell as the representative of the British viceroy and governor-general of India. The British pledged not to interfere in Bhutan's internal affairs as long as Bhutan accepted British advice on external affairs. The British were concerned that China wanted to expand along the northeastern frontier of India and would use Bhutan as a base of intrigue and operations. Ugyen Wangchuck sought good relations with the British for several reasons. He had been impressed with British military success in storming one of the Tibetan dzongs. He wanted protection against the Chinese who already claimed Bhutan as part of their imperial designs. He realized that the British were stronger than the Chinese, whose empire was already in decline. If he wanted to keep Bhutan independent, it would be better to have the friendship of Britain.

Ugyen Wangchuck was successful in opening a period of coexistence with the British in India. There were a few other treaties involving border questions. One was an agreement about the capture and possession of elephants found in the territory along the border.

In his government inside Bhutan, he showed wisdom. He treated his enemies and those of his father with mercy. When a powerful family plotted to murder him, instead of killing the family members, he banished the ringleader of the plot to a distant valley away from good communication. He introduced a system of education patterned along Western lines that would permit some of his subjects to qualify for the examinations needed to gain access to foreign education. Because of this, several young men received technical training in India in the mid-1920s. He built and renovated monasteries and temples throughout the country. He knew the history and legends of his country. He appointed his relatives and friends to be officials and maintained strong centralized control over them.

One of the strong leaders under Ugyen Wangchuck was Kazi Ugyen Dorji. The Dorji family was to have a close association with all of the Dragon Kings. The mother of the present king came from that family. Kazi Dorji met Ugyen Wangchuck in 1890, and the two men discovered a relationship through their paternal grandfathers. They became close friends. Kazi Dorji was a trusted supporter of the new king. Ugyen Wangchuck gave Kazi Dorji administrative authority over the whole of southern Bhutan and made him district officer of the Ha territory in western Bhutan. Both of these assignments were made hereditary in the Dorji family, as long as the person holding office served faithfully. Also, *gongzim*, or chief chamberlain, the highest office at that time, was given to Kazi Dorji in 1908. While not explicitly made hereditary, the king expressed the wish that descendants of the Dorji family be given this rank. For ninety-five years, there has been a close collaboration between the Wangchuck and Dorji families. Since the queen of the third king was from the Dorji family, the present king belongs to both families.

JIGME WANGCHUCK: CONSOLIDATOR

When Ugyen Wangchuck died on August 21, 1926, his eldest son, Jigme Wangchuck succeeded him. An attempt was made by religious leaders to recapture secular power by performing religious ceremonies to bring divine wrath on the new ruler and by seeking support from Indians and Tibetans. However, the people of Bhutan and the British stood by the king. Jigme Wangchuck consolidated power. He appointed relatives to official posts in order to be sure of their loyalty. He continued development policies. Internal peace was secured.

The British were very careful to give no offense to the Bhutanese, although it would have been possible for them to have

Jigme Wangchuck

incorporated the country into India as part of the British Empire. Instead the British even stopped Westerners from visiting Bhutan, since the Bhutanese took offense at such intrusions. This status that the British accorded to Bhutan was of the greatest importance when the British left India in 1947.

In the turmoil that followed the establishment of the nation of India, the Bhutanese became very concerned about imperialistic designs that India may have had on incorporating Bhutan into India. Some thought was given to putting together a Himalayan kingdom with neighboring Sikkim and Tibet. However, this idea did not materialize, and in 1948 Jigme Wangchuck sent a delegation to the capital of India to discuss relations between Bhutan and India. India agreed not to interfere in the internal affairs of Bhutan, if Bhutan would agree to be guided by the advice of the Indian government as it had by the British. In addition, India agreed to pay Bhutan a subsidy of 500,000 rupees and to return to Bhutan thirty-two square miles (eighty-two square kilometers) of territory. The two countries agreed to imports of war materiel from India while prohibiting export of these items by Bhutan. The Indo-Bhutanese Friendship Treaty of

Jigme Dorji Wangchuck, with his wife and three children, in 1958

1949, while obligating Bhutan to seek India's advice on foreign policy, did not provide for Indian control of Bhutanese foreign policy nor make advice binding. Also it was silent on the defense and integrity of Bhutanese territory.

JIGME DORJI WANGCHUCK: INNOVATOR

Jigme Wangchuck died in 1952 and was succeeded by his eldest son, Jigme Dorji Wangchuck. This third king was to institute many reforms and to bring his country into many international organizations, including the United Nations. In the twenty years of his reign, the political and administrative system was restructured, and intensive efforts were made to introduce modernization through educational, technological, and economic means. While these changes produced tension and strain, their necessity for Bhutan to remain independent is broadly recognized.

The new king was concerned about preserving the cultural heritage of Bhutan. He established schools for painting, singing, dancing, sculpture, and language. He opened a national museum at Paro. He, himself, had received higher education in India and

England; spoke Hindi, English, Nepali, and a little French; and read very widely.

Jigme Dorji Wangchuck was the one who, building on the tradition of the old *Tshogdu*, the National Assembly, turned it into a popular legislature where freedom of speech was respected. He introduced the basis of a cabinet system of government. He established a judicial system separate from the executive. He introduced land reform and gave a considerable portion of his private lands to the government. He changed from a barter to a money economy. He abolished serfdom, punishment by mutilation, and capital punishment (except for treason), granted civil rights to the people of Nepalese origin who had settled in the country, and worked to improve the position of women.

The king gave up power from the monarchy by renouncing his right to veto legislation passed by the National Assembly. On his motion, the National Assembly was granted the right to dismiss the king if he acted against the welfare of the people. Since the monarchy had been instituted by vote of the National Assembly, he decided to subject the monarchy to a vote of confidence every three years. If the king failed to get a two-thirds majority, he had to abdicate in favor of the next person in the line of succession to the throne. In the first vote taken by secret ballot, 135 members voted for the continuance of the king, 2 were opposed, and 1 abstained. In May 1971, the king was confirmed a second time with a vote of full confidence. After the death of Jigme Dorji Wangchuck, the confidence vote was discontinued because the Assembly considered it unnecessary.

Some attempts were made to reestablish one of the competing religious offices. The Tibetan lamas sought a new reincarnation. However, with the failure of such attempts in 1952 and 1962, the position fell into disuse. The establishment of a national religion based on the foundation of Padma Sambhava, preached by the Drukpas, and headed by a Bhutanese lama elected by the Bhutanese religious council, has served to keep religious matters under the control of the Bhutanese (not the Tibetans). It also served to keep secular matters under the control of the king.

During Jigme Dorji Wangchuck's reign, three Five-Year Plans for modernization were designed. The result has been increases in road building, transportation services, communication facilities, schools, hospitals, model farms, agricultural and animal husbandry research, forest usage and conservation, new industries, improved trade, and development of power.

In external affairs, the king fostered good relationships with India by exchanging visits of heads of state and then ambassadors. In 1962, Bhutan became a member of the Colombo Plan (an organization of nations in South and Southeast Asia for receiving economic aid on a cooperative basis). In 1969, the nation was admitted to the Universal Postal Union. On September 21, 1971, Bhutan was unanimously voted into membership in the United Nations. Ambassador Yost of the United States and president of the Security Council commented in the debate in Council: "In recent years not less than three different United States Ambassadors have visited Bhutan. They have all been impressed by the beauty of the country and by the determination which it is demonstrating in its efforts to achieve economic development while simultaneously preserving Bhutan's rich traditions and ancient culture."

The movement away from isolation and toward modernization was undoubtedly hastened by the fear of Chinese aggression. As China moved into Tibet in the early 1960s, refugees poured into

Bhutan bringing tales of bad treatment and atrocities. Roads were built originally for military reasons, but they, together with advances in communication, have opened the country to new development. Two factors have held back the nation; foreign currency needed for imports, and trained leadership.

Leadership is a key problem. Jigme Dorji Wangchuck needed public servants skilled in dealing with the Bhutanese culture and with foreigners. Because the king had a heart condition that often necessitated his being out of the country for medical treatment, he had to rely on others. Few persons had had access to expensive foreign education, so the supply of persons with the necessary qualifications was limited. While foreign experts were employed in limited numbers, the Bhutanese, after years of protection through isolation, had a natural suspicion of these persons.

JIGME PALDEN DORJI: PRIME MINISTER

Many persons felt that the king was especially fortunate in having a member of the Dorji family, Jigme Palden Dorji, the queen's brother, as his prime minister. In 1958 at the time of the king's first heart attack, Jigme Dorji was given the rank of *lonchen*, or prime minister, and extensive powers for internal management of the country. In 1963 when the king had a more severe second heart attack, Jigme Dorji was made regent. He was active in carrying out the modernization plans of the king.

On April 5, 1964, Jigme Dorji was assassinated. Behind his death is a story of palace politics. Some persons have tried to account for the assassination by family conflict between the Wangchucks and the Dorjis or by dissension between the modernists and the traditionalists. Both theories have defects. The

Jigme Palden Dorji

two leading families in Bhutan had worked together for many years. While Jigme Dorji was certainly a modernist who might have attracted enemies from among those who favored more traditional policies, the persons implicated in the plot were also reformers.

The king and his wife, Aji Kesang Dorji, had a son and daughters. The king also had a Tibetan mistress called Yangki by whom he had several illegitimate sons. Yangki wielded a good deal of influence at court. For example, she used government transportation for trade and private purposes to such an extent that supplies between the border and the capital of Bhutan were often sidetracked. Jigme Dorji transferred the trucks from the army to a civilian transportation department and required special orders for nongovernmental use. This order did not sit well with the army officers who were trying to win favor through Yangki.

The April 5 assassination occurred as Jigme Dorji was relaxing in the evening with some of his family and friends playing cards.

Someone shot through the window ten feet (three meters) to the rear of Jigme Dorji's chair. Later rumors described a plot to wipe out his whole family. The prime minister's last words were reported to be: "Tell my King that I served him as best I could" and a Buddhist prayer. The assassination had occurred at one of the border towns, and police dogs were borrowed from India to try to track the killer. A noncommissioned army officer was caught. He confessed and implicated two army officers including one who was the head of the army and the uncle of the king.

The king, who was in Switzerland for medical treatment, returned immediately and on April 14 ordered the arrest of forty persons. A trial took place. The uncle was found guilty on May 16 and executed the following day. The other army officer, who appeared to be telling too much about the conspiracy, committed suicide earlier with a dagger that had been left conveniently within his reach. The official story was that the army officers had feared that the prime minister had intended to take over power and kill the king and that they had feared being replaced by younger officers who were being brought into the army.

The gun used in the assassination was a pistol that the king had given to his Tibetan mistress. Yangki loaned it to the assassin. Her father was thought to be behind the plot, which was rumored to have involved not merely the death of Jigme Dorji, but of Dorji's whole family. Apparently Yangki and her father believed that the Western physician that Jigme Dorji had recommended to the king was plotting to kill the king. Yangki was from an immigrant family from Tibet without influence prior to her becoming the royal mistress in 1961. If anything happened to the king, her power would be lost. Yangki's father went to the king's uncle and convinced him of a Dorji plot against the king. However, there seemed to be no policy difference between the Yangki faction and the Dorji faction. It was a power play. The role of Yangki and her father was kept out of official records, but the king's uncle was executed.

Although the king returned to Bhutan, his ill health did not permit him to govern on a full-time basis. He appointed the brother of Jigme Dorji, Lhendup, as the acting prime minister, and he relied heavily on his younger half-brother, Namgyal Wangchuck.

Up until the time of the assassination of her brother, the queen was unaware of the mistress. The king had forbidden anyone, on threat of death, to tell her. Her family had shielded her from the information. Now, however, with the news that the pistol had been the gift of the king to his mistress, the queen and the crown prince believed themselves to be in peril. The crown prince was smuggled out of Bhutan, and the queen moved out of the palace to her mother's home. Meanwhile, the mistress was not punished in any way, and indeed was reported to have been seen wearing the queen's ceremonial headdress.

The king returned to Switzerland for medical treatment. According to one of the rumors that circulated, the king had given orders to have the mistress "accidentally" killed. Yangki, fearing for her life, planned to flee to India until the king returned. Unfortunately, she was arrested, searched, and detained at the border. News was cabled to Switzerland to the king, who was not pleased with this treatment of his mistress. He ordered special protection for his half-brother whom the king thought was in danger. Lhendup Dorji, the acting prime minister, tried to obtain an audience with the king in Switzerland, but he was refused. Believing he had lost the confidence of the king, he resigned. Then

Lhendup Dorji, his sister, and several army colonels fled Bhutan for refuge in Nepal.

A footnote to this bit of history lies in the invitation that Lhendup Dorji had extended to the American movie actress, Shirley MacLaine, to visit Bhutan. She was there when word was received that Lhendup had fled and some of his supporters were being arrested. Lhendup's secretary and another Bhutanese official were sent word to leave the country and get Ms. MacLaine out. All might have gone well, except that the army at the border had orders to arrest the secretary. Ms. MacLaine and the other Bhutanese tried to protect him. They were detained overnight. While the three were sleeping, the guards tried to drag away the secretary. Ms. MacLaine reports in her book, *Don't Fall Off the Mountain,* that she jumped up. She rushed at the guards and waved her arms. She crossed her eyes and stuck out her tongue. She screamed. In a nation where belief in evil spirits is common, it is no wonder that the guards dropped the man. Eventually, through the intervention of others, the three were permitted to leave the country. The secretary said that he owed his life to the willingness of Ms. MacLaine to stand up for him and to refuse to leave him behind.

In 1965, there was an attempt on the life of the king. One night, when he was walking alone, a grenade was thrown at him. He escaped injury because he had heard an unusual sound and had thrown himself to the ground. The assailant was tracked, and it was found that a cook who had been employed by Tashi Dorji, sister of the queen, was staying with the assailant. The cook under torture confessed that Tashi Dorji had plotted to kill the king. However, when the cook was reexamined in the queen's presence and under a terrifying Bhutanese oath that promised disaster to a liar and his descendants, the cook stated that he had no knowledge of the incident and had not met Tashi Dorji for over ten years. That the Dorji family should be suspect was not surprising, because under the old Bhutanese code of values, if Jigme Dorji had been killed by the king, it would have been an act of piety to revenge Jigme Dorji by killing the king. However, the circumstances of the attempt were such—the king was alone, his guards were not alert, and the assassin had a clear shot at the victim—that the failure to make a kill raised the question of whether the anti-Dorji party had not been trying to frame the Dorji family.

Tension between the king and queen deepened. The king's sisters served as his official hostesses. His mistress assumed a position of power at the court. However, the king had no plans to change the line of succession. The king groomed the crown prince to assume power. He had his son sit with him when he gave audiences, met with the Royal Council, or went on state visits. His two eldest daughters were appointed his personal representatives to the important departments of planning and finances. At last, there was a reconciliation with the queen.

In March 1972, four months before the king's death, the crown prince was appointed the *Tongsa ponlop*, the governor of the territory of Tongsa. Like the investiture of the prince of Wales for the British crown, the appointment to govern Tongsa, the ancestral home of the Wangchucks, was the sign that he was to be the next king. Also in that year, the king left instructions for the crown prince that were countersigned by several of the top Bhutanese officials in which he indicated that his affair with Yangki was a "blunder," warned the prince not to give Yangki's children any government service or status, specified that her

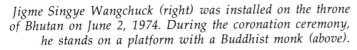

Jigme Singye Wangchuck (right) was installed on the throne of Bhutan on June 2, 1974. During the coronation ceremony, he stands on a platform with a Buddhist monk (above).

children were not to be considered royal but instead illegitimate, stated that he had given them adequate wealth, and recommended that after his death the children should stay outside the country for a few years. However, the mistress would be heard of again during the reign of the next king.

The king was on a trip to Nairobi for medical treatment, and perhaps to fulfill a wish to shoot a lion in Africa, when he died. He had lived four years longer than his physicians had thought possible nine years before. His son, Jigme Singye Wangchuck, succeeded him.

JIGME SINGYE WANGCHUCK

The new king had the blood of both the Wangchuck and the Dorji families through his father and mother. While being kept close to his Bhutan roots, he had been given the advantage of a modern education. His father gave him personal instruction on the art of being a king. On June 2, 1974, he was installed on the throne when he placed on his shoulders a sacred scarf of his great, great, grandfather. His uncle and aunt, Lhendup and Tashi Dorji, returned from exile. The United States ambassador to India brought as gifts a telescope, a piece of moon rock, and as a personal gift, a Polaroid camera. The new king is reported to have said that he would be happy if Bhutan remained a free, sovereign kingdom and if his people remained happy, united, and self-sufficient.

On taking the throne, Jigme Singye Wangchuck announced that he recognized the authority of the head abbot in the sphere of religion and did not intend to make any competing claim. Nevertheless, the king does exercise indirect influence by virtue of his position.

A challenge to the new king took place in 1974 in the form of a Tibetan conspiracy. Yangki, the late king's mistress, had married one of the retainers of the late king and had been permitted to settle in Bhutan on property she had been given. However, a plot was uncovered to assassinate the king and replace him with one of Yangki's sons. This plot was said to have been organized by the brother of the Dalai Lama—a Yellow Hat. Yangki and her family fled to India.

Jigme Singye Wangchuck has followed the policies of the other kings in bringing modern advantages to his country at a pace that does not jeopardize Bhutanese culture. He has extended his country's relationships with other nations. He has been concerned for developing his nation's rich resources in a way that also conserves them for the future.

Chapter 5

DEVELOPMENT OF AN UNDERDEVELOPED COUNTRY

Bhutan is rich in natural resources—its forests—yet the income per person is about $120 a year—one of the lowest in the world. The population of Bhutan is low relative to the resources available, and the people for the most part have enough land, food, and housing.

It is important to develop the natural resources of the country, but there are at least three problems. First, the rugged mountains and the swift rivers make it difficult to get into the areas where some of the resources are located. Thus, costs of getting these materials to market are high. Second, there are not enough trained leaders to carry out the development. Bringing in too many foreigners may make the Bhutanese people angry and threaten independence. Third, in order to open up some industries, machinery manufactured in other countries must be bought. But Bhutan has a limited amount of credit.

Other countries have had problems in their development efforts. There are places in the Himalayas where forests have been cut back so far that erosion of the land has taken place. Storms

Women gather brush that they will use for firewood.

and mud slides have taken away good soil. Wood, once plentiful, is now scarce. In some nations, education has been pushed beyond the availability of white collar jobs for the graduates. The result has been an educated but unhappy group of people who are unable to find work they have trained to do—a group of people that have become politically active.

The Bhutanese, with their history of isolation from other nations, distrust outsiders. They are conservatives and value their traditions of many centuries. Yet they are now vulnerable to modern tactics of warfare and to the world political tensions in a way that they were not before. But they need the advantages of modern medicine and conveniences. How can Bhutan develop its country and respect the wishes and life-style of its people?

Typical houses and fields of the Paro valley

AGRICULTURE AND ANIMAL HUSBANDRY

Agriculture is the most important segment of the economy of Bhutan. It contributes about half of the gross domestic product of the nation, one-fourth of the export earnings, and employment for about 95 percent of the total population. Farming is labor-intensive—people working the land without much equipment. The production of food is primarily for use by the farmers. Livestock is important for hauling things and for milk and meat products. Some commercial crops have been started where roads permit access to markets—cardamoms (used as a spice or in medicine) and oranges in the south and potatoes and apples in the interior valleys.

Only about 3 percent of the total land area is used for agricultural purposes, with an additional 10 to 12 percent used for seasonal or permanent pasture. Often the fields have to be painstakingly built in terraces up the sides of hills. Usually the

Left: Terraced fields are built on the hillsides.
Right: A farmer plowing his field with animal power

terraces are irrigated, but in the south they may be watered by
rain. Sometimes land is used that would be better left alone
because of the problems of erosion and loss of topsoil. Also, there
is a practice called *tsheri*, which involves clearing forestland and
cultivating it temporarily. This practice can be harmful.
Pastureland is of importance in the northern belt and in the areas
above and between the valleys.

   Most of the cultivated land is farmed by the owners.
Traditionally, land owned by the monasteries was worked by
farmers who shared the crop with the monks. Much of this land
has been redistributed. The land is fairly well distributed with
ownership being legally limited to 25 acres (10 hectares), but
seldom exceeding 10 acres (4 hectares). In a survey of twelve
villages covering 120 households, 82 households owned less than
4 acres (1.6 hectares), 30 owned between 4 and 10 acres, and 4
owned more than ten. The average farm size was 4 acres. Only 4
families were landless. Farm size is thought to be somewhat larger
in the south and east, but in the east the land is dry farmed

Harvesting rice

(relying on rainfall) and needs more acreage. Grazing land has been communally owned with traditional rights determining access. However, the idea of letting persons build fences in order to provide incentive to investing in improvements in the land is being considered.

In the past Bhutan was self-sufficient in the production of grains—even exporting some to Tibet. However, with the increase in the population, with nonfarming populations growing, and with some rise in the consumption per person, demand has exceeded supply. The government has had to import food—mainly rice. Crops marketed within the country are usually exchanged through barter, not for cash.

The main cereal crops are rice, maize, wheat, barley, and buckwheat. Cereals are the main source of both calories and protein in the diet. Oilseeds and pulses (vegetables like peas and beans) have a limited part in agriculture. Mustard seed is gaining in importance. Soya is grown largely for export. Pulses are a cash crop in the south. Chilies are the main vegetable crop grown in home gardens.

The most important recent development in agriculture has been the introduction of commercial farming in an economy that before was almost entirely subsistence farming. The main cash crop is the potato. Orchards have increased with the building of roads and marketing services. Because of the high cost of starting orchards, investment in this type of agriculture has been by wealthy farmers, government employees, and business concerns. The development of oranges and cardamoms in the south has resulted from farmers seeking a cash crop to add to their subsistence farming.

Cultivation practices have changed very little over the centuries. There is good potential for increased production with the introduction of modern equipment and new crop varieties. Most of the labor is provided by family members with almost no paid agricultural labor except in the south. Labor shortages do limit the intensities and yields of crop. In the off-season, compulsory and voluntary labor obligations to the government may be met through communal projects such as house construction and establishment and maintenance of irrigation systems. The country's variations in elevation and climate provide good opportunities for timing production to meet seasonal demand in the markets of neighboring countries. Also, the isolation of the various valleys in the country has kept disease problems low. Some new specialty crops such as asparagus, mushrooms, and vegetable seeds will depend on the expansion of commercial farming that will require strong technical and marketing support.

Animal husbandry is important to the rural economy. Cattle are used as draft animals and for milking purposes. Most of the milk is consumed as cheese, curd, or butter. Most farmers also keep a few pigs and chickens. In the north, a small segment of the

Above: Yaks graze in the summer in the alpine pastures of the north. A yak herder (right)

population maintain herds of yak and sheep on the summer alpine pastures and migrate below the snow line during the winter months. In the south, sheep and goats are herded, and horses are used for transportation purposes. Crossbreeding programs and veterinary services have halted the decline in the numbers of some animals such as the yak. However, pasture limits for the sheep and yak create problems of overgrazing, if these animals increase in large numbers.

Agriculture has been an increasingly important target of government development plans. Progress has been made in supplying support services such as test farms, research, and extension work, in promoting irrigation and land development programs, and in encouraging commercial farming. However, the shortage of trained people, the mountainous territory, the scattered population, the need for good marketing and credit systems, and conservative attitudes often make development planning difficult. Bhutan faces important questions about the

Bhutanese farm women

amount of land that should be devoted to agriculture in comparison to forestry and to what extent farm machinery should be used without disrupting the existing economy.

FORESTRY

Forests are a very beautiful resource of Bhutan and very important to the economy. Directly, they account for about 16 percent of the gross national product. In addition, about half of the industrial units are based on wood products. About 9 percent of government receipts are based on income and taxes from forests. Yet the government has cut back on this income in order to conserve the forests.

The government has centralized control over the forests to protect and to make the best use of this resource. Several problems exist. In the southern foothills and in parts of the east, too many trees have been cut in areas next to roads without adequate planting of new trees. Hillsides without trees are vulnerable to landslides and erosion. On the other hand, in the northern parts of the country there are forests that are overaged. Because of lack of access to the area, they cannot be worked profitably. In other areas, trees have been cut selectively producing a forest of trees of various ages. Usually the best forest management practices require all the trees from a certain area to be cut and then new trees of a high value species to be planted to reforest the area with an even-aged forest. The government is working to train its citizens for careers in forestry.

Because of the value of wood products in neighboring countries that are poor in forests, Bhutan has a bright future in developing industries working in products such as veneer, plywood, furniture, and particleboard. Twenty-seven sawmills, three veneer mills, a pencil slat factory, a tea chest factory, and a match factory are privately owned. In addition, the government is developing other industrial uses of wood products and wants to maximize export earnings from this resource consistent with sound conservation practices.

INDUSTRY AND MINING

Manufacturing accounts for only 3.3 percent of the gross national product—very low even for a developing country. Moreover cottage industries account for a quarter of this total. The small population with low income may help to explain why the market within Bhutan is so small. Food processing, distillery operations, and cement account for two-thirds of industrial production. Most of this total and two-thirds of industrial employment come from three large companies owned in whole or in part by the government. The largest private sector operation is involved in processing citrus fruit into jams and canned juices with markets in India and Bhutan. There are about sixty small or medium-scale private industries producing consumer goods such as soap, candles, furniture, and processed foodstuffs.

Problems in developing industries come from the limited domestic market, lack of dependable supplies and power, and lack of manpower. Non-Bhutanese managers and also unskilled labor are required. The Bhutanese do not seem to like factory work. The government has tried to promote industrialization by the Bhutanese, but it has prohibited direct private investment by foreigners in order to keep control of its resources. However, outside investment has been welcomed in government-owned projects.

Mining operations are limited by inaccessibility of deposits, high extraction and processing costs, and a lack of power. Slate and marble are used within the country, and dolomite chips, lime, and coal are exported to India. The Penden cement factory was the first modern large-scale industry established in Bhutan. This operation has developed profitably, with both domestic and export markets. The government is looking into other factories and mining operations that can be developed for a profit.

TOURISM

The beauty of Bhutan's scenery and the fascinating culture of the nation attract foreign tourists. However, Bhutan has been very careful in developing tourism. In 1974 overseas tourists were first permitted to visit the country on a regular basis. The country has adopted a high-priced, all-inclusive tour strategy. In this way the

Garden of the Paro Hotel

country avoided some of the problems of neighboring areas where travelers on low budgets, often seeking drugs, gathered in certain towns. With hiking and fishing tours, organized groups travel under supervision along set itineraries in order to minimize the environmental impact. Recently there has been concern about the lack of respect that tourists showed for holy sites by photographing prohibited Buddhist images and even touching some of them. Therefore, a decision was made to ban these sites from tourists and to emphasize tours featuring scenic beauty instead.

About twenty-five hundred foreign visitors travel to Bhutan each year. In spite of the restrictive policy, tourism was the main hard currency foreign exchange producer for the government. Hotels have been built, and personnel have been trained. The seasonal nature of travel in the country has meant that hotel facilities are sometimes underutilized. The government has tried

One of Druk-Air's planes

to move commercial operations associated with tourism out of the government budget and into a separate organization. The first airline, Druk-Air, made its first regular flights between Calcutta, India, and Paro in 1984. The ninety-minute flight, the comfortable and attractive hotels, and the trips possible on good roads increase the potential for tourism in this country.

ENERGY AND POWER

With wood from the forests so readily available, it is not surprising to find that fuel wood is used by most people for their household needs. Moreover, the people of Bhutan consume a lot of energy when compared with neighboring countries such as Nepal where wood is becoming scarce. However, wood is not a very efficient source of energy.

For commercial uses, energy sources have been coal, petroleum, and electricity. The cement factory has been operated entirely with coal. Gasoline and diesel fuel are used in transportation. Kerosene is used for lighting. Petroleum products have to be imported, and the prices can be quite high in the north-central parts of the country after transportation costs. However, electricity generated from the mountain rivers represents the great power potential for this country.

Recently the big Chukha hydroelectric project was completed, which utilizes the water of the Wong Chu river in western Bhutan. This project is the largest single investment undertaking in the country. India agreed to finance the entire project—60 percent grant and 40 percent loan—in return for which Bhutan, which retains sole ownership, agreed to sell surplus power to India at a negotiated rate. The potential income to Bhutan and the potential power source for the country makes this project very attractive. From 1967 when the very first hydropower plant was installed, through the period when the country got along with six small hydroelectric stations and six diesel generating stations, to the present, Bhutan has made great progress in developing its water potential.

COMMUNICATION

Until the early 1960s, to get a message from one part of Bhutan to the other, the message was routed by hand along the network of trails. Now, however, communications within the country are far different. Bhutan has a comprehensive postal system. Telephone service has been more of a problem because of obsolete equipment and lack of maintenance, but new systems are being installed. Wireless networks (either voice or Morse code) have been even more widely used than telephones. A radio service broadcasts in three regional languages and in English. The wide audience for these broadcasts is used to strengthen national ties and to support development efforts. An official weekly bulletin and a quarterly magazine are published by the government in several languages.

Stamp collectors love the varied and unique stamps Bhutan has designed. Sales of the stamps have brought in significant amounts of foreign currency. Bhutan was the first country in the world to have a three-dimensional stamp. It commemorated space travel. The country was first again in printing a stamp on metal foil. Also stamps depicting sacred scroll paintings have been printed on silk.

MONEY AND BANKING

Use of money instead of barter is still fairly recent in Bhutan, and barter still is very important in rural areas. Taxes were paid in goods and through labor. Coins were issued during the 1950s, but only in the 1960s with the expansion of trade with India did the use of money become widespread. Until 1974, the India rupee was the medium of exchange. Then Bhutan issued *ngultrums* as the official currency. The Bank of Bhutan was established in 1968. Lending has grown rapidly, mostly for trade and industrial uses rather than for rural or personal purposes. Because of the need for capital expansion, development of internal and external investment is important.

Recently the World Bank did a study of Bhutan. It found that the development is fundamentally sound. In spite of shortages of technical, managerial, and even manual labor, in spite of the rugged physical conditions, and in spite of needs exceeding the financing currently available, it concluded that the future for Bhutan is bright. The country has good natural resources and is well managed.

After a landslide, a crew works to clear the mountain road.

TRANSPORTATION

With the mountains and rivers of Bhutan, road building is difficult. With the twists and turns required to get up a hillside, actual road distances are usually several times the straight-line distances. Moreover, maintaining these roads is not easy in a land of snow, flooding rivers, and mud slides.

At first the Bhutanese declined assistance in building roads as part of their protection through isolation. However, by the late 1950s, roads were seen as necessary for military defense and the development of the economy. At first, compulsory labor at road building was employed. However, this work took the people away from agriculture. In 1959, Bhutan accepted the offer of help from India through the Border Roads Organization, which brought in

A group of traders traversing the mountains

large numbers of contract laborers from India. The acute shortage of graduate Bhutanese engineers is being helped as young people graduate from technical schools and return from training abroad. The difficulties of maintaining the roads are aided somewhat by the still low number of vehicles in the country and by the fact that the rugged terrain limits the size of the trucks that can use the roads.

In a country like Bhutan, foot and mule tracks are still important. With the swift mountain streams that are full in the spring with the melt off of snow, bridges are essential. Often a detour of several days walking is necessary to cross a river. The government has a program to construct foot suspension bridges and improve existing trails.

Ropeways are a cost-effective way to move some products in mountainous areas. Timber and minerals are moved this way in Bhutan. Waterways are not practical because the rivers move too swiftly. There are no railways. However, air transportation and the development of airstrips are receiving support. There are now Bhutanese pilots, and others are in training.

Chapter 6

GROSS NATIONAL HAPPINESS

While some nations concentrate on economic growth so completely that their people have a difficult life, King Jigme Singye Wangchuck has said that he is not so much interested in the gross national product as the gross national happiness of his country. How can a nation utilize its human and natural resources to maximize the happiness of its people today and also in the future? Religion, style of government, educational opportunities, health conditions, and conservation of plant and animal resources—all play a role in the well-being of the citizens of a country.

RELIGION

Religion is obviously a very important part of Bhutanese life. The state religion of Bhutan is the Drukpa sub-sect of *Kagyupa*, a branch of Mahayana Buddhism. Buddhism, which comes to Bhutan from its origin in India, teaches "four noble truths":

Above: A dzong, with homes clustered nearby, dominates this valley. Mantras are printed on flags (right) or engraved on prayer wheels (below).

Young monks chanting prayers

existence is suffering, the origin of suffering is desire, suffering ends when desire ends, and the way to end desire is to follow the "noble eightfold path." That path involves right resolve, right speech, right conduct, right living, right effort, right belief, right contemplation, and right ecstasy. A person's goal should be to escape from existence into nonexistence, or *nirvana*. In Mahayana Buddhism, the goal is not just a personal escape, but also involves helping others to attain this nonexistence. A *bodhisattva* is a person who has attained the self-purification required to enter nirvana but who, out of compassion for others, remains in existence to work for others.

Since these Buddhists believe in reincarnation, a good life now filled with merit will help a person to be born into a better life the next time. Elaborate ceremonies are designed to help a person who has just died to continue to make the right choices for the next life.

Mantras, or sacred syllables, are thought to have great power. These mantras are used in meditation, in prayers, and in inscriptions cut into rocks. They also are put on flags and into prayer wheels. As the flags flap and the wheels turn, the message of the mantra is sent out.

65

Chortens (above) contain relics of holy men. The Memorial Chorten (right) at Thimphu is dedicated to Jigme Dorji Wangchuck. The interiors of chortens contain elaborate artifacts such as paintings (below) or gold Buddhas (below right).

Many beautiful temples are found in Bhutan with images of Buddha and pictures of male and female divinities. Also, there are other buildings called *chortens* that contain the bones or other relics of holy men. In addition to the funerals, the lamas or monks recite scripture, cast horoscopes, handle other ceremonies, teach doctrine, and perform masked dances. The dances help to teach people about religion and to deal with the spirits. The monks and nuns keep their heads close shaven and wear red robes. Contributions by lay persons to the clergy are given as a sign of respect and as a way of gaining merit.

In some parts of the country, elements of the earlier Bon religion are still very strong. Beliefs in omens and demons are common. Magical ceremonies are used to appease the demons. Lamas are consulted to determine the best day for starting something, such as a trip. If an omen is observed that is interpreted as unfavorable, the traveler will go home and wait for another time. Some of the seasonal festivals associated with agriculture may be tied to practices that existed before the coming of Buddhism.

In the south, the Hindus are in the majority. Various Hindu gods and goddesses are worshiped in temples and with festivals. Often there is a mixture of Buddhism, Hinduism, and Bon in the religious practices of different cultural groups in Bhutan.

GOVERNMENT

Bhutan is a monarchy with a king called the druk gyalpo. With the establishment of the present line of kings in 1907, the first two monarchs held absolute power and worked to unify the country with a strong central government. The third king, Jigme Dorji

Wangchuck, gave up some of that power in order to provide a constitutional monarchy, which he felt would better serve the needs of his country during his reign. His son, the present ruler, has followed this policy.

In 1953, the king established the National Assembly, called the *Tshogdu*. Originally this body, with about 130 members representing the people, the monks, and certain government officials, was only a group for the king to consult. It had no binding power. Then in 1968 the king took the step of making the Assembly's decisions final. He retained the right to address the Assembly personally when he had serious problems with actions of the Assembly. Then the king went even further in 1969 giving the Assembly the power to remove the king or any public official with a vote of no confidence. In 1973 at the death of the late king, this provision was repealed by the Assembly. The idea was considered too radical.

The membership of the Assembly is now about 150, because of the addition of government officials with the expansion of the administrative offices. The legislature consists of 100 representatives elected for three-year terms on the basis of one vote per one household, a speaker elected by secret ballot by the Assembly, 10 representatives of the monks elected for a three-year term on a regional basis, and 40 government officials who hold membership in the Assembly as long as they have their positions in the government. The Assembly meets twice a year, in the spring and fall, for sessions lasting several weeks. There is free debate in the sessions. All matters of policy are open for discussion. Most of the focus has been on development programs and domestic issues. Heads of government departments must report to the Assembly at least once a year.

A Royal Advisory Council, called the *Lodoi Tsokde*, was established by the king in 1965. The Council is always in session, advises the king, and monitors the way the National Assembly resolutions are being implemented. It is made up of nine members who must be approved by the National Assembly. Two members are appointed by the king, two monks are selected by the Assembly from a slate prepared by the monastic institution, and five regional representatives are chosen by the Assembly. The chair is appointed by the king from Council members.

Then there is a Cabinet of the high administrative officials. Until the 1960s, the administration of the government was fairly simple and could be handled by a small number of persons. However, with the many new development projects, administration has become more complex, and new officers have been appointed to manage the work.

The judicial system of the country goes back to the laws established by the Shabdrung Ngawang Namgyal in the seventeenth century. While there have been modifications since that time, the Buddhist framework is still in place. In the past the law was administered by the district governors and local leaders with a few cases of a serious nature being heard by the king. In 1968, a separate set of judges was established. The High Court is made up of six judges—four appointed by the king and two elected by the National Assembly. District courts were set up with judges appointed from government workers, other than the district official. Village leaders still handle local disputes. The king can overturn a decision of the High Court only if legal principles have not been followed. The country still has no laws for corporations. Most corporations or official groups are formed by the process of the king giving them charters.

The country is divided into 17 districts along historical lines and geographical natural barriers. Each district is administered by a district officer appointed by the king and reporting to the ministry of home affairs. With decentralization of some of the development programs, the importance of district government has increased. Some of the larger districts are subdivided even further so that there are units consisting of about three to five hundred families. There are about 188 of these units with a head chosen by the villagers. This person is the link between the people and the district officials on questions such as taxes and labor service.

There are no political parties in the country. The factions that have existed appear to be based on power and personal interest, rather than on policy considerations. So far, palace politics have been the more usual form of transfer of power. The more educated Bhutanese appear to agree on many policy issues, and political interest has not been strong at the village level in most parts of the country.

As for the army, Bhutan has had a great fighting tradition over the centuries. Armies were raised when a threat appeared. However, in 1952, it was decided to create a regular military force. Officers have been trained, and males are subject to conscription. The force has been kept small so as not to drain labor from other segments of the economy.

In international relations, the king is continuing to attend international meetings and to extend diplomatic ties with more countries. However, Bhutan cannot establish permanent diplomatic missions in other countries without spending more foreign currency than would be desirable now.

Although the monks have lost most of the secular power they once had, they are an important unifying factor with a voice in

The dzong in Punakha

many of the high-level government bodies. The structure of the
monastic government has continued over the centuries. There are
about thirty-three hundred monks. From these, hundreds are
chosen to be members of the Central Monk Body. The high abbot
is chosen from among the high lamas and holds the position
indefinitely. He has full power over religious affairs including
Buddhist organizations that are not of the Drukpa sect. In each
district, except those in the south that are predominantly Hindu,
there is a lama appointed from the Central Monk Body with
responsibility to conduct district religious ceremonies, keep up the
monasteries, run the monastery schools, and preside over the
District Monk Body. Ties between religious and secular officials
are close, since both share the administrative building, the dzong.

Economic power of the monks has declined. Until 1968, the
monasteries collected taxes in goods and services directly as well
as rents in goods and services from tenants on the sizable

Monks at a monastery gather for the evening meal.

monastery lands. In 1968, the government replaced the monastery taxes with direct payment by the government to the monastery. In 1982, the government began purchasing monastery land for redistribution to the farmers who for the most part owned none. Most of this money is being invested in income-producing development projects. The government still must provide free public labor for the construction and maintenance of the monasteries.

The prestige of the monks is still very high. It used to be considered desirable for at least one son of a family to become a monk. Until the establishment of other educational opportunities, it was the one route for some families to provide training and advancement for a child. Now, recruitment is more difficult. However, a smaller and better-educated clergy may prove to be a better managed force for social service and strengthening national values.

EDUCATION

Historically, only some of the monks and a few of the
government officials could read or write. Until the 1960s there
was almost no formal education, except for the teaching of
religion and the classical Dzongkha language in the monastic
schools. Few citizens had studied outside Bhutan. Since that
decade, a formal education system has been established and a
significant number of students have been sent abroad for
specialized training. Much progress has been made, but the
Bhutanese recognize that much remains to be done. By the end of
the 1970s, only 10 percent of the adults could read and write, and
enrollment in schools was only 21 percent of the age group for
primary education and 2.5 percent for secondary schools.

The education system consists of two years of pre-school (lower
and upper kindergarten), five years of primary (Classes I through
V), five years of secondary (Class VI through X), and two years at
junior college. While the primary schools are day schools in local
communities, there are central schools where students can live in
order to get education from lower kindergarten through Class X.
Classes are taught in English, by teachers who have studied in
India or have learned English from their teachers. However, the
teaching of Dzongkha, the official language, is required. Some
specialized education is provided for teacher training and for
technical courses. Also, there are monastic schools, art schools,
and a business skills school.

The government controls and manages the schools providing
free textbooks and supplies, free meals, and board, and for
students abroad, tuition and living allowances. The government is
committed to providing free, universal, but not compulsory

Primary schoolchildren (left)
and secondary students (above)

primary education. Because villages may be a distance from the schools and because the children are needed by their families to work in the fields during certain periods, it may be hard for some youngsters to get to school for an education.

Students take examinations at the end of the fifth, eighth, and tenth years of class to determine whether they are eligible for further education. Also, at the end of the fifth and eighth years, the government transfers students between schools in different regions to foster national integration. After the exam at the Class V stage, only 1,500 are eligible to continue to the secondary school. Those not in the eligible group may go to technical schools, join the army, return to their villages, or apply for on-the-job training programs. Since the children who stop their training at age eleven or twelve when they leave the Class V are likely to forget some of what they have learned, some attention is being given to having refresher courses and reading materials in local communities to help these youngsters remember their studies. After the Class VIII exam, only the best 600 students continue. The Class X exam determines which of 120 students can be admitted to junior college, after which only about 100 qualify for education abroad.

As of 1982, there were not enough qualified students to meet the quotas for the next stage of education. Since educated and skilled citizens are needed, the government must be careful to see that students are encouraged to continue their education.

HEALTH

Like education, health needs have a high priority in the development plans of Bhutan. Life is not easy in this country with its extreme climate patterns and the difficulty of travel to receive medical attention. The average life span is short, and the infant mortality rate is high. Communicable diseases are a common feature of life. Gastrointestinal infections are the most common cause of death—especially for young children. Influenza and pneumonia are next. Other troubles come from parasites, skin diseases, tuberculosis, malaria, and goiter.

Since the 1960s, modern health services have been introduced in increasing quantities. The government carries the cost of public health care along with a contribution of 1 percent of the salary of civil servants and with free labor from rural citizens for construction and upkeep of local health buildings. There is only one general hospital in the country—Thimphu Hospital in the capital. In 1980, there were nineteen specialized hospitals, thirty-seven dispensaries, and fifty basic health units. The basic health units are important in getting health services out to the people where they live. They are staffed by health workers. There are shortages of physicians and other medical personnel in the country, though efforts are being made to train such people and to expand the number of the basic health units.

Preventive medicine through better sanitation, hygiene, and nutrition also holds promise. Only 8 percent of the population has regular access to safe water. Improved water availability and better waste disposal will help in reducing disease. As for food, while people generally have enough good food to eat, parasitic disease often prevents bodies from utilizing the food that is eaten. Deficiencies of iodine and iron in the diet—factors in the deaths of infants—are being remedied by the distribution of iodized salt and iron tablets.

ANIMAL AND PLANT CONSERVATION

Just as the government is working hard to provide improved conditions for the human population, so also is it sensitive to the animal and plant life in Bhutan. Bhutan is rich in the variety of animals and plants within its borders. In the northern parts of the country, there are national parks where snow leopards, musk deer, and black bears live. In the southern national parks, tigers, elephants, and rhinoceroses can be found. Bhutan is home to twenty endangered species. One species of monkey, the golden langur, can be found only in Bhutan.

In order to preserve these animals and the forests and vegetation on which they depend, action must be taken. Forests must be protected. Hunting in conservation areas must be stopped. Musk deer are targets because the musk they produce can be sold for use in perfume or medicine. Snow leopards are killed because they sometimes attack cattle. Investigation of animal attacks and greater knowledge of the wildlife are needed. Fires set

Left: A kapok tree   Right: A snow leopard

by poachers or just carelessly left by local people sometimes spread out of control and have destroyed territory in the conservation areas.

How can Bhutan, with all its other needs, deal with the conservation requirements it has? When the United Nations help was not forthcoming, some private international groups such as the World Wildlife Fund have provided funds, training, and advice to help the country. Projects such as "Operation Tiger" in the Manas Tiger Reserve have been especially successful in preserving the areas in which tigers are found. Money for elephants, jeeps, and radio equipment have been supplied for this reserve. Also conservation groups have been able to provide advice about legislation and training.

A Royal Society for the Protection of Nature in Bhutan has been established. The purpose of this organization is to develop conservation programs and to help educate the public about the importance of preserving natural resources.

Chapter 7

LIFE OF THE
DRAGON PEOPLE

What is life like in this "Paradise of the South"—another name for Bhutan? The people of Bhutan really represent three or four cultural groups who live in different parts of the nation with different land and climate conditions. Therefore, there may be considerable variation in life-styles.

Some experts divide the Bhutanese into three main groups: the Bhote (from Tibet), Nepalese (from Nepal), and various other tribal groups. According to this classification, the Bhote are in the majority, the Nepalese are about 25 percent of the population, and the tribal groups make up about 15 percent. Some other analysts add a fourth group of a small number of Bhutanese nationals at the southern border with India, who are culturally like their neighbors who live along the flatlands of India that adjoin Bhutan. Still other writers describe the Indo-Mongoloid people of southeastern Bhutan as separate from the tribal groups.

Women in traditional dress

THE BHOTES

The Bhotes are the largest group and are concentrated in western and central Bhutan. Most of the social and political leaders of the country are from this group. Many of the elite came to Bhutan from Tibet in the eighth century A.D. Tibetan refugees have entered the country at many other times. After the recent Chinese invasion of Tibet, a large influx of Tibetans created a refugee problem for Bhutan.

The newly arrived Tibetans had the custom of wearing their hair long, while most Bhutanese (both men and women) wear short hair. Now with the influence of Western styles, some women are letting their hair grow longer. The Bhutanese are generally tall and athletic in appearance. True to their Mongolian origins, they have small elongated eyes and broad cheekbones. The early visitors to Bhutan described them as a handsome people. Independence and cheerfulness are qualities attributed to the

Most men wear scarves that can be wrapped around their heads for warmth at night.

Bhotes. Both men and women who are farmers work long and hard in their fields raising crops.

Their dress is well suited for life in a mountainous area. The women wear beautifully woven fabrics with colorful and intricate designs. The *kira* is a long piece of cloth that is wrapped around the body and attached to the shoulders with a pair of silver brooches. At the waist, women wear a wide belt. Usually a small jacket will be worn over this outfit. When women and men go into a temple, they wear a scarf over their shoulders as a sign of respect. The color of the scarf may give an indication of the rank of the person.

The men's dress is a long robe called a *go*. Often it will be plaid. During the daytime, it is fastened up with a belt so that it comes about to the knees. At night, the robe will be let down to provide a comfortable robe for sleeping. Men rarely wear hats, but will carry a scarf to wrap around their heads at night. The only pocket they will have is in a fold in the clothing under the robe.

Left: Men laboriously hand painting a house in traditional designs
Right: Red chili peppers drying on a roof weighted down by rocks

Traditionally every man carried a long knife, which he could use for protecting himself, cutting trees, or digging holes. Men may go barefoot, or wear sandals or woolen Tibetan boots.

Farmers often will live in small settlements or in isolated homes. In larger towns, the houses will cluster around the dzongs, which have provided protection in the past. The houses may be painted with attractive designs and are built with timber and thick pounded mud walls to keep out the cold. Most are two stories but sometimes go as high as four. If the family owns animals, the livestock will be kept on the ground floor while the family lives above. The roof made from wooden slats is anchored by heavy rocks. Often red chili peppers are put out on the roof to dry for use in cooking later.

Inside the house the family will have a shrine at which they can worship. In a poor family, the shrine may be a small Buddhist image or a painting. In a rich family, a whole room may be set aside as the shrine and furnished with a carved and painted altar, lamps, incense burners, and other religious items.

The houses traditionally had windows with shutters—not glass. They were heated by a wood fire in a large bowl of bronze or iron placed in the center of the room. It could get smoky and sooty at times. Beautifully decorated low tables are common, but chairs and beds are unusual in the villages, where people prefer to sit and sleep on the floor.

Usually the family consists of one husband and one wife. Traditionally a man might have many wives and a woman might have many husbands. Where population is sparse, where numbers of females and males may be unequal in a community, and where mountains and streams make visits to a neighboring village difficult, these customs are understandable. Now a wife may have only one husband, but a husband may have a maximum of three wives with the permission of the previous wives. Women can marry at age sixteen and men at age twenty-one. A newly married couple may live with her family, his family, or on their own—depending on where the need for farming is greatest. Usually there is no formal wedding ceremony, and only recently have marriages been registered by law. Divorce is easy and fairly common. In Bhutan, the important unit is the larger family including grandparents, aunts, and uncles, all of whom may look after the children.

As for food, the ordinary villager may not be able to afford meat often, and may rely on a dish of rice, potatoes, a vegetable, and some chilies. A meat soup with herbs sometimes begins the morning and midday meals. Meat curry with rice and potatoes spiced with chili pepper is a common dish. The red chilies were introduced from South America by the Portuguese. Potatoes were

Bhutanese usually buy goods and produce in open-air markets, which are especially busy on Sundays (right).

brought in the eighteenth century by the English. The garlic, onion, and ginger seasonings were added by the Bhutanese only in the 1950s, but now they are popular. Yak meat is eaten fresh, dried, or powdered for bouillon. The yak also supplies milk from which butter is made. Pork, chicken, eggs, and beef also contribute to the diet in lesser degrees. A butter tea made by brewing tea leaves, butter, and salt is a popular beverage, though it is more like a soup than the tea to which Westerners are accustomed. A fermented drink is *chang* (sometimes called beer by foreigners), which can be made from different types of grain. Cheese is popular. There is a form that comes in little chunks that can be chewed for hours. Also chewing the habit-forming areca nut that produces a red juice that stains the mouth and teeth is a custom. Vegetables can include mushrooms, young ferns, and even orchids. Orchards have added delicious fruit to the meals. Also, a good-luck pastry is served that is rolled into different shapes and patterns.

THE INDO-MONGOLOID PEOPLE AND TRIBAL GROUPS

Just as the United States has its tradition of the "Wild West" where life is a little freer than on the sedate East coast, so also Bhutan has its "Wild East." Here live a number of groups speaking different languages, having different dress, and somewhat different customs. Perhaps some of these people fled to the more rugged country in the east as new populations came into Bhutan from other countries over the centuries. Nevertheless, these groups are closely linked to the Bhotes because they share a common religion taught by the lamas, although in the east there is often a strong element of the older Bon religion.

The language problem has been greater in the east because often the dialects spoken in one valley have become so different from those in the next valley that the people understand each other only with difficulty. The introduction of a standardized language taught in schools will help this problem over the generations.

Land is cleared by burning the vegetation. Then the people grow rice on it for several years only to abandon the area when the soil no longer produces well. Cattle, pigs, and goats are important for home use, market, and religious sacrifices.

Houses are made of stone and wood. Sometimes the houses are built on stilts or piles on the slopes of the hills. If water is not adequate at the site, bamboo conduits may be used to funnel water from a nearby stream to the settlement.

Often the dress of the people may be quite different from the dress of the Bhotes. For example, to the east in the Sakteng valley live a people called "Dakpas." The women, who keep their hair long, wear traditional dress consisting of a red-and-white silk poncho, a red silk jacket decorated with animal designs, a red

A young girl from Nepal

wool cape, and perhaps a braided black wool jacket. The men wear trousers of leather or cloth over which are big white wool breeches, topped by a red wool jacket, and sometimes a sleeveless outer garment of leather and felt. Both men and women wear earrings decorated with turquoise. However, the most distinctive part of their dress is their hat. It is a flat disc of felt made from yak hair on which are five taillike downspouts for the water to drain off to keep the head dry. Herding yak and sheep and spinning and weaving wool are important activities in this group.

THE NEPALESE

Recent immigrants to Bhutan are the Nepalese. They came first in the late nineteenth and early twentieth centuries. These people arrived from neighboring Nepal seeking better living conditions. They have settled in southern Bhutan where they are in the majority. These people have a religion that is predominantly

Hindu. They have caste and family ties to Nepal and India. They have been influenced by Indian political ideas, and some have lacked the same loyalty to the monarchy that was predominant in other parts of Bhutan.

The government has tried various approaches to the "Nepalese problem." Further immigration was prohibited in 1959. At first, the government tried to restrict the Nepalese to the south and to cut down their interaction with other parts of the country. However, that policy tended to make the Nepalese second-class citizens. It was not desirable to have an unhappy population along the border with India in an area of the country where development projects could lead to rapid economic growth. Now the government has adopted the policy of integration. Hindu religious holidays are celebrated throughout the country along with Buddhist ones. Intermarriage between southern and northern Bhutanese is encouraged with financial help for the couples. Children of secondary school level are sent to boarding schools in different parts of the country. While contract labor from outside Bhutan is allowed into the country for temporary work on development projects, new immigration is being strictly controlled.

In the south where climatic conditions are different, bamboo and thatch houses are common. Nepali is spoken and used in schools along with the other required languages. The women wear the sari—a cloth sixteen feet (five meters) long that is draped and pleated at the waist to form a skirt with one end draped over the blouse at the shoulder. The men wear trousers and jackets with a Gurka cap (a cloth cap with a flat top). The caste system of separating different social levels may control the choice of marriage partners and other social relationships.

Tourists being served afternoon tea in a hotel

The food of the Nepalese who live in Bhutan is closer to that of India. They like rice with different curries. Eating beef is forbidden by the Hindu religion, and some people do not eat any meat. Sweet tea, rather than the butter tea of the Bhotes, is the most popular beverage.

THE INDIANS

In a narrow strip along the southern border are a group of people who are linked culturally with India. Given the difficulty of travel up to central Bhutan, it is understandable that in culture, language, and economic ties this group should develop close contacts with the neighboring Indian states of Bengal and Assam. These people are Hindu and are part of the caste system where social rank passes in families. They farm intensively, producing wet and dry rice, millet, barley, and maize. They live in mud and thatch houses and eat the rice and curry dishes common to India.

Above: Musicians with typical long brass horns
Right: A dramnyen

SINGING, DANCING, AND FESTIVALS

When the Bhutanese want to relax, they turn to singing, dancing, and festivals. The songs are of different types. Some are for the monks, some are from Tibet, and some are folk songs from particular valleys. Often they are accompanied by musical instruments such as the flute, the drum, and a seven-stringed instrument called a *dramnyen.*

Sometimes storytellers, called *manips,* come to the village to repeat religious tales. They carry a kind of cabinet with them that has different scenes picturing their stories.

Dancing by both men and women is popular. Traditionally they dance separately. The women have very sedate, slow movements, but some of the men's dances are quite wild and ferocious.

Festivals are colorful two- and three-day events. The Bhutanese have their own calendar with months measured by phases of the moon. The New Year, which falls at either the beginning or the end of February, is the biggest celebration. Dances then are performed usually by specially trained monks. Like stained-glass windows in churches, the dances were a way of teaching religion to a people who could not read or write. However, the dances have an even deeper function in that they are believed to be a way of controlling and influencing the spirits. The dance steps and patterns are very complicated, and they have been handed down over the generations without changes. Some of the dances are believed to have originated in the dreams and visions of the lamas where the gods and spirits danced in a heavenly kingdom. Beautiful robes, elaborate masks, and the sound of cymbals and long brass horns combine to fix the attention of the watchers.

The Drum Dance of Dramitse represents a vision of heavenly beings at the palace of the Guru Rimpoche. The dancers wear masks representing different animals—deer, tigers, elephants, crocodiles—and carry decorated drums. Their costumes are of multicolored silk with skirts of various colored scarves. The drum symbolized the essence of religion that defeats the demons. The "Black Hat" dancer is magnificently costumed in brocade robes and an elaborate black hat. The dance has two meanings: a portrayal of the assassination of a Tibetan king in A.D. 842, who persecuted Buddhists; and a conquering of and offering to the earth deities. In some of the dances, skulls and death are emphasized as a reminder that the good and bad deeds of a person will influence destiny on rebirth. A lighter note is introduced by the clowns who joke with the audience and mimic the serious dancers.

Ceremonial masks (above and below left) are worn by festival dancers. Clowns (below right), as they do all over the world, introduce a comic note to the proceedings.

Dancers at the Tshechu Festival in Thimphu

The Bhutanese love their festivals. Usually, they will bring along picnics in baskets so they can continue to watch the dances all day. They laugh at the clowns. One of the highlights of many festivals is the raising of a huge picture of the Guru Rimpoche on a special wall inside a dzong. These pictures are silk sewed on a background sheet. They look like paintings. The people believe that looking at such pictures can heal them of suffering caused by false beliefs. Of course, many of the audience do not understand the details of the dances and the religion, but they believe it is more important to have faith than to understand.

The courtyard of the Punakha Dzong (left) and a close-up of its painted woodwork (right)

ARTS AND CRAFTS

The architecture of dzongs and temples has been much admired. The West learned of their beauty through the diary and drawings of Samuel Davis, the British surveyor who journeyed to Bhutan in 1783. Dzongs were built without nails, being mortised and dovetailed in construction. The white walls on the outside have a red band under the eaves. Often the woodwork is painted with beautiful designs. The same traditional style of construction and design was used in 1955, when the king ordered new buildings added to the Thimphu Dzong.

In Bhutan today, you can see beautiful statues in the temples. Bronze casting was done in foundries in the dzongs as early as the sixteenth century. Figures of the Buddha and some of the Bon deities were made by the Bhutanese. In order to cast these statues, a figure was molded in beeswax or clay. The image would then be cut into halves and baked in terra-cotta to form the molds into

Wall painting inside a dzong

which the molten bronze would be poured. Some of the
sculptures were made in clay and then gilded, painted, and
dressed in splendid robes. These works of art were commissioned
by persons wishing to gain religious merit. It was thought that the
larger the statue, the more the merit. Sometimes, clay statues were
covered by thin plates of metal except for the face.

Painting also was used to teach about the lives of important
persons. A central figure in a ritual pose would be surrounded by
divine beings and scenes from the life of the person portrayed.
These paintings are often stylized, but use bright colors. Another
kind of wall painting depicts the demonic world showing
magicians, witches, wild animals, and demons. The artist had
greater freedom in portraying hell than in painting deities where
position and even color were governed by tradition. The wall
paintings were created by coating a moist wall with a mixture of

*Painting (left) with a central figure surrounded by divine
beings, and a wood chest (right) with an intricate painted design*

lime and gum. This surface was polished with something like a
shell. The figures were drawn with ink and charcoal and then
colors were applied in several coats by brush. Finally, to
strengthen the color, this picture was covered with a varnish
consisting of glue, lime, and more color. The colors came from
minerals and organic materials.

Bhutan also was famous for its wood carvings. The many forests
of the country provide a ready supply of materials for carving.
The statues portray religious themes. Wood chests and tables are
often painted with intricate pictures and designs.

Metalwork also is used to produce articles of a religious nature.
Bhutanese bells are highly prized. Swords, daggers, teapots, and
jars also are among the works of art of the metalworkers. Jewelry
is very popular with the Bhutanese.

A loom (left) used to weave textiles (right) in detailed patterns

Hand looming of wool, silk, and cotton textiles is done in almost every home. Often this means spinning the yarn, dyeing it, and then weaving it in traditional detailed patterns. The fabrics are beautiful. In addition to meeting the clothing needs of the people, they are an attractive souvenir for the foreign tourist. Basket and bamboo weaving is also a common craft for making containers for food, water, hats, and arrows.

SPORTS

While soccer, basketball, volleyball, badminton, tennis, table tennis, darts, shot put, and wrestling are popular, the national sport of Bhutan is archery. In 1984, Bhutan first fielded a team of archers at the Olympic Games. In the days that dzongs were defended with bow and arrow, the Bhutanese were considered the best archers in the Himalayas.

Although a year-round sport, the village competitions usually take place during cold weather when the harvests are in. The day-

An archery contest (left) and children taking a break from a game of basketball (right)

long tournaments, with intermissions for eating and drinking, are very competitive. The targets are placed from 325 to 350 feet (99 to 106 meters) from the archers. The team stands around the target and dodges the arrows. An archer making a very good shot may be rewarded then and there with the gift of a white scarf. Dances of joy by the winning team may follow, or the losing team may dance and whoop it up to chase away the evil spirits. Magic may be practiced to help a team win. Women are not allowed to touch the bows, but they come to dance and sing, often making sarcastic comments about the unlucky shots while cheering on the home team.

The bows and arrows are made of bamboo and require physical strength. The bows are 6 feet (1.8 meters) in length. The bow string may be made from the fiber of a plant, like a stinging nettle,

Festival dancers

and is stronger than the best nylon of the same thickness. For contests the arrows are tipped with copper. In war, barbed steel was used.

The love of the Bhutanese for archery can be illustrated by an incident in the life of the third king. As a prince visiting London in 1950, he decided that he had to have an archery contest on the Bhutanese New Year's Day. He took his bow and arrows to Picadilly Circus in the heart of London. When one of his arrows went astray into the bedroom window of a house, one of his attendants scaled up the drain pipe, entered the window, and returned with the arrow. It was with some relief to those charged with the care of the prince when he returned to Bhutan.

The life of the dragon people is filled with hard work, but also with fun. Bhutan has preserved for the world an ancient culture with beautiful music, dance, art, and crafts.

Chapter 8

MAPS OF THE UNIVERSE

On temple walls in Bhutan are found some fascinating maps of the universe called *mandalas*. The mandala is a sacred map of the universe that represents the potential achieved by an enlightened person. It is a diagram that is believed to have great power and is used in meditation.

With its newly trained scientists and its ownership of a moon rock, Bhutan also possesses the scientific maps of the universe. Just as a map of the country showing differences in rainfall is not in conflict with a map of the nation showing where different cultural groups live, so also the religious and scientific maps need not be in conflict. Both can be used by people to enrich their lives.

MAJOR SETTLEMENTS IN BHUTAN

The visitor to Bhutan by air will land on the airstrip in the Paro valley. It is a beautiful place near the Himalayas and the holy Mount Chomolhari. The Paro Chu river meanders through rice and wheat fields.

The courtyard of the Paro Dzong (left) and a seventh-century monastery near Paro

The Paro Dzong was one of the strongest forts in Bhutan. It was built on the site of a temple founded by Padma Sambhava in the ninth century. When the dzong was burned down in 1907, the enormous wall hanging about 100 by 150 feet (30 to 46 meters) picturing Padma Sambhava was saved. This wall hanging is unrolled and hung on the monastery wall for several hours at the New Year's Day festival. One of the watchtowers of this fort was restored and now houses the National Museum.

This valley also is the location of several other holy sites. The Takstang Monastery, the Tiger's Nest, is perched high on a cliff that makes for a thrilling climb. It was here that Padma Sambhava meditated in a cave. One of the country's oldest temples, the Kyichu Lakhang, dating from the seventh or eighth century, lies across the river. The valley is home to other dzongs and temples of historic importance.

Top: The Paro Chu river valley
Above: Urban transportation in Paro
Left: A scene on Paro's main street

Thimphu, the capital of Bhutan

The National Secretariat Building in Thimphu (left) and worshipers outside the memorial chorten to Bhutan's late king (right)

Thimphu, the capital of Bhutan since 1960, is in the valley of the Wang Chu river. The largest city in Bhutan, it is at an elevation of over 7,500 feet (2,286 meters). The main Secretariat Building, the *Tashichhodzong*, is the location of all ministries, the National Assembly Hall, the office of the king, and the throne room. It is the summer residence of the Monk Body and the religious chief, the je khempo. While there is a yearly festival in the courtyard of this dzong, the famous wall hanging there is displayed only once in twenty-five years. A two-story-high statue of Buddha, wall paintings, and copies of Buddhist scriptures are some of the treasures of this dzong.

The white memorial chorten to the late king, His Majesty Jigme Dorji Wangchuck, contains a collection of paintings and statues of religious significance. Pilgrims walk around this building swinging their prayer wheels.

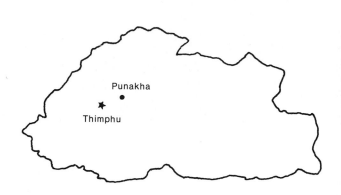

The Punakha valley

On a ridge five miles (eight kilometers) from the city is the Simtokha Dzong, built by Ngawang Namgyal in 1627. It houses the Dzongkha Language and Religious University.

The town of Thimphu has many shops. Here one can buy brick tea, horseshoes, cooking oil, and clothing fabrics. The Handicraft Emporium run by the government sells many of the traditional craft items for tourists. Here also is the post office where Bhutan's famous stamps may be purchased.

Punakha was the capital until it was moved to Thimphu. Punakha is situated in the valley of the Pho Chu and Mo Chu rivers. It is in a temperate climate. Crops of rice and fruits such as mangoes, bananas, and oranges are cultivated here.

In 1637, Ngawang Namgyal built the fortress at the junction of the two rivers. The Punakha Dzong contains many important temples, including one in which the embalmed body of the Ngawang Namgyal lies in state. No one except the king and certain high lamas may enter the burial chamber. It is the seat of religion, and rituals are carried on as they were in the seventeenth century.

Above: The post office in Thimphu
Below: The Mo Chu and Pho Chu rivers meet at Punakha.

*The Tongsa Dzong (above) and
some of its interior decoration (right)*

South of Punakha, in an area known for slate carving and
bamboo weaving, is the Wangdiphodrang Dzong that is situated
on top of a ridge between the Sankosh and Tangchu rivers. This
fortress guards the gateway to central and eastern Bhutan. A
bridge over to the fortress was made entirely of wood from fir
trees without any metal parts. Wooden pegs were used to hold it
together. It has withstood three hundred years of weathering. This
town has been selected as the site of a national agricultural
research center.

Tongsa, one of the most impressive of all the dzongs, was the
home of the ruling Wangchuck family. The present king was
installed as governor of Tongsa by his father as an indication that
this son was to inherit the throne. The dzong is very old and
houses at least twenty temples, each marked by a golden symbol
on the roof over the altar. The strategic location of this dzong on
the Mangde River and in the center of the country on the passage
between east and west added to the prestige of the rulers of this
area.

The Ha Dzong is in the heart of a fertile valley.

Bumthang, the historic area associated with Padma Sambhava's healing the Indian ruler of a serious disease, is today a center for industrial and educational development in Bhutan. Apple orchards are being encouraged here.

Clear over to the east of the nation is the Tashigang Dzong built on the heights overlooking the Manas River. An important market is held at the junction of the trade routes between Tongsa and southern Bhutan and India.

The Ha Dzong, in the western part of the country, is located in the fertile and densely settled valley that has been controlled by the Dorji family. Winters are very cold here because the mountains hide the afternoon sun. During the winter, many migrate with their cattle south to a warmer climate.

Chimakothi is the third-largest settlement in the country and is close to the Chukha Hydropower Project on the Wang Chu river.

Thimphu
Bumthang
Tongsa
Chimakothi
Tashigang
Phuntsholing

A view of Phuntsholing

The second-largest community is Phuntsholing, on the southern border. It is the gateway for the main land route from India into Thimphu and Paro. More than half of the manufacturing establishments are in this town. It also is an administrative center for development planning.

THE FUTURE

Bhutan has done a remarkable job in utilizing modern ideas and techniques, while preserving its ancient culture. In only several generations, the nation has gone from an isolated group of local rulers with an agricultural barter economy to a country that has designed and implemented development plans and is a full partner in the United Nations. It is a nation where change is evaluated in terms of the gross national happiness of its people.

MAP KEY

Black Mountain Range	A3, B3, C3
Bumthang (district)	A3, A4, B3, B4
Bumthand (district capital)	B4
Bumthang (river)	B4, C4
Chamka Chu (river)	A4, B4
Chimakothi	C2
Chirang (district)	C2, C3
Chukha	C2
Chuzom	B2
Daga (district capital)	C2
Dagana (district)	B2, C2, C3
Damphu (district capital)	C3
Dechheling	C4
Deothang	C5
Drukyel	B1
Gasa (district)	A2, A3, B2, B3
Gasa (district capital)	A2
Gaylegphug (district)	C2, C3, C4
Gaylegphug (district capital)	C3
Gedu	C2
Gyetsa	B3
Ha (district)	B1, B2, C1, C2
Ha (district capital)	B1
Ha Chu (river)	B1, B2
Kulong Chu (river)	A5, B5
Kuru Chu (river)	A4, B4, C4
Laya	A2
Lhuntsi (district)	A4, A5, B4
Lhuntsi (district capital)	B4
Lunana	A3
Manas (river)	B5, C5, C4
Mo Chu (river)	A2, B2
Mongar (district)	B4, B5, C4, C5
Mongar (district capital)	B4
Nanglam	C5
Pagli	C1
Paro (district)	A1, A2, B1, B2, C1, C2
Paro (district capital)	B2
Paro Chu (river)	B1, B2, C2
Pema Gatsel (district)	C4, C5
Pema Gatsel (district capital)	C5
Pho Chu (river)	A3, B3, B2
Phuntsholing	C2
Punakha	B2
Samchi (district)	B1, C1, C2
Samchi (district capital)	C1
Samdrup Jonkhar (district)	C4, C5, C6
Samdrup Jonkhar (district capital)	C5
Sankosh (river)	B2, B3, C3, C2
Sarbhang	C3
Shemgang (district)	B3, B4, C3, C4
Shemgang (district capital)	B3
Sibsoo	C1
Simtokha	B2
Tashi Yangtsi	B5
Tashigang (district)	A5, B4, B5, B6, C5
Tashigang (district capital)	B5
Thimphu (district)	A2, B2, B3, C2
Thimphu (national capital)	B2
Tongsa (district)	B3, B4, C3
Tongsa (district capital)	B3
Tongsa Chu (river)	B3, C4
Torsa (river)	B1, C1, C2
Wangdiphodrang (district)	A3, B2, B3, C2, C3
Wangdiphodrang (district capital)	B2
Wong Chu (river)	C2

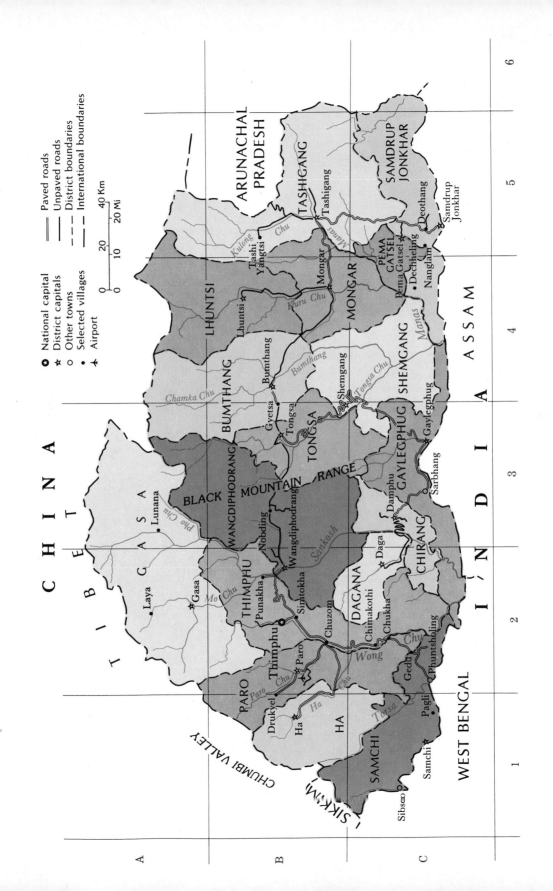

CHINA

TIBET

CHUMBI VALLEY

SIKKIM

WEST BENGAL

INDIA

ASSAM

ARUNACHAL
PRADESH

GASA

Lunana

Laya

Gasa

Pho Chu

Mo Chu

PARO

THIMPHU

Punakha

Drukyel

Paro

Ha

HA

Thimphu

Simtokha

Paro Chu

Ha Chu

Torsa

Wong Chu

Chuzom

Gedu

Phuntsholing

Pagli

Sibso

Samchi

SAMCHI

Chimakothi

Chukha

DAGANA

Daga

Damphu

CHIRANG

Sarbhang

GAYLEGPHUG

Gaylegphug

WANGDIPHODRANG

BLACK MOUNTAIN RANGE

Nobding

Wangdiphodrang

Sankosh

BUMTHANG

Chamka Chu

Gyetsa

Bumthang

TONGSA

Tongsa

Tongsa Chu

Bumthang

Shemgang

SHEMGANG

Manas

LHUNTSI

Lhuntsi

Kuru Chu

Tashi
Yangtsi

Kulong Chu

MONGAR

Mongar

Manas

TASHIGANG

Tashigang

Chu

PEMA
GATSEL

Pema Gatsel

Dechheling

Nanglam

SAMDRUP
JONKHAR

Deothang

Samdrup
Jonkhar

Paved roads
Unpaved roads
District boundaries
International boundaries

40 Km
20 Mi

20
10
0
0

● National capital
☆ District capitals
○ Other towns
• Selected villages
✦ Airport

Artisans painting the exterior of a monastery

MINI-FACTS AT A GLANCE

GENERAL INFORMATION

Official Name: Druk-Yul (Kingdom of Bhutan)

Capital: Thimphu

Official Language: Dzongkha, a Tibetan dialect

Government: Bhutan is a constitutional monarchy with a king and a National Assembly. There are about 150 members in the Assembly. The legislature consists of 100 representatives elected for 3-year terms. A 9-member Royal Advisory Council, established in 1965, is always in session to advise the king and monitor the National Assembly.
In the judicial system, the High Court has six judges. District courts have judges appointed from among government workers. The country is divided into 17 districts. There are no political parties.
Bhutan became a member of the United Nations in 1971.

Religion: Buddhism is predominant. The state religion is the Drukpa subsect of Kagyupa. In the south, the Hindus are in the majority.

Flag: The flag is divided diagonally with yellow on the left and orange on the right. A white dragon is in the center.

Money: The basic unit is the ngultrum. In 1988, 15.06 ngultrums were equal to one U.S. dollar.

Weights and Measures: Bhutan uses the metric system.

Population: 1,532,000 (1988 estimate); 5 percent urban, 95 percent rural

Cities:
Thimphu 23,000
Phuntsholing 18,000
(Population figures based on 1988 estimates.)

113

GEOGRAPHY

Highest point: Kula Kangri, 24,783 ft. (7,554 m) above sea level

Lowest point: 150 ft. (46 m) above sea level

Mountains: Bhutan is a rugged, mountainous country. The landscape consists of a succession of lofty and rugged mountains. The Black Mountain range almost divides the country in half between east and west. Towering peaks reach a height of 24,000 ft. (7,315 m).

Rivers: Rivers run from north to south and form fertile valleys. A series of parallel streams intersect the country, beginning with the Sankosh River and its tributary, the Pho Chu. Farther west are the Paro Chu and Wong Chu, which join to form the Raidak before it flows through the Sinchu La Pass into India. Still farther west are the Torsa and the Jaldhaka rivers, which rise in the Chumbi valley and in Sikkim, respectively.

Climate: Climate changes with elevation, slope, and exposure. Three climatic regions can be distinguished. A little above sea level in the valleys and the Duars plain, the climate is humid and subtropical, with heavy rainfall. Between 5,000 and 15,000 ft. (1,524 and 4,573 m) the winters are cool and the summers are warm (often hot) and rainy, with excessive precipitation on the southern slopes. The northern, and highest, region along the Himalayas contains snow-covered peaks. The high valleys from 12,000 to 18,000 ft. (3,657 to 5,486 m) are rather dry areas used for grazing cattle and yaks in the summer.

Greatest Distances: North to south: 110 mi. (177 km)
East to west: 200 mi. (322 km)

Area: 17,950 sq. mi. (46,500 km²)

NATURE

Trees: Thick forests grow on the sun-drenched southern slopes of the mountains. Oak and birch predominate. Most of the areas at the foot of the mountains are covered with dense vegetation. Sal, magnolia, and rhododendron trees intermingle with tangled undergrowth. The southern part bordering India is mostly covered with savanna and bamboo jungle.

Animals: Elephants, bears, leopards, tigers, deer, and other wild animals inhabit the areas at the foot of the mountains. In the northern national parks, snow leopards, musk deer, and black bears live. In the southern national parks, tigers, elephants, and rhinoceroses live. Bhutan is home to twenty endangered species. Conservation groups are developing programs of education. Leeches are a major source of annoyance to man and beast.

EVERYDAY LIFE

Food: The ordinary villager relies on a diet of rice, potato, vegetables, and some chilis. A meat soup with herbs and meat curry with rice and potatoes spiced with chili pepper are common. Yak meat is eaten fresh, dried, or powdered for bouillon. Pork, chicken, eggs, and beef are other less common options. Orchards add a variety of fruit to Bhutanese meals.

Butter tea and a fermented drink called *chang* are popular.

Housing: Compact villages along the Indian border house most of Bhutan's Hindus. Houses are generally rectangular, made of mud blocks and stones. They are built on high ground for protection against snakes, wild animals, and floods. In the small villages of the mid-Himalayan valleys, people live in houses of oblong stone blocks that have pine-shingle roofs. In the high, northern mountain valleys people live in small villages protected by stone walls.

Holidays

> Beginning or end of February, New Year's
> August 8, Independence Day
> December 17, National holiday

Culture: Bhutan is famous for its beautiful temples, wall paintings, wood carvings, and metalwork on religious themes.

Hand looming of textiles is done in almost every home. Bamboo and basket weaving are popular crafts.

The Bhutanese enjoy singing, dancing, and festivals. Songs are often accompanied by musical instruments such as the flute, the drum, and a seven-stringed instrument called the *dramnyen*.

Sports and Recreation: The national sport of Bhutan is archery. Soccer, basketball, volleyball, tennis, badminton, table tennis, darts, shot put, and wrestling are popular also.

Communication: Bhutan has a comprehensive postal system and stamp collectors enjoy the varied and unique stamps that Bhutan has issued. There are about 300 mi. (483 km) of telephone lines. Wireless connects all main administrative centers. Communication has been improving since the 1960s. A radio service broadcasts in 3 regional languages, plus English, to a wide audience.

The government publishes a weekly bulletin and a quarterly magazine in several languages.

Transportation: There are no railroads, and travel has been primitive. Druk-Air, the national airline, now offers air service between Paro (near Thimphu) and both Calcutta, India, and Dhaka, Bangladesh. Flights to New Delhi are pending. Fairly good mountain roads connect Bhutan with India. Within most of the country, however, travel is by foot or pack animal. About 1,375 mi. (2,293 km) of roads have been constructed. The highway from the western border of India to Thimphu was completed in 1962. A 300-mi. (483-km) road links Paro with Tashigang, and a 100-mi. (161-km) road from the Assam border to Tashigang was opened in 1965.

Schools: Only 18 percent of the adult population is literate. In 1984 less than 45,000 students between the ages of 7 and 11 attended school; 3,608 students between 12 and 16 attended secondary school; and less than 2,500 students are enrolled in vocational training or teacher-training schools. English is taught, but Dzongkha, the official language, is required. Specialized education is provided for technical and teacher training; there are also monastic schools, art schools, and a business-skills course.

Health: Special food-handling methods are essential. Only 8 percent of the population has access to safe water. Gastrointestinal diseases are common and the most common cause of death—especially in young children. Influenza, pneumonia, parasites, skin diseases, tuberculosis, malaria, and goiter also are prevalent.

Life expectancy is 47 years. Medical equipment and professionals are in short supply. There is only one general hospital; but there are 19 specialized hospitals, 37 dispensaries, and 50 basic health units.

ECONOMY AND INDUSTRY

Principal Products:
Agriculture: barley, fruit, rice, vegetables
Handicrafts and industries: blankets, leatherwork, pottery, preserved fruit, textiles
Mining: coal

IMPORTANT DATES

2000 B.C.—From artifacts discovered, Bhutan was probably inhabited by a Stone Age culture

A.D. 850—Guru Padma Sambhava, a Buddhist monk from India, brought his faith to both Bhutan and Tibet

8th century—Tantric Buddhism is introduced

12th century—Gyalwa Llhanangpa, a lama, establishes a sect that applies the *dzong* system to Bhutan; Phajo-Drukgom-Shigpo brings the *Drukpa,* or Red Hat, sect to Tibet

Early 1500s—Descendants of early invaders control Bhutan; Thangthong Gyalpo builds iron chain suspension bridges

1600s—Bhutan becomes a separate state; a Tibitan lama takes charge; Ngawang Namgyal unifies Bhutan under one government and one religion and repels invasions by outsiders

17th century—Drukpa sect becomes dominant; Doopgein Skeptoon comes to power

1768—Sonam Lhendup, called Shidar, becomes prime minister and puts down the power of the clergy

1774—Treaty gives British East India Company access to Bhutan to cut lumber, opening the door for British trade missions and intelligence gathering

1864—Anglo-Bhutanese War

1865—Treaty of Sinchula ends Anglo-Bhutanese War; Britain gains control of Bhutan

1869—Civil war

1877—Civil war

1880—Civil war

1885—Civil war

1907—Ugyen Wangchuck makes himself first king and gives Bhutan its first effective central government

1910—Treaty of Punakha; British Indian government takes control of Bhutan

1926—Jigme Wangchuck becomes king

1949—Indo-Bhutanese friendship treaty, used to guide Bhutan in external relations

1952—Jigme Dorji Wangchuck becomes king; eventually brings Bhutan into many international organizations, including the United Nations

1959—China claims part of the country

1960s—Bhutan undertakes modernization, abolishes slavery and caste system, emancipates women, and institutes land reform

1972—Jigme Dorji Wangchuck dies; is succeeded by his son Jigme Singye Wangchuck in 1974

1986—Bhutan forges closer relationship with China

1987-91—Five-year plan to develop badly needed skills for trade and industry

IMPORTANT PEOPLE

Aji Kesang Dorji, wife of Jigme Dorji

Jigme Palden Dorji (-1964), became prime minister in 1957; regent in 1963; assassinated in 1964

Kazi Ugyen Dorji, trusted supporter of King Ugyen Wangchuck; became chief chamberlain in 1908

Lhendup Dorji, acting prime minister during the reign of King Jigme Dorji Wangchuck

Tashi Dorji, sister of Queen Aji Kesang Dorji

Siddhartha Gautama (c. 563-c. 483 B.C.), founder of Buddhism

Gushi Khan, Mongol leader; attempted to invade Bhutan in the 17th century

Sonam Lhendup, prime minister in 1768; called Shidar

Gyalwa Llhanangpa, lama forced out of Tibet into Bhutan in 12th century

Ngawang Namgyal (-1651), united Bhutan against the Drukpas in 1616; unified the country under one government and one religion

Phajo-Drukgom-Shigpo, lama; brought Drukpas sect to Bhutan

Guru Padma Sambhava (8th century A.D.), Buddhist monk from India who came to Bhutan; called "Precious Teacher"; known as Second Buddha

Doopgein Skeptoon, 17th century monk; builder of forts, provided code of law including provisions for protection of peasants

Jigme Wangchuck (-1952), king from 1926 to 1952

Jigme Dorji Wangchuck (1929-1972), king from 1952 to 1972; developed modernization plans; worked to preserve cultural heritage of Bhutan; turned National Assembly into popular legislature; introduced cabinet system of government

Jigme Singye Wangchuck, became king in 1974

Namgyal Wangchuck, half-brother of King Jigme Dorji Wangchuck

Ugyen Wangchuck (-1926), became first king in 1907 and served until 1926; knight commander of Indian empire

A portable shrine on sale at a Sunday market

INDEX

Page numbers that appear in boldface type indicate illustrations

administrative system, 36
Africa, 45
agriculture, 38, 49, **49**, 50, **50**, 51, **51**, 52, 53, 54, 61, 67, 106, 108, 116
air travel and airplanes, 17, 58, **58**, 62, 99
Anglo-Bhutanese War, 28, 117
animal husbandry, 38, 49, 52
animals, **9**, 12, 14, 15, 21, 45, 49, **50**, 52, 53, **53**, 63, 76, 77, **77**, 82, 85, 86, 90, 115
annexation, 28
appearance of people, 80
archaeology, 20
archery, 96, 97, **97**, 98
architecture, **5**, 93
area, 114
aristocrats, 22
army, 9, 40, 41, 43, 70, 74
art, **18**, 19, 73, 93, **93**, 94, **94**, 95, **95**, 98, **112**
Asia, 7, 8, 11, 13, 23, 38
Assam Duars, 28
Assam, India, 20, 28, 88
assassination, 39, 40, 41, 42, 44, 46, 90
automobiles, 14
bamboo, 15, 23, 85, 87, 96, 97, 106
Bank of Bhutan, 60
banking, 60
barter (trade), 37, 51, 60, 108
Bell, C.A., 32
Bengal Duars, 28
Bengal, India, 27, 28, 88
Bhotes (people from Tibet), 79, 80, **80**, 85, 88
Bhutan, derivation of name, 7
Bhutanese, **5**, 7-9, **10**, 20, 26-30, 32, 34, 35, 38, 39, 43, 44, 46-48, **54**, 56, 61-63, 70, 73, 79, 80, 84, **84**, 89, 90, 92, 93, 95, 98
"Black Hat" dancer, 90
Black Mountain range, 15
bodhisattva, 65
Bogle, George, 27
Bon religion, 20, 21, 67, 85, 93
border disputes, 28, 29
Border Roads Organization, 61

borders, 7, 17, 33, 40-43, 61, 79, 87, 108
boundary markers, 20
bridges, 8, 22, 23, **23**, 62, 106
British, 26-29, **29**, 30-35, 44, 93
Buddha, 21, **66**, 67, 93, 103
Buddhism and Buddhists, 7-9, 20-22, 24, **45**, 57, 63, 65, 67, 69, 71, 82, 87, 90, 103, 113, 116, 118
Bumthang, 107
business, 17
Cabinet and cabinet system, 37, 69
Calcutta, India, 17, 58
capital of Bhutan, 17, 19, 40, 75, 103, 113. *See also* Thimphu
capital punishment, 37
caste system, 87, 88, 118
cattle, 14, 52, 76, 85, 107
caves, 21
central authority, 23, 25
central Bhutan, 59, 80, 88, 106
central council, 24. *See also* lenchen
Central Monk Body, 71
cereal crops, 51
ceremonies, religious, 34, 65, 67, 71
chang (a drink), 84
chanting, **65**
charters, 69
chief chamberlain, 34
children, **4**, **16**, 19, **36**, 72, 74, **74**, 75, **78**, **80**, 83, 87, **89**, **97**, **109**
Chimakothi, 107
China, 7, 8, 13, 33, 38, 117, 118
Chinese, 7, 33, 38, 80
Chomolhari, Mount, 99
chortens (memorials), **66**, 67, 103
Chukha hydroelectric project, 59, 107
cities, major, 113
civil authority, 24
civil rights, 37
civil war, 25, 29, **29**, 117
clergy, 67, 72
climate, 13, 15, 17, 52, 75, 79, 87, 104, 107, 114
clothing (dress), **4**, **80**, 81, **81**, 85-

87, 90, 96, 104
coal, 56, 58, 116
code of values, 44
college, 73, 75
Colombo Plan, 38
commerce, 27
communal projects, 52
communication, 17, 20, 30, 33, 38, 39, 59, 60, 115
conscription (military service), 70
conservation, 9, 38, 46, 54, 55, 63, 76, 77
conservatives, 48, 53
constitutional monarchy, 68, 113
Cooch Behar, 25, 26, 29
coronation ceremony, **45**
costumes, 90, **91**
cottage (home) industries, 55
Council, king's, 32
courts, 69
crafts, 93, 95, **95**, 96, **96**, 98, 104, 116
crops, 8, 50-52, 104
crown prince, 42, 44
cultivation, 15, 52
cultural groups, 79, 99
culture, 8, 9, 20, 31, 36, 38, 39, 46, 56, 79, 98, 99, 108, 115
customs, 19, 83, 85
"Dakpas" (people in eastern Bhutan), 85
Dalai Lama (a holy man), 23, 46
dancing, 36, 67, 89, 90-92, **92**, 97, 98, **98**
dates, important, 116-118
Davis, Lieutenant Samuel, 27, 93
defense, 9, 36, 61
development projects, 39, 47-51, 53, 55, 60-62, 68-70, 72, 75, 87, 107, 108
diet (food), 51, 84
disease, 27, 52, 75, 76, 107
distances, greatest, 114
District Monk Body, 71
Don't Fall Off the Mountain, 43
Dorji, Aji Kesang, 40, 118
Dorji family, 33, 34, 39, 41, 42, 44, 45, 107

Dorji, Jigme Palden, 39, 40, **40**, 41, 42, 44, 118
Dorji, Kazi Ugyen, 33, 34, 118
Dorji, Lhendup, 42, 43, 46, 118
Dorji, Tashi, 43, 44, 46, 118
Dragon Kings, 31, 32, **32**, 33-35, **35**, 36, **36**, 37-40, **40**, 41-45, **45**, 46
"Dragon people," 79, 80, **80**, 81, **81**, 82, **82**, 83, 84, **84**, 85, 86, **86**, 87, 88, **88**, 89, **89**, 90, **91**, 92, **92**, 98
dramnyen, (musical instrument), 89, **89**
dress (clothing), **4**, **80**, 81, **81**, 85-87, 96
drugs, 57
Druk-Air, 58, **58**
druk desi (prime minister), 24
druk gyalpo (king), 31, 67
Drukpas (Red Hat sect of Buddhism), 22, **22**, 23, 38, 63, 71, 113, 117
Druk-yal ("Land of the Thunder Dragon"), 7. *See also* name, official
Drum Dance of Dramitse, 90
dry territory, 14
Duars (hill passes), 28, 29, 32
Duars plain, 15
dzong, 22, 23, 33, **64**, **71**, 82, 92, 93, **93**, **94**, 96, 100, **100**, 103, 104, **105**, 106, **106**, 107
Dzongkha language, 17, 73, 104, 113
Dzongkha Language and Religious University, 104
dzongpons (district chiefs), 24
earthquakes, 13, 19
eastern Bhutan, 50, 54, 106, 107
East India Company, 26, **26**, 27, 117
economic development, 38
economy, 26, 37, 49, 52, 54, 61, 63, 70, 71, 88, 108, 116
education, 9, 32, 33, 36, 39, 46, 48, 63, 72, 73-75, **74**, 77, 107
elective office, 25
electricity, 58, 59
elephants, 15, 33, 76, 77, 90

elevation, 12, 52, 103
employment, 49, 55
energy, 58, 59
England and English, 17, 37, 59, 73, 84
environment, 57
equator, 11, 12
erosion, 47, 50, 55
everyday life, 115
executive branch of government, 37
exports, 35, 49, 51, 55, 56
external affairs, 32, 33, 38
farmers and farming, **10**, **15**, 38, 49, **49**, 50, **50**, 51, **51**, 52, 53, **53**, **54**, 72, 81-83, 88
festivals, 89, 90, 92, **92**, **98**, 103
fires, 19, 76, 77, 83
five-year plan, 38, 118
flags, 7, **64**, 65, 113
flat land, 8, 11, 79
floods, 23, 61
flowers, 14
food, 47, 49, 51, 52, 55, 76, 82-84, **84**, 88, 115
foreign relations, 25, 33, 36, 39, 56, 57, 73, 75, 96
forests, 7, 12, 15, 47, 50, 54, 55, 76, 95
forest usage, 38, 50, 54, 55
fortresses and forts, 9, 22, 25, 26, 100, 104, 106
"four noble truths," 63, 65
freedom of speech, 37
French, 37
frontiers, 28, 33
fruit, 49, 52, 56, 84, 104
fuel, 58, 59
Gautama, Siddhartha, 20, 118
Gelugpas (Yellow Hat sect of Buddhism), 23, 46
geography, 114
geology and geologists, 11-13, 17
ghosts, 28
go (men's robe), 81, **81**
gods, 28
gongzim (chief chamberlain), 34
gorges, 17
government, 22, 23, 30, 33, 35, 37, 40, 52-58, 62, 63, 67-76, 87,

104, 113
governors, 24, 25, 29, 30, 32, 44, 106. *See also* penlops
grains, 51, 84, 88, 89
grants, 32
gross national happiness, 63-77, 108
gross national product, 49, 54, 55, 63
Gushi Khan, 118
Gyalpo, Thangthong, 22, 23, 117. *See also* master engineer
Ha Dzong, 107, **107**
Ha territory, 34
Handicraft Emporium, 104
harvest, 96
Hastings, Warren, 26, 27, **27**
head abbot, 23, 46, 71. *See also* je khempo
health, 75, 76, 116
hereditary monarch, 30, 31, 34
"The Hidden Holy Land," 8, 19, 21
High Court, 69, 113
high lamas (holy men), 71, 104
highest point, 114
highways, 9
hills, 8, 15, 28, 32, 49, **50**, 54, 55, 61, 85
Himalayan kingdom, 35
Himalayan mountains, 7, 8, 11, 13, 22, 47, 96, 99
Hindi and Hindu, 37, 67, 71, 87, 88, 113
historical objects, **18**
holidays, 115
holy men, **66**, 67. *See also* Dalai Lama and high lamas
holy sites, 57, 100
horses, 9, 53
hospitals, 38, 75
hotels, 57, **57**, 58, **88**
households, 50, 58, 68
houses and housing, 47, **49**, 52, **64**, 82, **82**, 83, 85, 87, 88, 98, 104, 106, 115
humidity, 15
hunting, 76
hydroelectric power, 9, 17, 59
hygiene, 76
immigrants and immigration,

41, 86, 87

imports, 35, 39, 58

income, 47, 54, 55, 59

independence, 9, 23, 27, 33, 36, 47, 80

India, 7, 8, 11, 13, 15, 17, 20, 28, 29, 32, 33, 35, 36, 41, 42, 46, 56, 58-63, 73, 79, 87, 88, 107, 108

Indians 13, 17, 20, 28, 30, 34, 87, 88, 107

Indo-Bhutanese Friendship Treaty, 35, 36, 117

Indo-Mongoloid people, 79, 85, 86

industry, 38, 47, 54-56, 60, 107, 116

innovator, 36

integration, 87

intermarriage, 87

internal affairs, 35

international relations, 70

invaders and invasion, 8, 23, 80

iron, 23, 76, 83

irrigation, 50, 52, 53

isolation, 9, 17, 38, 39, 48, 52, 61, 108

je khempo, 23, 103. *See also* head abbot

jobs, 48, 74

judges, 69

judicial system, 37, 69, 113

jungle, 15

Kagyupa (a religious sect), 63

kapok tree, **77**

Khan, Gushi, 23

kidnapping, 28

Kingdom of the Thunder Dragon, 9

kings, 9, 20, 23, 26, 30-32, **32**, 33-35, **35**, 36, **36**, 37-46, **40**, **45**, **46**, 67-70, 90, 93, 98, 103, 104, 106, 113, 117

kira (clothing), 81

knight commander of the Indian Empire, 30

Kula Kangri (highest point), 114

Kyichu Lakhang, 100

Kyichu river, 23

lamas (holy men), 22, **22**, 30, 37,

38, 67, 71, 85, 90. *See also* Dalai Lama and high lamas

land, 13, 28, 32, 37, 47, 49-51, 53, 54, 61, 72, 79, 85

"Land of the Hidden Treasures," 21

land reform, 37, 118

landslides, 55, 61, **61**

language, 17, 23, 36, 37, 59, 60, 73, 85, 87, 88, 104, 113

latitude, 12

laws, 9, 24, 25, 69

Laya, **6**

leaders and leadership, 29, 33, 34, 39, 47, 69, 80. *See also* kings

legends, 20, 33

legislation, 37

legislature, 37, 68

lenchen (central council), 24

Lhasa, Tibet, 23, 30

Lhendup, Sonam, 25, 117, 118. *See also* Shidar

lifespan, 75, 116

life-styles, 79

Llhanangpa, Gyalwa, 22, 117, 118

local rule and rulers, 20, 23, 69, 108

Lodoi Tsokde (Royal Advisory Council), 69

lonchen (prime minister), 39

London, England, 98

lowest point, 114

machinery, 47, 54

MacLaine, Shirley, 43

Maharaja (king), 32

Maharajaship, 30

Mahayana Buddhism, 63, 65

Manas River, 107

Manas Tiger Reserve, 77

mandalas (maps of the universe), 99, **99**

Mangde River, 106

manips (storytellers), 89

mantras (sacred syllables), **64**, 65

manufacturing, 55, 108

maps of Bhutan:
   political map, **111**
   regional map, **1**
   topography, **2**

maps of the universe, 99, **99**. *See also* mandalas

marketplaces, **84**, 107, **119**

marriage, 87

masks, 90, **91**

master engineer, 22. *See also* Gyalpo, Thangthong

meat, 49, 83, 84, 88

medicine, 27, 48, 49, 76

meditation, 21, 65, 99

megaliths (stone pillars), 20

Memorial Chorten, **66**, 66

men, 80, 81, **81**, 82, **82**, 83, **84**, 86, 87, 89, **97**

milk, 49, 52, 84

minerals, 12, 32, 56, 62, 95

mining, 23, 32, 55, 56, 116

ministry of home affairs, 70

missions, trade, 27-30

mistress, 40-42, 44-46

Mo Chu river, 104

modern ways and modernization, 31, 36, 38, 39, 46, 48, 52, 108, 118

modernists, 39, 40

monarchy, 30, 31, 37, 67, 87, 113. *See also* hereditary monarch

monasteries, **5**, 21, **21**, 22, 23, 33, 50, 71, 72, **72**, 73, 100, **100**, **112**

monastic government, 71

money, 37, 60, 72, 77, 113

Mongolian, 23, 80

Monk Body, 103

monks, 7, 20, 25, **45**, 50, **65**, 67-72, **72**, 73, 89, 90

moon rocks, 46, 99

mountains, **6**, 7-9, 11, 13, 14, **14**, 15, 17, 22, 47, 53, 59, 61, **61**, 62, **62**, 81, 83, 114

mud slides, 48, 61

mules, **9**, 62

music, 98

musical instruments, 89

musicians, 89, **89**

Museum, National, **18**, 19, 36

mutineers, **29**

myths, 20

Nairobi, Kenya, 45

name, official, 113. *See also* Druk-yal

Namgyal, Ngawang, 23, 24, **24**, 25, 69, 104, 117, 118

nation, 30, 35, 43, 46, 48, 49, 56, 63, 79, 99, 107, 108

National Assembly, 37, 68, 69, 103, 113. *See also* Tshogdu

National Museum, 100

national religion, 38

national unity, 29

natural resources, 47, 60, 63, 77

nature, 114, 115

neighboring countries and neighbors, 9, 17, 23, 26, 29, 35, 52, 55, 57, 58, 79, 83, 86, 88

Nepal, 25, 26, 43, 58, 86, 87

Nepalese, 37, 79, 86, **86**, 87, 88

"Nepalese problem," 87

Nepali (language of Nepal), 37, 87

New Year, 90, 98, 100

ngultrums (currency), 60

nirvana (nonexistence), 65

"noble eightfold path," 65

northern Bhutan, 13, 14, **14**, 15, 27, 50, 52, **53**, 55, 59, 76, 87

nutrition, 76

Olympic Games, 96

open trade, 29

"Operation Tiger," 77

"oral history," 19

orchards, 52, 107

overgrazing, 53

Pacific Coast, 11

paintings, **18**, 36, **66**, 92, **93**, 94, **94**, 95, **95**, 103

"Paradise of the South," 79

parks, 76

Paro, 17, 29, 30, 36, 58, **101**, 108

Paro Chu river, **16**, 99

Paro Chu river valley, **101**

Paro Dzong, 100, **100**

Paro Hotel, **57**

Paro National Museum, **18**, 19. *See also* National Museum

Paro valley, **15**, **49**, 99

peace, 34

peace treaty of 1774, 26, 27

peaks, mountain, 13, 14, **14**

peasants, 25

Penden cement factory, 56, 58
penlops, 24. *See also* governors
people, **4**, **5**, **9**, **16**, 17, **18**, 19, **22**,
    25, 37, 46-48, **48**, 49, **50**, **51**, **53**,
    58, 61, **61**, 62, **62**, 63, **64**, **65**, 68,
    70, **72**, 75, 76, 77, 79, 83, **84**, 85,
    86, **86**, 88, **88**, **89**, **91**, 92, **92**, 99,
    101, 108
people, important, list of, 118
peppers, 51, 82, **82**, 83
perfume, 76
persecution, 23, 90
Phajo-Drukgom-Shigpo, 22,
    117, 118
Pho Chu river, 104
Phuntsholing, **108**, 113
plains, 7
plants, 52, 84
plate tectonics, 11
plateaus, 12, 13
poachers, 77
Polaroid camera, 46
political parties, 70, 113
political system, 36
politics, 20, 39, 48
population, 9, 15, 17, 32, 47, 49,
    51, 53, 55, 76, 79, 85, 87, 113
porters, 14
Portuguese, 83
postal system, 59
power, hydroelectric, 9, 17, 38,
    56, 58, 59
power, political or religious, 24,
    25, 30, 34, 37, 39, 41, 42, 44,
    65, 67, 68, 70, 71, 99
prayer, 41, 65, **65**
prayer wheels, **18**, **64**, 65, 103
"Precious Teacher," 21. *See also*
    Rimpoche, Guru and
    Sambhava, Padma
pre-history, 20
primary schools, 73, 74, **74**
prime minister, 24, 25, 27, 28,
    30, 39, 41, 42. *See also* druk
    desi
prince of Wales, 44
products, principal, 116
pulses (vegetables), 51
Punakha, **16**, **71**, 104, 106
Punakha, Treaty of, 32, 117

Punakha Dzong, **93**, 104
Punakha valley, **104**
queen, 34, 39, 42-44
radio, 17, 59, 77
radioactive elements, 12
railways, 62
rain and rainfall, 15, 50, 51, 99
raja (ruler), 26
recreation, 115
Red Hat sect of Buddhism, 22,
    22, 63, 117. *See also* Drukpas
reformers, 40
reforms, 36, 37
refugees, 8, 38, 80
regent, 39
reincarnation, 24, 25, 37, 65, 90
relics, 23, **66**
religion, 20-23, 38, 46, 63, **64**, 65,
    65, **66**, 67, 73, 85, 86, 88, 90, 92,
    104, 113
religious ceremonies, 34, 65, 67,
    71, 90, **91**, 92, **92**
religious council, 38
religious institutions, 24
religious sects, 22, 23. *See also*
    Gelugpas and Drukpas
resources, 9, 46, 47, 54. *See also*
    natural resources
revolt, 28
rice, 15, 51, **51**, 83, 85, 88, 99, 104
Rimpoche, Guru, 21, 23, 90, 92.
    See also "Precious Teacher"
    and Sambhava, Padma
rituals, 20, 21, 104
rivers, 9, 12, 15, **16**, 17, 23, 47,
    59, 61, 99, 100, 103, 104, 106,
    107, 114
roads, **16**, 17, 32, 38, 39, 52, 54,
    58, 61, **61**, 62
rocks, 12, 13, 46, 65, **82**, 99
rope bridges, **23**
Royal Advisory Council, 44, 69.
    See also Lodoi Tsokde
royal family, 22. *See also*
    Wangchuck family
Royal Society for the Protection
    of Nature, 77
rule and rulers, 20, 23, 25, 26,
    28, 34, 106, 108
rupees, 28, 29, 35, 60

Russians, 26
Sakteng valley, 85
Sambhava, Guru Padma, 20, 21, **21**, 38, 100, 107, 116, 118. *See also* Rimpoche, Guru and "Precious Teacher"
Sangladip, an Indian prince, 20
sanitation, 76
Sankosh River, 106
Saunders, Dr. Robert, 27
scarf, sacred, 46
schools, 17, 22, 32, 36, 38, 62, 71, 73, 85, 87, 116
scientists, 12, 13, 99
sea level, 12, 13, 15
seal of Bhutan, 7, **8**
seas, 12, 13
secondary schools, 73, 74, **74**, 87
secret ballot, 37
Secretariat Building, 103, **103**. *See also* Tashichhodzong
sects, religious, 22, 23, 63. *See also* Gelugpas and Drukpas
secular matters, 38
secular power, 34
Security Council, United Nations, 38
semitropical land, 7
serfdom (slavery), 37
settlements, 99, 107
shabdrung (local ruler), 23-25, 30, 69
Shidar, 25, 117. *See also* Lhendup, Sonan
shopping, **84**, 104
shrines, 82, 83, **119**
Sikkim, 29, 35
Simtokha Dzong, 104
Sinchula, Treaty of, 29
singing and songs, 36, 89, 97
Skeptoon, Doopgein, 25, 117, 118
slate, 56, 106
slavery, 37, 118. *See also* serfdom
snow, 14, **14**, 23, 53, 61, 62
snow leopards, 76, **77**
soil, 48, 85
South America, 83
southeastern Bhutan, 79
southern Bhutan, 15, 34, 49, 50-

54, 67, 71, 76, 79, 86-88, 107, 108
southwestern Bhutan, **15**
speech, freedom of, 37
spices, 49
spirits, 24, 25, 43, 67, 90, 97
sports, 96, 97, **97**, 98, 115. *See also* recreation
spring, 62, 68
stamp collecting, 60
Stone Age, 20, 116
stones, 12, 20, 85
stories of Bhutan, 19, 21, 89
storms, 8, 47
storytellers, 89. *See also* manips
streams, 22, 83, 85
subtropical land, 15
succession, 37, 44. *See also* hereditary monarch
summer, 14, 15, 53, **53**, 103
Switzerland, 7, 41, 42
Taktsang Monastery, 21, **21**, 100
Tangchu river, 106
Tashichhodzong, 103, **103**. *See also* Secretariat Building
Tashigang Dzong, 107
taxes, 54, 60, 70-72
tea, 28, 32, 55, 84, 88, **88**
teachers, 20, 21, 22, **22**, 73. *See also* lamas
temperate zone, 15
temples, **5**, 7, 21, 33, 67, 81, 93, 99, 100, 104, 106
termas (treasures), 21
terraces, 8, 49, **50**
territories and territory, 7, 8, 14, 17, 22, 26, 29, 33-36, 44, 53, 77
Tethys, an ancient sea, 12, 13
theocratic ruler, 23
Thimphu, capital of Bhutan, **66**, **102**, 103, 104, 108, 113. *See also* capital
Thimphu Dzong, 93
Thimphu Hospital, 75
throne, 37, **45**, 46, 103, 106
thunder, 7-9
Thunder Dragon, 7, 9
Tibet, 7, 8, 13, 14, 20, 22, 23, 25-27, 29, 30, 35, 38, 51, 79, 80, 89
Tibetan, 17, 23, 30, 33, 34, 37, 38,

40, 41, 46, 80, 82, 90, 113
Tibetan Autonomous Region of the Peoples Republic of China, 7
Tibetan plateaus, 13
"Tiger's Nest." 21, **21**, 100. *See also* Taktsang Monastery
timber, 9, 26, 32, 62, 82
Tongsa, 107
Tongsa Dzong, 106, **106**
Tongsa ponlop (governor of Tongsa), 44
Tongsa territory, 29, 44
tourism and tourists, 56, 57, 58, **88**, 96, 99, 104
towns, 13, 23, 41, 57, 82, 104, 106, 108
trade, 8, 27, 29, 32, 38, 40, 60
trade missions, 27-30
trade routes, 8, 9, 107
traders, **62**
traditions, 19, 38-40, 48
trails, 17, 59, 62
transportation, **9**, 17, 20, 38, 40, 53, 58, 59, 61, 62, **101**, 116
travel, 17, 75, 88
tribal groups, 79, 85, 86
treason, 37
treasures, 21. *See also* termas
treaties, 26-29, 32, 33, 35, 36, 117
Treaty of Punakha, 32, 117
Treaty of Sinchula, 29, 117
trees, 12, 14, 54, 55, **77**, 82, 106, 114
Tshechu Festival, **92**
tsheri (clearing forests), 50
Tshogdu, 37, 68. *See also* National Assembly
Turner, Captain Samuel, 27
unexplored regions, 12
unification, 7, 23, 29, 67
United Nations, 9, 36, 38, 77, 108, 113, 117
United States, 38, 46, 85
unity, national, 29
Universal Postal Union, 38
valleys, **6**, 14, 15, **15**, 17, 23, 50, 52, **64**, 85, 89, 100, 103, 104, **104**, **105**, 107, **107**
vegetables, 49, 51, 52, 83, 84
vegetation, 15, 76, 85
veneer, 55
veterinary services, 53

veto power, 37
viceroy, 32
villages, 17, 50, 70, 74, 83, 96
voting, 37, 68
Wang Chu river, 103, 107
Wangchuck family, 39, 44, 45, 106. *See also* royal family
Wangchuck, King Jigme, 31, 34, 35, **35**, 36, 117, 118
Wangchuck, King Jigme Dorji, 31, 36, **36**, 37-39, **66**, 67, 68, 103, 106, 117, 118
Wangchuck, King Jigme Singye, 31, 45, **45**, 46, 63, 68, 106, 118
Wangchuck, Namgyal, 42, 118
Wangchuck, King Ugyen, 29, 30, 31, 32, **32**, 33, 34, 117, 118
Wangdiphodrang Dzong, 106
war, 25, 28, 35, 48, 98, 117
wastelands, 32
water, 13, 28, 50, 59, 76, 85, 86, 96
watershed, 15
weather, 8
weaving, 96, **96**
weights and measures, 113
welfare, 32, 37
West Virginia, 7
western Bhutan, 34, 59, 80, 106, 107
Western world, 33, 35, 41, 84, 93
White, John Claude, 30, 31
"Wild East," 85
"Wild West," 85
winter, 15, 53, 107
women, **36**, 37, **48**, **51**, **54**, **78**, 80, **80**, 81, 83-87, 89, 97, **109**, 118
Wong Chu river, 59
wood, 48, 54, 55, 58, 83, 85, 106
wood carvings, 95, **95**
work, 48, 81, 98. *See also* employment
World Bank, 60
World Wildlife Fund, 77
yak herder, **53**
yaks, 14, 53, **53**, 84, 86
Yangki, 40, 41, 42, 44, 46
Yellow Hat sect of Buddhism, 23, 46. *See also* Gelugpas
Yost, ambassador of United States, 38
zones, three, 13-15

About the Author:

Leila Merrell Foster is a lawyer, United Methodist minister, and clinical psychologist with degrees from Northwestern University and Garrett Evangelical Theological Seminary. She is the author of books and articles on a variety of subjects.

Dr. Foster's love of travel began early as she listened to her mother and older sister read aloud travel and adventure stories. As a youngster, she enjoyed the family trips through which she learned geography, geology, history, art, agriculture, and economics in a very pleasant manner.

When she traveled recently in Bhutan, she found this country to be one of great scenic beauty with an ancient culture. The great fortress-monasteries and the masked dancers she saw made her want to learn more of the history of this nation. She discovered a fascinating people who in a few generations have moved from an isolated barter economy to become a member of the United Nations seeking to develop resources wisely.

Better Homes and Gardens®

Beautiful
CROSS-STITCH

DESIGNS AND PROJECTS
INSPIRED BY THE WORLD AROUND YOU

Meredith® Books
Des Moines, Iowa

Beautiful CROSS-STITCH

Editor: Carol Field Dahlstrom
Writer: Susan M. Banker
Graphic Designer: Angie Haupert Hoogensen
Cross-Stitch Designer: Barbara Sestock
Copy Chief: Terri Fredrickson
Copy and Production Editor: Victoria Forlini
Editorial Operations Manager: Karen Schirm
Managers, Book Production: Pam Kvitne,
Marjorie J. Schenkelberg, Rick von Holdt
Contributing Copy Editor: Margaret Smith
Contributing Proofreaders: Chardel Blaine,
Jessica Kearney Heidgerken, Colleen Johnson
Photographers: Andy Lyons Cameraworks, Scott Little
Technical Illustrator: Chris Neubauer Graphics, Inc.
Editorial and Design Assistants: Kaye Chabot,
Mary Lee Gavin, Karen McFadden
Technical Assistant: Judy Bailey

Meredith® Books
Editor in Chief: Linda Raglan Cunningham
Design Director: Matt Strelecki
Executive Editor, Food and Crafts: Jennifer Dorland Darling

Publisher: James D. Blume
Executive Director, Marketing: Jeffrey Myers
Executive Director, New Business Development:
  Todd M. Davis
Executive Director, Sales: Ken Zagor
Director, Operations: George A. Susral
Director, Production: Douglas M. Johnston
Business Director: Jim Leonard

Vice President and General Manager: Douglas J. Guendel

Better Homes and Gardens® **Magazine**
Editor in Chief: Karol DeWulf Nickell

Meredith Publishing Group
President, Publishing Group: Stephen M. Lacy
Vice President-Publishing Director: Bob Mate

Meredith Corporation
Chairman and Chief Executive Officer: William T. Kerr

In Memoriam: E. T. Meredith III (1933-2003)

Cross-Stitch
A MASTERPIECE
OF STITCHES

Many times cross-stitchers tell us their fabric is their canvas and with tiny stitches they create their beautiful cross-stitch masterpieces. Like a painter, they find the inspirations for the themes that fill their fabric canvas in the world around them. Maybe it is a beautiful flower garden or landscape scene. Perhaps it is the view from a balcony in a far off land. The idea for a motif might be as simple as seeing the smile of a young child.

In this book of cross-stitch designs and projects, we have tried to capture many of the inspirations around you and translate them into beautiful motifs to stitch. You'll find designs influenced by nature, travel, children, other cultures, and more. We've also given you ideas for transforming your stitched pieces into items that you can use every day. You'll find lovely samplers to display on your wall, as well as tote bags, bookmarks, paperweights, baby bibs, tablecloths, and more. We know you'll enjoy this treasury of timeless designs as you create your own cross-stitch masterpieces.

Carol Field Dahlstrom

Cross-Stitch
CONTENTS

CHAPTER ONE • *Pages 8–35*
EARTH'S GARDENS

Capture the splendor of Mother Nature's flowers, vegetables, and fruits in beautiful cross-stitch.

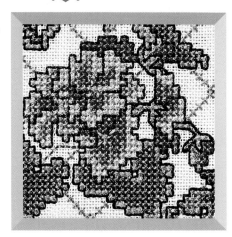

CHAPTER TWO • *Pages 36–57*
CUTE AS A BUTTON

Playful motifs stitched in bright colors, baby animals stitched in natural colors, and much more fill this chapter.

CHAPTER THREE • *Pages 58–95*
AROUND THE WORLD

Stitch inspiring designs influenced by Asian, Mexican, Russian, and Scandinavian cultures.

CHAPTER FOUR • *Pages 96–115*
BIRDS AND INSECTS

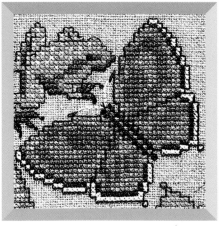

From ladybugs to dragonflies, geese to flamingos, this chapter invites you to stitch nature's most interesting neighbors.

CHAPTER FIVE • *Pages 116–133*
COUNTRY FAVORITES

Get out your needle and floss to stitch roosters, quaint buildings, baskets, and all that's country at heart.

CHAPTER SIX • *Pages 134–163*
THE GREAT OUTDOORS

Choose from an imaginative selection of designs to stitch for outdoor enthusiasts— from fishermen to cowgirls.

CHAPTER SEVEN • *Pages 164–193*
HOLIDAYS

Celebrate Valentine's Day, Easter, Halloween, Thanksgiving, and Christmas by stitching seasonal motifs.

CHAPTER EIGHT • *Pages 194–213*
BORDERS AND EMBELLISHMENTS

This chapter offers dozens of accent designs and borders to enhance your cross-stitch projects.

CHAPTER NINE • *Pages 214–221*
CROSS-STITCH BASICS

Ensure your cross-stitch success with tips, techniques, and specialty stitches from the pros.

HELPFUL GUIDES

HOW TO USE THIS BOOK • *Pages 6–7*

INDEX • *Pages 222–223*

SOURCES • *Page 224*

HOW TO USE
THIS BOOK

*H*undreds of wonderful cross-stitch designs and dozens of projects...where do you start?

There are so many options in this book to feed your love of cross-stitch that you may be a bit overwhelmed. Not to worry!

Each of the samplers (or plates) has a common theme. You can stitch the sampler as it is shown, stitch a part of it, or combine the motifs in any arrangement you wish.

Before you stitch, browse through the book to become familiar with the projects. Make note of the projects that you are eager to complete. If you prefer a different color scheme than any shown, change the embroidery floss colors to those you want.

You have permission to make photocopies (see *page 2*) of the charts and keys for your own use (to mark with changes, enlarge for ease of reading, or to make a project more portable). When you change floss colors or make other design alterations, record them on a photocopy to plan your stitching and to recall the changes in case you want to stitch the design the same way again.

PERSONALIZE
YOUR PROJECTS

As you look through the book, you'll see that some designs have few floss colors and will stitch up quickly. Other patterns use many colors and have considerable backstitching. Consider your stitching experience and time available when selecting a project.

Projects are easy to simplify. Change all the backstitching to one color, substitute one color for two or more colors when there are subtle differences, or eliminate portions of the design.

Each project includes a complete materials list to finish the project as shown in the photograph. A count of cross-stitch fabric other than that listed will alter the finished

size of your design. You also may want to alter the way an item is finished. Each project is accompanied by step-by-step stitching and finishing instructions.

If you've never cross-stitched before or could use a refresher, read the Basics Section on *pages 214–221*. These pages include the following information:
• how to get started
• how to stitch
• how to secure threads
• how to make specialty stitches
• how to choose and prepare materials
• how to press and clean
• how to frame
Once you master the basics, you can complete any project in this book!

FRAME THEM CREATIVELY

Take note of the interesting framing ideas used for some of the samplers. Extra touches make a world of difference in how your cross-stitch looks hanging on the wall. Such embellishments as paint, shells, unusual mats, feathers, and rope give you choices.

Before taking your stitched piece to a professional framer, clean and press it. If it is stitched on light-color fabric, have the framer mount it on white before framing. Otherwise, the mounting color will show through the threads and make the colors appear washed out.

It's time to enjoy this inspirational book of cross-stitch designs that has been lovingly put together lovingly by a team of cross-stitch enthusiasts—just like you!

When the stitching is complete and it's time to frame or finish your stitchery, select from dozens of projects and more than 100 additional finishing ideas designed to spark your imagination. There are thousands of possibilities!

As you look through the book, keep a list of finishing ideas that pique your interest. If you're a cross-stitcher at heart, you probably have a stitching wish list already started.

EARTH'S GARDENS

You'll find them along roadsides,
in your backyard, and growing
gracefully in unexpected places.
Mother Nature's gardens are
sprinkled all around. To capture
their beauty, this chapter helps
you pick a pretty bouquet of
designs to stitch.

Inspiration

EARTH'S BOUNTY

*N*atural gifts abound. Fruits, vegetables, and flowers make the world an even more beautiful place, and these treasures are wonderful inspirations for cross-stitch designs. Below is a sample of earth's bounty, so real looking that you can almost smell the ripe, plump strawberries and feel the glossy-smooth skin of the eggplant. Whether you stitch the entire plate or only portions of it, your work will reflect a love of nature.

EARTH'S BOUNTY

SAMPLER

MATERIALS

FABRIC
*14-inch square of 14-count
light oatmeal Aida*

FLOSS
*Cotton embroidery floss in colors
listed in the key, page 14*

SUPPLIES
*Embroidery hoop; needle
Mats and frame*

INSTRUCTIONS

Tape or zigzag stitch the fabric edges. Find the center of the chart and the center of the fabric; begin stitching there. Use two plies of floss to work cross-stitches over one square of fabric. Work the remaining stitches using the plies indicated in the key.

Press the stitchery from the back. Mat and frame as desired.

continued on page 14

EARTH'S BOUNTY

ANCHOR		DMC	
CROSS-STITCH (2X)			
876	⊞	163	Celadon green
119	★	333	Deep periwinkle
118	◎	340	Dark periwinkle
1025	◉	347	Salmon
351	◀	400	Mahogany
879	◆	501	Dark blue-green
204	‖	563	Seafoam
874	◣	676	Light old gold
890	⊕	680	Dark old gold
256	◇	704	Chartreuse
326	◈	720	Bittersweet
295	−	726	True topaz
307	✳	728	Dark topaz
358	▶	801	Coffee brown
906	♥	829	Bronze
035	☆	892	Carnation
340	✖	919	Dark copper
339	∼	920	Medium copper
274	▢	928	Slate green
905	▲	3021	Brown gray
263	✚	3051	Gray-green
036	╱	3326	Light rose
267	✖	3346	Hunter green
031	⊞	3706	Watermelon
118	▤	3746	Darkest periwinkle
1015	▦	3777	Terra-cotta
279	∟	3819	Moss green
1049	‖	3826	Dark golden brown
363	∧	3827	Pale golden brown
308	◰	3852	Straw
1003	♡	3853	Autumn gold
002	•	3865	Winter white

ANCHOR	DMC	
BACKSTITCH (1X)		
119	333	Deep periwinkle – words, blueberries
1025	347	Salmon – petunia
683	500	Deep blue-green – leaves
256	704	Chartreuse – strawberry stems
906	829	Bronze – tool straps, sunflower
339	920	Medium copper – nasturtium
844	3012	Khaki – cherry, strawberry, flower stems
267	3346	Hunter green – pepper stem

ANCHOR	DMC	
BACKSTITCH (1X)		
279	3819	Moss green – leaf veins
1049	3826	Dark golden brown – sunflower
236	3799	Charcoal – all other stitches
STRAIGHT STITCH (2X)		
256	704	Chartreuse – strawberry stems
295	726	True topaz – strawberry detail
844	3012	Khaki – cherry stems
LAZY DAISY STITCH (2X)		
256	704	Chartreuse – small leaves
FRENCH KNOT (2X wrapped twice)		
307	728	Dark topaz – petunia center

MORE PROJECT IDEAS

- Stitch the designs on plastic canvas to use for garden markers.
- To express your thanks to a favorite teacher, stitch the apple on a note card.
- Use small-count waste canvas to stitch the watering can on the front of a T-shirt to wear for gardening.
- Stitch the strawberry motif on black fabric and make it into a striking brooch or pincushion.
- Embellish a gingham apron with fruit and vegetable designs.
- Stitch motifs on cross-stitch fabric to cover a gardening album.
- Stitch the words on ribbon Aida banding to make an extra-special gift bow.
- Spruce up kitchen accessories, such as hot pads, towels, and bread cloths, with stitched fruits and vegetables.
- Stitch the flower-filled watering can and frame it for a special friend who enjoys gardening.

EARTH'S BOUNTY

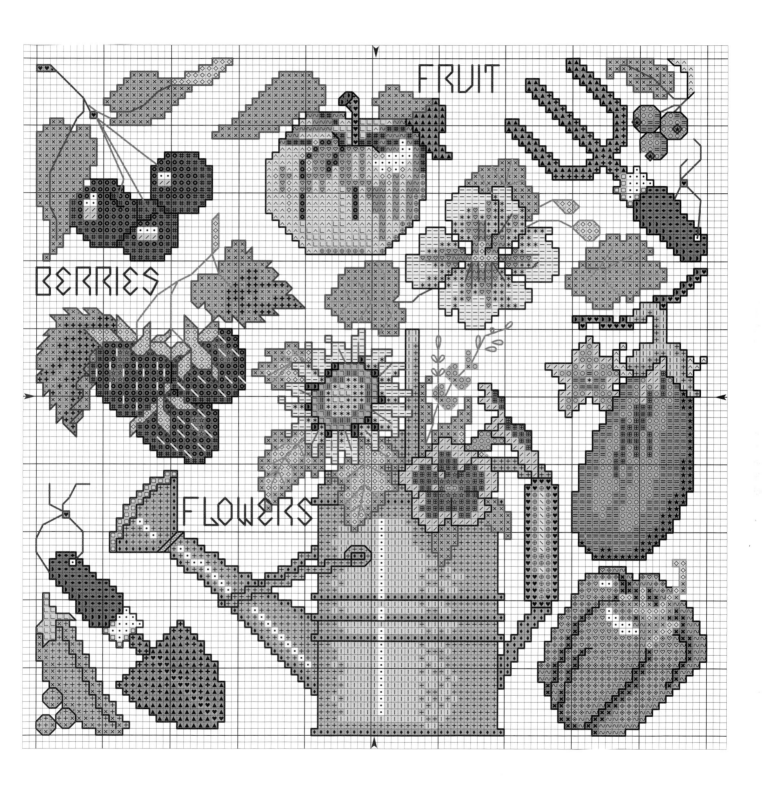

EARTH'S BOUNTY

 TRAY

MATERIALS

FABRIC

*7×11-inch piece of 14-count
raw linen Aida*

FLOSS

*Cotton embroidery floss in colors
listed in the key, opposite*

SUPPLIES

*Embroidery hoop; needle
Tray with insert for cross-stitch,
such as Sudberry House
Mat*

INSTRUCTIONS

Tape or zigzag stitch the fabric
edges. Find the center of the
chart. Measure 4 inches from one

short end of fabric; begin
stitching there. Use two plies of
floss to work cross-stitches over
one square of fabric. Work the
remaining stitches using the plies
indicated in the key. Press the
stitchery from the back.

Mat the completed stitchery
to fit into the tray. Insert glass,
mat, and stitchery in the tray as
directed by the manufacturer.

EARTH'S BOUNTY

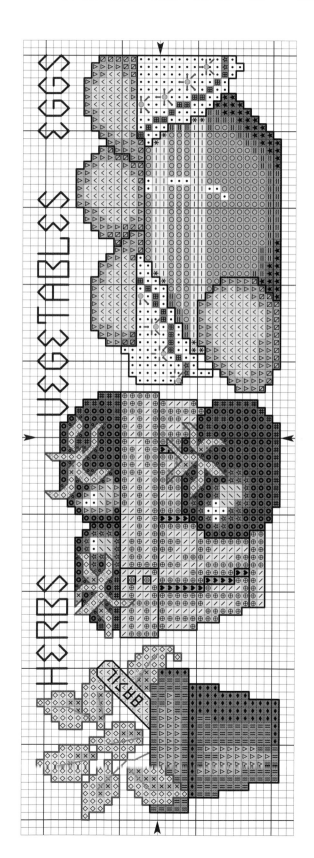

ANCHOR   DMC

CROSS-STITCH (2X)

118	3746	Darkest periwinkle
1049	3826	Dark golden brown
363	3827	Pale golden brown
002	3865	Winter white

BACKSTITCH (1X)

119	333	Deep periwinkle – "HERBS", "VEGETABLES", "EGGS"
683	500	Deep blue-green – leaves
295	726	True topaz – bowl detail
844	3012	Khaki – stems
279	3819	Moss green – leaf veins

ANCHOR   DMC

CROSS-STITCH (2X)

119	333	Deep periwinkle
118	340	Dark periwinkle
1025	347	Salmon
351	400	Mahogany
1046	435	Caramel
874	676	Light old gold
890	680	Dark old gold
256	704	Chartreuse
295	726	True topaz
307	728	Dark topaz
906	829	Bronze
035	892	Carnation
1002	977	Light golden brown
036	3326	Light rose
267	3346	Hunter green
031	3706	Watermelon

ANCHOR   DMC

CROSS-STITCH (2X)

236	3799	Charcoal – all other stitches

STRAIGHT STITCH (2X)

326	720	Bittersweet – flowers

FRENCH KNOT (1X wrapped twice)

307	728	Dark topaz – flower centers

17

JUST ROSES

*R*oses of every color and type are romantic. Whether you have a single stem, a bouquet, or a garden full of these lovely flowers, roses deliver sweet scents and sentiments. The designs in the plate below can be stitched for borders and silhouettes. Stitched completely as shown, this rose-filled sampler will delight anyone who loves these endearing, time-honored flowers.

Sampler
JUST ROSES

SAMPLER

MATERIALS
FABRIC
*14-inch square of 28-count raw
Cashel linen*

FLOSS
*Cotton embroidery floss in colors
listed in the key, page 22*

SUPPLIES
*Embroidery hoop
Needle
Mats and frame*

INSTRUCTIONS
Tape or zigzag stitch the fabric
edges. Find the center of the
chart and of the fabric; begin
stitching there. Use two plies of
floss to work cross–stitches over
two threads of fabric. Work the
remaining stitches using the plies
indicated in the key.

Press the stitchery from the
back. Mat and frame as desired.

continued on page 22

Sampler Key

JUST ROSES

ANCHOR		DMC
CROSS-STITCH (2X)		
059	▲	150 Dusty rose
041	✖	335 Rose
011	◘	351 True coral
008	⧅	352 Light coral
374	♦	420 Hazel
232	II	452 Shell gray
266	#	470 Medium avocado
265	✕	471 Light avocado
254	○	472 Pale avocado
324	⊕	721 Medium bittersweet
323	✶	722 Light bittersweet
298	✱	725 Topaz
301	I	744 Medium yellow
307	◈	783 Christmas gold
268	★	937 Moss green
880	−	951 Medium blush
055	⧄	962 Dark pink
185	=	964 Light aqua
244	✚	987 Medium forest green
242	☆	989 Light forest green
1020	/	3713 Salmon
074	▽	3716 Medium pink
120	◇	3747 Periwinkle
122	+	3807 Blue-violet
386	:	3823 Pale yellow
9575	∾	3824 Melon
1072	◗	3849 Teal green
347	⊞	3856 Mahogany

ANCHOR		DMC
BACKSTITCH (2X)		
059	/	150 Dusty rose – rosebud
011	/	351 True coral – flower veins
374	/	420 Hazel – yellow rose
254	/	472 Pale avocado – yellow rose detail
301	/	744 Medium yellow – left middle flower center
838	/	926 Slate green – rugosa roses ribbon
861	/	935 Pine green – yellow rose leaves (2X); small yellow border rose (1X)
236	/	3799 Charcoal – all other stitches

ANCHOR		DMC
BLENDED NEEDLE BACKSTITCH		
362 266	/	437 Caramel (2X) and 470 Medium avocado (2X) – rugosa rose stem
254 266	/	472 Pale avocado (2X) and 470 Medium avocado (2X) – rosebud stem
298 301	/	725 Topaz (2X) and 744 Medium yellow (2X) – top left flower center
STRAIGHT STITCH (2X)		
374	/	420 Medium hazel – thorns
120	/	3747 Periwinkle – flower petals
LAZY DAISY STITCH (2X)		
265	0	471 Light avocado – leaves
055	0	962 Dark pink – flower
FRENCH KNOT (2X wrapped twice)		
298	●	725 Topaz – flower centers

MORE PROJECT IDEAS

- *Stitch the sampler to finish as a decorative pillow top.*
- *Omit the central motifs from the sampler and fill in the space with names and dates for a wedding sampler.*
- *Stitch small blooms on perforated paper for personalized name cards.*
- *Accent a brooch with one of the large rose motifs.*
- *Stitch the center rose trio on opposite ends of a dresser scarf.*
- *Stitch the ribbon and rose silhouette on a blouse collar or pocket.*
- *Create a Victorian-style tote from the sampler, finishing the bag with dainty fabrics, lace, and button accents.*
- *Use waste canvas to stitch roses to sheet borders and pillowcases.*
- *Stitch the large yellow rose on an eyeglasses case.*
- *Make a set of button covers using the small designs.*
- *Stitch a rose in the corner of a plain cosmetics bag.*
- *Trim towels by stitching roses on banding, then machine-stitching the band to the towels.*
- *Stitch a rose on perforated paper to make a thank you or birthday card.*

JUST ROSES

JUST ROSES

PURSE

MATERIALS

FABRIC
*7×10-inch piece of 28-count raw
Cashel linen*

FLOSS
*Cotton embroidery floss in colors
listed in the key, opposite*

SUPPLIES
*Embroidery hoop; needle
Tracing paper; pencil; ruler
⅓ yard pink silk fabric; iron
Thread; scissors; pins
10-inch square of fleece
9×18-inch piece of lining fabric
10-inch square of fusible interfacing
Seed beads in pink and green;
1¼ yard pink cording
Fabric glue; button*

INSTRUCTIONS
Tape or zigzag stitch the linen edges. Find the center of the chart and the center of the fabric; begin stitching there. Use two plies of floss to work cross-stitches over two threads of fabric. Work remaining stitches using plies indicated in the key. Press the stitched piece from the back.

JUST ROSES

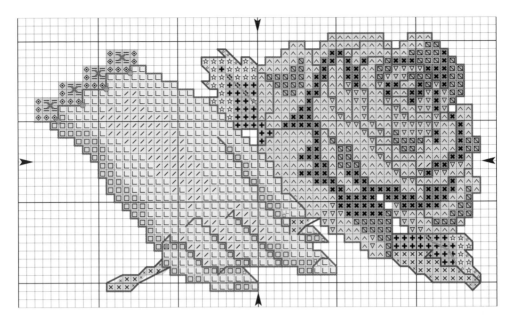

ANCHOR		DMC	
CROSS-STITCH (2X)			
041	✖	335	Rose
265	✕	471	Light avocado
1012	☐	754	Peach
307	◈	783	Christmas gold
881	∟	945	Dark blush
055	◪	962	Dark pink
185	═	964	Light aqua
244	✚	987	Medium forest green
242	☆	989	Light forest green
649	⋀	3689	Mauve
1020	⟋	3713	Salmon
074	▽	3716	Medium pink

ANCHOR		DMC	
BACKSTITCH (2X)			
374	⟋	420	Hazel – hand, rose
301	⟋	744	Medium yellow – leaf veins
861	⟋	935	Pine green – leaf
FRENCH KNOT (2X wrapped twice)			
1072	●	3849	Teal green– ring and bracelet detail
BEAD			
	✕	561	Ice green Mill Hill Glass Bead – bracelet detail

Draw a 7-inch circle onto tracing paper. Draw a 1-inch grid in the circle. Layer a 10-inch piece of pink silk fabric on the fleece. Pin the pattern to the silk fabric; machine-quilt on the circle and grid. Remove paper. Allowing a ¼-inch seam, cut out the circle.

Cut silk fabric for back and two lining pieces the same size as the purse front. Fuse interfacing to back piece. Draw a 6½×4-inch rectangle on tracing paper. Fold paper in half crosswise and round the bottom corners. Open paper and use it for the flap pattern.

Line the cross-stitch design. Bind the curved edge with silk bias. Stitch pink beads to the quilting intersections.

Determine flap placement on front and back pieces. Trim off top edge of quilted circle. Stitch flap to back piece. Right sides together, stitch purse front to back along curved edge. Clip seam around curve; turn.

Stitch lining pieces together along curve. Allowing 24 inches for handle, glue cord along curve. Hand-stitch the lining to the purse top at the straight edges. Sew on a button and floss loop closure.

JUST ROSES

SCISSORS CASE AND PINCUSHION

MATERIALS

FABRIC

3×6-inch piece and 7-inch square of 28-count rose evenweave

FLOSS

Cotton embroidery floss in colors listed in the keys, opposite

SUPPLIES

Embroidery hoop; neelde

Thread; scissors; ruler
Tracing paper, pencil, and
¼ yard of peach silk for scissors case
6-inch square of fleece, 5-inch squares
of calico fabric and fusible interfacing,
1 yard of ⅝-inch-wide gathered dark
gold satin ribbon, and cotton batting
for pincushion

INSTRUCTIONS

Tape or zigzag stitch the evenweave edges. For each design, find the center of the chart and the fabric; begin stitching there. Use two plies of floss to work cross-stitches over two threads of fabric. Work the remaining stitches using the plies indicated in the key. Press the finished stitchery from the back.

For the scissors case, trace the shape of scissors to tracing paper. Shape the pattern into a triangle, adding a ¼-inch seam allowance.

For back flap, add 2¾-inch length along the top edge; round off top corners.

26

JUST ROSES

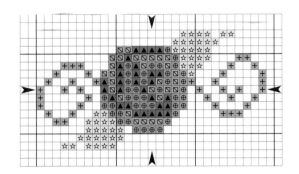

ANCHOR	DMC	
CROSS-STITCH (2X)		
059	▲	150 Dusty rose
324	⊕	721 Medium bittersweet
055	◨	962 Dark pink
242	☆	989 Light forest green
122	+	3807 Blue-violet

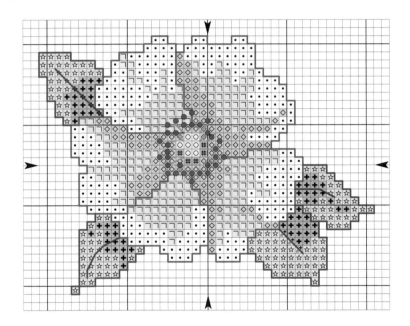

ANCHOR	DMC	
CROSS-STITCH (2X)		
002	·	000 White
266	⊞	470 Medium avocado
254	○	472 Pale avocado
234	⌐	762 Pearl gray
244	+	987 Medium forest green
242	☆	989 Light forest green
120	◇	3747 Periwinkle
BACKSTITCH (1X)		
838	/	926 Slate green – rose
861	/	935 Pine green – leaves, veins
STRAIGHT STITCH (2X)		
002	/	000 White – rose center
FRENCH KNOT (2X wrapped twice)		
1003	●	3853 Autumn gold – rose center

Cut one front and one back from peach silk fabric. Repeat for lining.

Cut out cross-stitch design, centering it on a 1¾-inch band. Fold under ¼ inch along each long edge; press. Fuse raw edges to back side.

Right sides together, stitch the back flap piece to the lining back flap piece. Clip into the seam allowance. Turn to right side; press.

Baste back pieces together along seam line. Right sides facing, stitch

front to lining along top edge. Turn to right side. Position cross-stitch band on front piece, approximately ½ inch from the top edge. Baste band to front. With right sides facing, stitch front to back. Clip curves. Turn to right side. To close case, insert flap into cross-stitch band.

For the pincushion, center the cross stitch design and draw a 4½-inch circle on the back. Machine-baste fleece to the wrong side of the cross-stitch piece along the circle. Fuse interfacing

to calico fabric. Cut out a 4½-inch circle of calico, which allows for a ¼-inch seam. Cut out top design ¼ inch past basting.

Pull basting thread to fit top circle to bottom circle. Stitch gathered ribbon along eased basting lines of top circle. Stitch top to bottom, right sides facing. Make a slit in the bottom circle. Turn to right side. Fill with cotton batting and shape the pincushion. Stitch the opening closed.

FLORAL FAVORITES

*R*ich, vibrant color catches the eye and sweet scents can be comforting or exhilarating to the senses. Perhaps flowers remind you of a garden experience from childhood. Whatever the reason, it seems almost everyone has a favorite blossom. The glorious sampler, below, is sure to include favorites that you will enjoy stitching.

Sampler
FLORAL FAVORITES

SAMPLER

MATERIALS

FABRIC
*14-inch square of 28-count
white Cashel linen*

FLOSS
*Cotton embroidery floss in colors
listed in the key, page 32*

SUPPLIES
*Embroidery hoop
Needle
Mats and frame*

INSTRUCTIONS

Tape or zigzag stitch the fabric
edges. Find the center of the
chart and the center of the
fabric; begin stitching there.
Use two plies of floss to work
cross-stitches over two threads of
fabric. Work the remaining
stitches as listed in the key.

Press the finished stitchery
from the back. Mat and frame
as desired.

continued on page 32

FLORAL FAVORITES

ANCHOR		DMC	
CROSS-STITCH (2X)			
110	✳	208	Lavender
119	◗	333	Deep periwinkle
041	☆	335	Medium rose
1030	◇	340	Dark periwinkle
117	⊕	341	Light periwinkle
066	▢	604	Cranberry
237	◈	703	True chartreuse
256	╱	704	Light chartreuse
326	✳	720	Dark bittersweet
324	=	721	Medium bittersweet
323	▽	722	Light bittersweet
298	✳	725	Medium topaz
303	⊕	742	Yellow
023	−	776	Pale rose
874	∟	833	Bronze
1044	▲	895	Hunter green
359	■	898	Coffee brown
026	◩	899	True rose
339	◆	920	Medium copper
274	▯	928	Slate green
186	✕	959	Aqua
206	△	966	Baby green
244	+	987	Forest green
077	‖	3687	True mauve
649	▢	3689	Light mauve
118	▦	3746	Darkest periwinkle
897	✚	3802	Antique mauve
891	∿	3822	Straw
002	·	3865	Winter white

ANCHOR		DMC	
BACKSTITCH (2X)			
401	╱	413	Medium charcoal – flowers 1, 8
683	╱	500	Blue-green – all leaves
237	╱	703	True chartreuse – stems 1, 9, tendril 4
256	╱	704	Light chartreuse – stem 1, leaf detail 3
359	╱	898	Coffee brown – stem 8
341	╱	918	Deep copper – flower 7, center 8
236	╱	3799	Dark charcoal – flower 2, 6, 9, 5
897	╱	3802	Antique mauve – flower 3, 4
002		3865	Winter white – leaf 2, flower 5

ANCHOR		DMC	
STRAIGHT STITCH (2X)			
326	╱	720	Dark bittersweet – flower detail 3
298	╱	725	Medium topaz – flower 6
303	╱	742	Yellow – flower 1, 3, 7
244	╱	987	Forest green – flower 3
002		3865	Winter white – flower 5
FRENCH KNOT			
256	●	704	Light chartreuse – flower 1 (2X wrapped three times)
324	●	721	Medium bittersweet – flower 1, 8 (1X wrapped twice)
295	●	726	True topaz – flower 7, 9 (1X wrapped three times)
244	●	987	Forest green – flower 3 (2X wrapped twice)
LAZY DAISY STITCH (2X)			
002		3865	Winter white – flower 5 center

FLORAL FAVORITES

FLORAL FAVORITES

TEA TOWEL

MATERIALS

FABRIC
*7×24-inch piece of 28-count
raw Cashel linen*

FLOSS
*Cotton embroidery floss in colors
listed in the key, opposite*

SUPPLIES
*Embroidery hoop; needle
¾ yard fabric for towel
⅛ yard contrasting fabric for band
Pins; 1½ yards of lace; thread*

INSTRUCTIONS

Tape or zigzag stitch the linen edge.
Find the center of the right-hand
row of the chart and the center
of the fabric; begin stitching there.
Use two plies of floss to work
cross-stitches over two threads of
fabric. Repeat the design on the
fabric. Work the remaining
stitches as listed in the key.

Press the stitchery from the
back. Trim the band to 3¼ inches
high. Press under ¼ inch along
each long edge.

Pin lace under each long edge.
Pin the lace-trimmed stitchery to
the contrasting band. Press under
long raw edges. Top-stitch band
to the towel. Hem towel edges.

Tea Towel Chart and Key

FLORAL FAVORITES

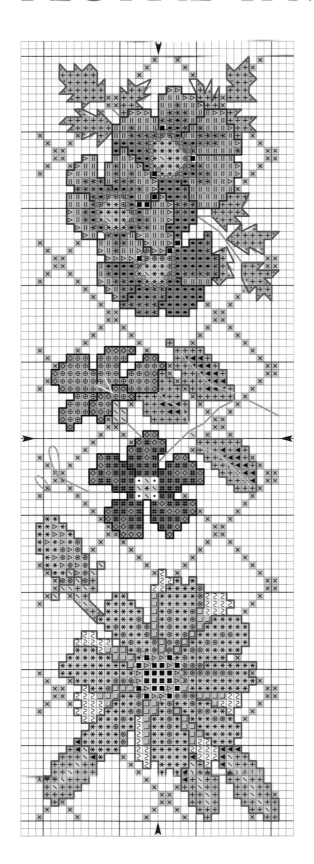

ANCHOR	DMC
CROSS-STITCH (2X)	
1030	340 Dark periwinkle
117	341 Light periwinkle
256	704 Light chartreuse
326	720 Dark bittersweet
324	721 Medium bittersweet
323	722 Light bittersweet
298	725 Topaz
303	742 Yellow
874	830 Bronze
1044	895 Hunter green
359	898 Coffee brown

ANCHOR	DMC
CROSS-STITCH (2X)	
339	920 Medium copper
186	959 Aqua
244	987 Forest green
118	3746 Darkest periwinkle
891	3822 Straw
002	3865 Winter white
BACKSTITCH (2X)	
683	500 Blue-green – all leaves
237	703 True chartreuse – right and center stems

ANCHOR	DMC
BACKSTITCH (2X)	
256	704 Light chartreuse – center leaf detail
359	898 Coffee brown – left flower
341	918 Deep copper – right flower
236	3799 Dark charcoal – center flower
STRAIGHT STITCH (2X)	
298	725 Medium topaz – center flower
002	3865 Winter white – center flower

ANCHOR	DMC
FRENCH KNOT	
295	726 True topaz – left flower (1X wrapped three times)
891	3822 Straw – right flower (1X wrapped twice)
LAZY DAISY STITCH (2X)	
237	703 True chartreuse – center small leaves

CUTE AS A BUTTON

𝒢et ready to ooh and aah
over the dainty and adorable
designs in this playful chapter.
Whether you love childlike
embroidered designs from days
past or stitchery of newborn
animals, you'll find it all in these
pages dedicated to children
around the world.

CHILDREN'S FAVORITES

Children love playful motifs—and that's the inspiration for the lively plate below. From a leapin' lamb to a kitten who can cook, these sweet designs will tug on your heartstrings. Created with a stamped-embroidery look, these colorful motifs stitch up quickly with French knot, lazy daisy, and straight stitch accents. Let these darling characters captivate your next stitching canvas!

CHILDREN'S FAVORITES

SAMPLER

MATERIALS
FABRIC
*14-inch square of 28-count
white Jobelan*

FLOSS
*Cotton embroidery floss in colors
listed in the key, page 42*

SUPPLIES
*Embroidery hoop
Needle
Mats and frame*

INSTRUCTIONS
Tape or zigzag stitch the fabric edges. Find the center of the chart and the center of the fabric; begin stitching there. Use two plies of floss to work cross-stitches over two threads of fabric. Work the remaining stitches using the plies indicated in the key.

Press the stitchery from the back. Mat and frame as desired.

continued on page 42

Sampler Key

CHILDREN'S FAVORITES

ANCHOR DMC

CROSS-STITCH (2X)

ANCHOR		DMC
403	■	310 Black
1025	♥	347 Salmon
235	#	414 Steel
398	╲	415 Pearl gray
1045	□	436 Caramel
1094	○	605 Cranberry
237	×	703 Chartreuse
295	|	726 True topaz
316	⊕	740 Dark tangerine
142	●	797 Royal blue
136	△	799 Delft blue
358	▲	801 Coffee brown
881	−	945 Blush
186	◇	959 True aqua
298	▽	972 Light tangerine
050	╱	3708 Geranium
066	+	3806 Light cyclamen
188	⧅	3812 Deep aqua

BACKSTITCH (2X)

ANCHOR	DMC
1025	347 Salmon – chef's apron tie, mouths, bear's tongue
235	414 Steel – girl's hat and apron, puppy, kitten
1045	436 Caramel – shoes, girl's hair, boy's shirt, bear
237	703 Chartreuse – chef's spoon
295	726 True topaz – butterfly, blocks, balloon
316	740 Dark tangerine – "LET'S COOK!", bird
142	797 Royal blue – boy's overalls, bird
136	799 Delft blue – boy's overalls, chef's hat and clothes
358	801 Coffee brown – boy's hair
228	910 Emerald – boy's hat, clown outfit, stems
186	959 True aqua – lamb
298	972 Light tangerine – balloon
050	3708 Geranium – bird's chest
882	3773 Rose-beige – skin
063	3804 Dark cyclamen – dress, apron, bows, ribbon, blocks
066	3806 Light cyclamen – balloon
188	3812 Deep aqua – puppy's eyes, kitten's jacket, blocks
403	310 Black – all other stitches

STRAIGHT STITCH (2X)

ANCHOR	DMC
403	310 Black – chef's whiskers and hair
295	726 True topaz – girl's hair
316	740 Dark tangerine – kitten, pom-pom
136	799 Delft blue – chef's hat
358	801 Coffee brown – clown dog, kitten, bear, butterfly
050	3708 Geranium – kitten's ears and nose
066	3806 Light cyclamen – hair bows

RUNNING STITCH (2X)

ANCHOR	DMC
237	703 Chartreuse – girl's apron

LAZY DAISY STITCH (2X)

ANCHOR	DMC
1025	347 Salmon – chef's apron tie
237	703 Chartreuse – leaves
136	799 Delft blue – chef's hat
063	3804 Dark cyclamen – kitten's bow
066	3806 Light cyclamen – hair bows, flowers
188	3812 Deep aqua – butterfly

FRENCH KNOT

ANCHOR	DMC
403	310 Black – eyes (2X wrapped twice); bear's nose (2X wrapped three times)
295	726 True topaz – flower centers (2X wrapped three times)
316	740 Dark tangerine – clown dog's collar (2X wrapped twice)
358	801 Coffee brown – butterfly (2X wrapped twice)
882	3773 Rose-beige – chef's nose (2X wrapped three times)
063	3804 Dark cyclamen – kitten's bow (2X wrapped twice)

LET'S
COOK!

CHILDREN'S FAVORITES

CASSEROLE COVER

MATERIALS
FABRIC
7×18-inch piece of 32-count antique white Belfast linen

FLOSS
Cotton embroidery floss in colors listed in the key, opposite

SUPPLIES
(for a 29-inch circumference casserole)
Embroidery hoop; needle
Scissors; 1¼ yards print fabric

4×15-inch piece of white cotton lining fabric
½ yard narrow cording
⅛ yard contrasting fabric for piping
Thread; pencil; ruler

INSTRUCTIONS
Tape or zigzag stitch the linen edges. Find the center of chart and of fabric; begin stitching there. Use two plies of floss to work cross-stitches over two threads of fabric. Work remaining stitches using the plies noted in the key.

Press the stitchery from the back. Center the design and cut the cross-stitch piece 4×15 inches (or half the circumference of the casserole plus ¼-inch seam allowances). Line the cross-stitch with white cotton. Cover the cording with contrasting fabric for piping. Raw edges together, stitch the piping to the sides and lower edge of the stitched design.

Place dish on print fabric and trace around the bottom. Add a ½-inch seam allowance and cut out the fabric shape. Measure the dish height and circumference, add 2 inches to each measurement for seam allowances and gathering, and cut out two fabric panels (front and lining). For the ruffle, cut a 2¾-inch bias strip two times the circumference of the dish, piecing as needed. Cut two 2×24-inch ties. Cut fabric to back stitchery flange. Cut two pieces of fabric for opposite side flange.

Right sides together, sew together the side seams of each panel for front and lining. Sew together the narrow edges of the ruffle strip to make a loop. Wrong sides together, fold the ruffle loop in half lengthwise and sew a gathering stitch along the raw edges. Sew the flanges by sewing them right sides together along the narrow sides and one long side. Turn to the right side and press. Pin the raw edges of the flanges to the top of the front panel, allowing approximately ½ inch space between each flange; baste in place. Gather the ruffle to fit the flanged edge; baste in place. Right sides together, fit the lining to the front panel over the flanges and ruffle; sew the pieces together catching the flanges and ruffle in the seam. Turn to the right side, adjust flange and ruffle, and press.

Baste and gather the lower edge of the front panel and lining to fit the bottom circle (or dish shape). Sew the pieces together. Fold tie in half lengthwise, wrong sides together; press. Turn the raw edges to the center, press, and stitch close to edges. Sew ties to opposite sides of cover between the flanges. Tie knots in the ends.

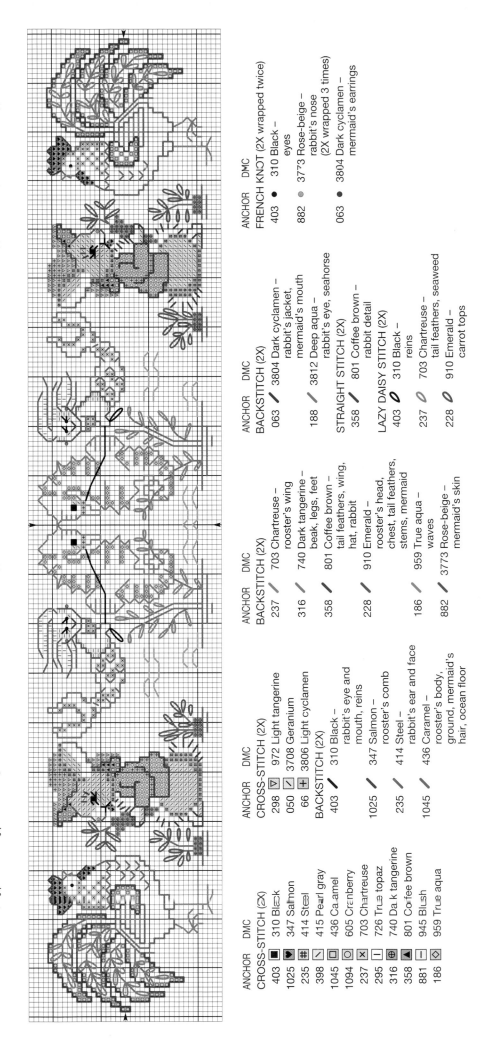

ANCHOR	DMC
CROSS-STITCH (2X)	
403 ■	310 Black
1025 ▶	347 Salmon
235 ▦	414 Steel
398 ╱	415 Pearl gray
1045 □	436 Caramel
1094 ○	605 Cranberry
237 ✕	703 Chartreuse
295 ▬	726 True topaz
316 ⊕	740 Dark tangerine
358 ◀	801 Coffee brown
881 ▮	945 Blush
186 ◇	959 True aqua

ANCHOR	DMC
CROSS-STITCH (2X)	
298 ▽	972 Light tangerine
050 ╱	3708 Geranium
66 ⊞	3806 Light cyclamen
BACKSTITCH (2X)	
403 ╱	310 Black – rabbit's eye and mouth, reins
1025 ╱	347 Salmon – rooster's comb
235 ╱	414 Steel – rabbit's ear and face
1045 ╱	436 Caramel – rooster's body, ground, mermaid's hair, ocean floor

ANCHOR	DMC
BACKSTITCH (2X)	
237 ╱	703 Chartreuse – rooster's wing
316 ╱	740 Dark tangerine – beak, legs, feet
358 ╱	801 Coffee brown – tail feathers, wing, hat, rabbit
228 ╱	910 Emerald – rooster's head, chest, tail feathers, stems, mermaid
186 ╱	959 True aqua – waves
882 ╱	3773 Rose-beige – mermaid's skin

ANCHOR	DMC
BACKSTITCH (2X)	
063 ╱	3804 Dark cyclamen – rabbit's jacket, mermaid's mouth
188 ╱	3812 Deep aqua – rabbit's eye, seahorse
STRAIGHT STITCH (2X)	
358 ╱	801 Coffee brown – rabbit detail
LAZY DAISY STITCH (2X)	
403 ◖	310 Black – reins
237 ◖	703 Chartreuse – tail feathers, seaweed
228 ◖	910 Emerald – carrot tops

ANCHOR	DMC
FRENCH KNOT (2X wrapped twice)	
403 ●	310 Black – eyes
882 ●	3773 Rose-beige – rabbit's nose (2X wrapped 3 times)
063 ●	3804 Dark cyclamen – mermaid's earrings

ANCHOR		DMC	
CROSS-STITCH (2X)			
1025	♥	347	Salmon
1045	☐	436	Caramel
237	☒	703	Chartreuse
BACKSTITCH (2X)			
1025	╱	347	Salmon – comb, GOOD MORNING
1045	╱	436	Caramel – body
237	╱	703	Chartreuse – wing
316	╱	740	Dark tangerine – beak, legs, feet
358	╱	801	Coffee brown – tail feathers, wing
228	╱	910	Emerald – head, chest, tail feathers

ANCHOR		DMC	
LAZY DAISY STITCH (2X)			
237	⟲	703	Chartreuse – tail feathers
FRENCH KNOT (2X wrapped twice)			
403	●	310	Black – eye

HOT PADS

MATERIALS

(for one hot pad)

FABRIC

8-inch square of 32-count antique white Belfast linen

FLOSS

Cotton embroidery floss in colors listed in the key, above or opposite

SUPPLIES

Embroidery hoop; needle; scissors ⅓ yard contrasting fabric for corner squares, back, and binding

⅛ yard print fabric for sashing
Thread; ruler; crochet hook
Cotton batting; ½ inch cabone ring
7½-inch square of white cotton fabric
Coordinating embroidery floss

INSTRUCTIONS

Tape or zigzag stitch the fabric edges. For each design, find the center of the chart and the center of the fabric; begin stitching there. Use two plies of floss to work cross-stitches over two threads of fabric. Work the remaining stitches using the plies indicated in the key. Press from the back.

Center the design and trim to 5 inches square. From contrasting fabric cut four 1¾-inch corner squares and one 7½-inch piece of batting and a backing square. Cut a strip 2×30 inches for binding, piecing as needed. Cut four 1¾×5-inch sashing rectangles from print fabric. Using ¼-inch seam allowances, piece the front.

Layer the pieced top, batting, and backing; baste edges. Bind the hot pad, mitering corners.

Single-crochet around cabone ring using 6-ply floss; stitch to hot pad. With contrasting floss, tie the corners of the patchwork.

CHILDREN'S FAVORITES

ANCHOR		DMC	
CROSS-STITCH (2X)			
403	■	310	Black
1025	♥	347	Salmon
237	✕	703	Chartreuse
316	⊕	740	Dark tangerine
142	◉	797	Royal blue
136	△	799	Delft blue
881	⊟	945	Blush
BACKSTITCH (2X)			
403	╱	310	Black – eyes, shoes
1025	╱	347	Salmon – apron ties
237	╱	703	Chartreuse – spoon handle
316	╱	740	Dark tangerine – LET'S COOK
136	╱	799	Delft blue – shirt, pants
358	╱	801	Coffee brown – eyebrows and mouth
882	╱	3773	Rose-beige – skin
STRAIGHT STITCH (2X)			
403	╱	310	Black – whiskers, hair
136	╱	799	Delft blue – hat

ANCHOR		DMC	
LAZY DAISY STITCH (2X)			
1025	⟁	347	Salmon – apron ties
136	⟁	799	Delft blue – hat
FRENCH KNOT (2X wrapped twice)			
316	●	740	Tangerine – exclamation mark
066	●	3806	Light cyclamen – nose (2X wrapped three times)

ANCHOR		DMC	
CROSS-STITCH (2X)			
1025	♥	347	Salmon
235	#	414	Steel
398	◣	415	Pearl gray
1045	▢	436	Caramel
1094	◎	605	Cranberry
316	⊕	740	Dark tangerine
358	▲	801	Coffee brown
298	▽	972	Light tangerine
050	⧄	3708	Geranium
066	+	3806	Light cyclamen
BACKSTITCH (2X)			
403	╱	310	Black – eye, mouth
235	╱	414	Steel – ear, face
1045	╱	436	Caramel – ground
358	╱	801	Coffee brown – hat, rabbit
228	╱	910	Emerald – stems
063	╱	3804	Dark cyclamen – jacket

ANCHOR		DMC	
BACKSTITCH (2X)			
188	╱	3812	Deep aqua – eye, LET'S EAT!
STRAIGHT STITCH (2X)			
358	▬	801	Coffee brown – rabbit detail
LAZY DAISY STITCH (2X)			
228	⟁	910	Emerald – carrot tops
FRENCH KNOT			
882	●	3773	Rose-beige – nose (2X wrapped three times)
188	●	3812	Deep aqua – exclamation mark (2X wrapped twice)

BABY ANIMALS

*W*ho can resist the innocent gaze or cooing sounds of a baby animal? These animals— whether in the barn, the wild, or the house—each need a place to call home. The plate below highlights some of mother nature's babies for you to stitch. Whether you have pets, enjoy watching bunnies in the backyard, or are a farm person at heart, these enchanting designs will appeal to the animal lover in you.

Sampler
BABY ANIMALS

SAMPLER

MATERIALS

FABRIC
*14-inch square of 28-count
dusty green linen*

FLOSS
*Cotton embroidery floss in colors
listed in the key, page 52*

SUPPLIES
*Embroidery hoop
Needle
Mats and frame*

INSTRUCTIONS

Tape or zigzag stitch the fabric edges. Find the center of the chart and the center of the fabric; begin stitching there.

Use two plies of floss to work cross-stitches over two threads of fabric. Work the remaining stitches using the plies indicated in the key.

Press the stitchery from the back. Mat and frame as desired.

continued on page 52

BABY ANIMALS

ANCHOR		DMC	
CROSS-STITCH (2X)			
002	▫	000	White
011	⊕	351	Coral
351	☆	400	Mahogany
372	=	422	Light hazel
874	⌐	676	Light old gold
590	⊞	712	Cream
295	−	726	True topaz
306	+	729	Medium old gold
308	✳	782	Christmas gold
137	◇	798	Delft blue
358	✚	801	True coffee brown
1050	▮	839	Dark beige-brown
906	▲	869	Dark hazel
338	◢	921	Copper
381	⋈	938	Deep coffee brown
1011	◣	948	Light peach
1001	○	976	Medium golden brown
382	■	3371	Black-brown
869			3743	Antique violet
882	♡	3771	Blush
1049	#	3826	Dark golden brown
363	▽	3827	Pale golden brown
901	╱	3829	Deep old gold
1003	‖	3853	Dark autumn gold
313	∧	3854	Medium autumn gold
379	✕	3863	Mocha-beige

ANCHOR		DMC	
BLENDED NEEDLE CROSS-STITCH			
1012	◺	754	Medium peach (2X) and
379		3863	Mocha-beige (1X)
914	◆	3859	Rosewood (2X) and
1007		3772	Cocoa (1X)
BACKSTITCH			
351	╱	400	Mahogany – chicks, duck, flowers (2X)
590	╱	712	Cream – dog eyes, shoe, bunny (2X)
358	╱	801	True coffee brown – cat whiskers (1X)
1050	╱	839	Dark beige-brown – goat, chicks, duck, pig (2X)
381	╱	938	Deep coffee brown – calf, kittens, colt, bunnies, dog (2X)
382	╱	3371	Black-brown – all other stitches (1X)

ANCHOR		DMC	
STRAIGHT STITCH			
002	╱	000	White – small highlight stitch in eyes (2X)
255	╱	907	Parrot green – grasses, stems (2X)
869	╱	3743	Antique violet – shoe (2X)
1007	╱	3772	Cocoa – calf mouth (3X)
SMYRNA CROSS-STITCH			
046	✳	666	True red – flowers (1X)
FRENCH KNOT (1X wrapped three times)			
137	●	798	Delft blue – flowers
382	●	3371	Black-brown – goat, dog eyes

MORE PROJECT IDEAS

- *Cut a mat from perforated paper and stitch a kitty in the corner to enhance a pet's photo.*
- *Stitch a chick on Aida to insert into a greeting card frame.*
- *Stitch the puppy and shoe for someone who loves dogs.*
- *Make an Easter trim by stitching chicks and bunnies on banding to wrap around a basket.*
- *Stitch a row of pigs on a baby bib.*
- *Make a brooch by stitching the horse motif on fine cross-stitch fabric and trim it with jute-like cording.*
- *Stitch the cows on a towel for a country kitchen.*
- *Alternate the bunny designs along the edge of a baby blanket.*
- *Use waste canvas to stitch the puppy and shoe on a sweatshirt front.*
- *For a special going-away card, stitch the duckling on white perforated paper with the inscription reading, "Waddle I do without you?"*
- *Stitch the kitty on perforated plastic and glue a magnet on the back for a refrigerator magnet.*

BABY ANIMALS

BABY ANIMALS

KITTY TREAT JAR TOPPER

MATERIALS
FABRIC
6-inch square of 28-count white Jobelan

FLOSS
Cotton embroidery floss in colors listed in the key, opposite

SUPPLIES
Embroidery hoop; needle
Pencil; scissors
Jar with lid
3×26-inch piece of bias-cut fabric
¼-inch-wide elastic
Fusible fleece
Thread
24 inches ribbon

INSTRUCTIONS
Tape or zigzag stitch the Jobelan edges. Find the center of the chart and the center of the fabric; begin stitching there. Use two plies of floss to work cross-stitches over two threads of fabric. Work remaining stitches using plies indicated in the key. Press from the back.

Trace the jar lid on the back of the cross-stitch and on fleece. On cross-stitch piece, cut ½ inch beyond the line. Cut out fleece on circle and fuse to back of cross-stitch.

Wrong sides together, press the fabric strip in half lengthwise. Machine-baste raw edges together. Stitch a casing for elastic ½ inch from the fold.

Pull basting threads to gather fabric to fit stitchery. Stitch in place. Insert elastic in casing and adjust to fit jar. Stitch seam closed, and trim excess elastic. Tie a ribbon bow over the elastic.

BABY ANIMALS

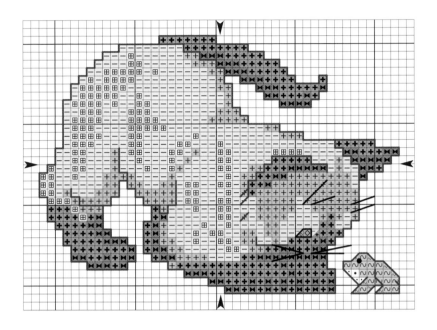

ANCHOR		DMC	
CROSS-STITCH (2X)			
002	•	000	White
874	−	676	Light old gold
590	⊞	712	Cream
306	+	729	Medium old gold
137	◇	798	Delft blue
358	✚	801	True coffee brown
255	∼	907	Parrot green
381	◪	938	Deep coffee brown
BACKSTITCH			
1050	╱	839	Dark beige-brown – kitten detail, frog (2X)
381	╱	938	Deep coffee brown – kitten (2X)
382	╱	3371	Black-brown – whiskers, eye (2X)
FRENCH KNOT (1X wrapped three times)			
382	●	3371	Black-brown – frog eye

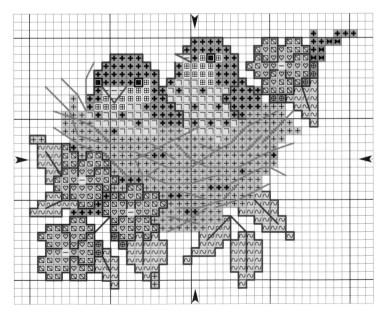

Album Cover—photo and instructions, page 56

ANCHOR		DMC	
CROSS-STITCH (2X)			
011	⊕	351	Coral
874	⌐	676	Light old gold
590	⊞	712	Cream
295	−	726	True topaz
306	+	729	Medium old gold
358	✚	801	True coffee brown
255	∼	907	Parrot green
381	◪	938	Deep coffee brown
1011	◨	948	Light peach
882	♡	3771	Blush
BACKSTITCH (1X)			
351	╱	400	Mahogany – flower
358	╱	801	True coffee brown – beaks (2X)
382	╱	3371	Black-brown – eyes
1050	╱	839	Dark beige-brown – all other stitches
STRAIGHT STITCH (2X)			
874	╱	676	Light old gold – nest
1050	╱	839	Dark beige-brown – leaf veins and stems

BABY ANIMALS

INSTRUCTIONS

Tape or zigzag stitch the linen edges. Find the center of the chart and the center of the fabric; begin stitching there. Use two plies of floss to work cross-stitches over two threads of fabric. Work the remaining stitches using the plies indicated in the key. Press the stitchery from the back.

Leaving ¾ inch around the design, trim the stitchery. Press under ¼ inch on each side. Center stitchery on fabric album cover; topstitch in place.

Cover the album with fabric, turning under and securing the edges with hand stitches.

Wrap ribbons around album cover to frame cross-stitch. Tack in place using hand stitches on the inside of the cover.

ALBUM COVER

MATERIALS
FABRIC
10-inch square of 28-count natural linen

FLOSS
Cotton embroidery floss in colors listed in the key, page 55

SUPPLIES
Embroidery hoop
Needle
Small album
⅓ yard fabric
Thread
Ribbon

BABY ANIMALS

BOOKMARK

MATERIALS

FABRIC

5-inch square of 28-count blue linen

FLOSS

*Cotton embroidery floss in colors
listed in the key and light blue*

SUPPLIES

*Embroidery hoop; needle; awl
2½×7-inch piece of rust suede
2¾×7¼-inch piece of tan suede
Scissors; fabric glue*

INSTRUCTIONS

Tape or zigzag stitch the linen edges. Find the center of the chart and the center of the fabric; begin stitching there. Use two plies of floss to work cross-stitches over two threads of fabric. Work remaining stitches using the plies indicated in the key. Press stitchery from the back.

Trim stitched fabric ½ inch beyond stitched area; remove four threads from each side. Cut round corners on the suede pieces.

Tack the stitched piece to the top of the rust suede with a cross-stitch in each corner using rust floss. Use blue floss to blanket stitch around the edge of the suede. If the suede is heavy, use an awl to puncture holes before stitching. Glue the rust suede centered on the tan suede. Let dry.

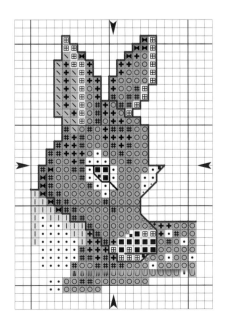

ANCHOR		DMC	
CROSS-STITCH (2X)			
002	·	000	White
590	⊞	712	Cream
358	✚	801	True coffee brown
381	◄►	938	Deep coffee brown
1001	○	976	Medium golden brown
382	■	3371	Black-brown
869	Ι	3743	Antique violet
1049	⊞	3826	Dark golden brown
BLENDED NEEDLE CROSS-STITCH			
1012	◹	754	Medium peach (2X) and
379		3863	Rose-beige (1X)
BACKSTITCH			
382	╱	3371	Black-brown – eye (1X)
381	╱	938	Deep coffee brown – all other stitches (2X)

AROUND THE WORLD

*T*ravel opens minds to
so many new things, including
patterns, styles, architecture, and
color combinations that sing of a
region's culture. May the diverse
sampling of projects on the
following pages prompt you to
stitch themed pieces of art
for gifts and home.

ASIAN SYMBOLS

*S*ymbols are used in Asian cultures to depict such feelings and traits as happiness and courage. Stitched on black, reminiscent of Asian styles, the select symbols on this sampler offer a wide range of designs, colors, and stitching options. The images below are accompanied by the words they represent. Choose symbols that are meaningful to you to stitch on a variety of projects.

ASIAN SYMBOLS

Sampler

SAMPLER

MATERIALS
FABRIC
*14-inch square of 28-count
black Jobelan*

FLOSS
*Cotton embroidery floss in colors
listed in the key, page 64*

SUPPLIES
*Embroidery hoop
Needle
Mats and frame*

INSTRUCTIONS
Tape or zigzag stitch the fabric
edges. Find the center of the
chart and the center of the
fabric; begin stitching there.
Use two plies of floss to work
cross-stitches over two threads of
fabric. Work the remaining
stitches as indicated in the key.

Press stitchery from the back.
Mat and frame as desired.

continued on page 64

ASIAN SYMBOLS

ANCHOR	DMC	
CROSS-STITCH (2X)		
002	⊡	000 White
059	◉	150 Dusty rose
041	⊞	335 Rose
101	✛	552 Violet
268	▲	580 Dark moss green
298	▽	725 Medium topaz
295	▢	726 True topaz
280	⊙	733 Olive
303	⊟	742 Yellow
275	⊟	746 Off-white
310	◈	780 Deep Christmas gold
137	✖	798 Delft blue
334	◉	900 Burnt orange
089	⊕	917 Plum
381	■	938 Coffee brown
186	▱	959 Aqua
292	⊓	3078 Pale topaz
086	◱	3608 Plum
279	◿	3819 Light moss green
176	◇	3839 Blue-violet
189	◆	3850 Bright green
308	✳	3852 Straw
1003	⊠	3853 Autumn gold

ANCHOR	DMC	
BACKSTITCH (1X)		
002	╱	000 White – butterfly, fish, dragon, bat
059	╱	150 Dusty rose – fan, dragon, phoenix
041	╱	335 Rose – fan
298	╱	725 Medium topaz – dragon, fan
310	╱	780 Deep Christmas gold – turtle, fan, phoenix
334	╱	900 Burnt orange – fish, dragon, phoenix
381	╱	938 Coffee brown – dragon, phoenix
086	╱	3608 Plum – dragon

ANCHOR	DMC	
BACKSTITCH (1X)		
176	╱	3839 Blue-violet – words
189	╱	3850 Bright green – phoenix
308	╱	3852 Straw – turtle, phoenix
1003	╱	3853 Autumn gold – dragon
STRAIGHT STITCH (1X)		
268	╱	580 Dark moss green – fan
FRENCH KNOT (2X wrapped three times)		
002	●	000 White – butterfly
381	●	938 Coffee brown – bat, turtle, phoenix

MORE PROJECT IDEAS

- *Use waste canvas to stitch a dragon on a T-shirt.*
- *Stitch a fan on perforated paper and embellish the flower center with seed beads for a greeting card.*
- *Stitch the Asian symbols along curtain hems.*
- *Make curtain tiebacks by stitching the butterfly on banding.*
- *Use waste canvas to stitch the turtle on a toddler's T-shirt.*
- *Stitch the fish on a black towel. Flank the design with a one-color motif for a decorative border.*
- *Stitch the bird on the center back of a denim jacket.*
- *Stitch the small symbols on a bookmark, using the words as a border.*
- *Add Asian influence to sleepwear by stitching the fan on a sleepshirt pocket or collar.*
- *Stitch the butterfly on perforated paper and attach it to a small dowel for a plant poke.*
- *Stitch the dragon on a child's duffel bag.*
- *Stitch the bird motif on the center of a hot pad.*

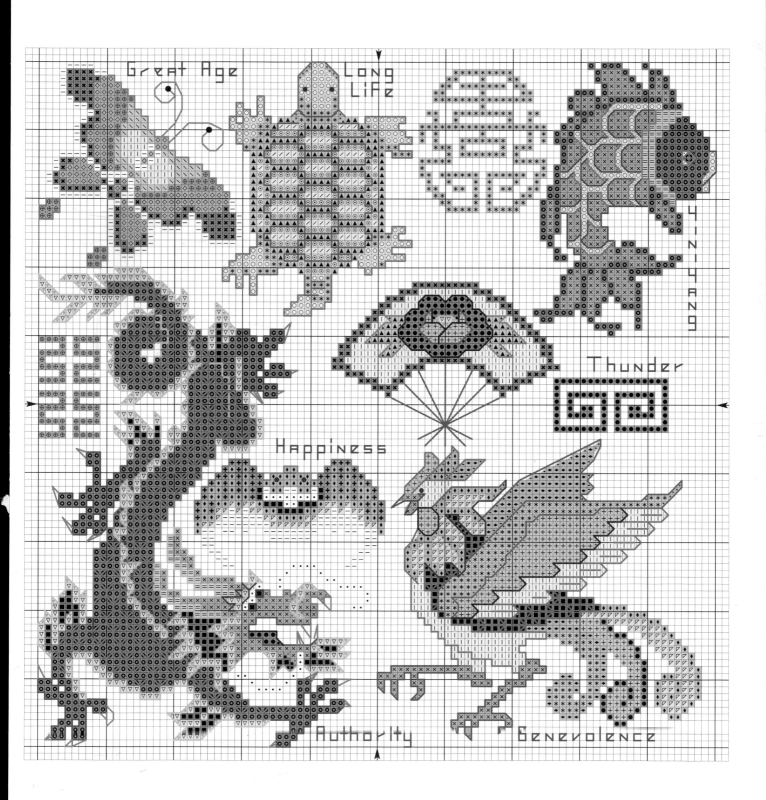

Great Age

Long Life

Yin Yang

Thunder

Happiness

Authority

Benevolence

ASIAN SYMBOLS

TABLE RUNNER

MATERIALS
FABRIC
14×28-inch piece of 14-count white Aida table runner

FLOSS
Cotton embroidery floss in colors listed in the key, opposite

SUPPLIES
*Embroidery hoop; needle
Ruler*

INSTRUCTIONS
Find the center of the chart. Begin stitching the border design at the center of one narrow side of the fabric at least 1¼ inches from the raw edge. Use two plies of embroidery floss to work cross-stitches over one square of fabric. Stitch the border design along the long edges, leaving room to stitch the trio of motifs along the second narrow edge.

Work the remaining stitches using the plies indicated in the key. Press the stitchery from the back.

Table Runner Chart and Key
ASIAN SYMBOLS

ANCHOR	DMC	
FRENCH KNOT (2X wrapped three times)		
298	⬤	725 Medium topaz – peony
310	⬤	780 Deep Christmas gold – beast
LAZY DAISY STITCH (2X)		
334	∅	900 Burnt orange – beast

ANCHOR	DMC	
BACKSTITCH (1X)		
298	╱	725 Medium topaz – peony, leaves
310	╱	780 Deep Christmas gold – beast
334	╱	900 Burnt orange – peony, leaves
089	╱	917 Plum – lotus
381	╱	938 Coffee brown – beast
279	╱	3819 Light moss green – leaves
176	╱	3839 Blue-violet – words

ANCHOR	DMC	
CROSS-STITCH (2X)		
002	⬤	000 White
059	⬤	150 Dusty rose
041	✚	335 Rose
268	◀	580 Dark moss green
295	○	726 True topaz
280	⊙	733 Olive
275	―	746 Off-white
307	☆	783 True Christmas gold
334	⊕	900 Burnt orange
089	⊞	917 Plum
381	■	938 Coffee brown
292	―	3078 Pale topaz
086	╱	3608 Plum
279	╱	3819 Light moss green

Courage

Rising

Thunder

Wealth

Courage Jar Lid

ASIAN SYMBOLS

COURAGE JAR LID

MATERIALS

FABRIC
*8-inch square of 28-count Christmas
red Jobelan*

FLOSS
*Cotton embroidery floss in colors
listed in the key, opposite*

SUPPLIES
*Embroidery hoop
Needle; scissors
Porcelain jar with lid for
stitchery insertion (available at
needlework shops)*

INSTRUCTIONS

Tape or zigzag fabric edges. Find
the center of the chart and the
center of the fabric; begin
stitching there. Use two plies of
floss to work cross-stitches over
two threads of fabric. Work
remaining stitches using plies
indicated in the key. Press the
stitchery from the back.

Trim and mount stitchery as
instructed by the jar manufacturer.
Insert the stitchery into the lid.

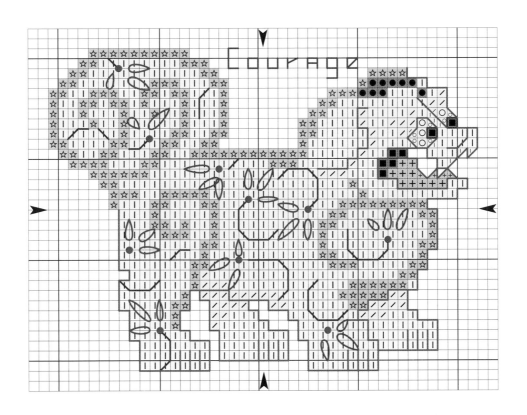

ANCHOR		DMC	
CROSS-STITCH (2X)			
059	●	150	Dusty rose
041	+	335	Rose
295	○	726	True topaz
307	☆	783	True Christmas gold
381	■	938	Coffee brown
292	I	3078	Pale topaz
279	/	3819	Light moss green
BACKSTITCH (1X)			
381	/	938	Coffee brown – eyes, stems (2X)
176	/	3839	Blue-violet – words
310	/	780	Deep Christmas gold – all other stitches
FRENCH KNOT			
(2X wrapped three times)			
010	●	700	Deep Christmas gold flower center
LAZY DAISY STITCH (2X)			
334	⊘	900	Burnt orange

Inspiration
ROSEMALING

Rosemaling is a distinctive form of decorative painting that originated in Finland, Norway, Sweden, and Denmark in the 1700s, with each country claiming its own style. As shown in the collection, opposite, rosemaling often decorates items made of wood as well as other home decor pieces, walls, and ceilings. Historically created from scrolling lines and fanciful flowers and leaves in bright colors, this cross-stitch reflects elegant rosemaling.

Sampler
ROSEMALING

SAMPLER

MATERIALS
FABRIC
*14-inch square of 28-count
natural linen*

FLOSS
*Cotton embroidery floss in colors
listed in the key, page 74*

SUPPLIES
*Embroidery hoop
Needle
Mats and frame*

INSTRUCTIONS
Tape or zigzag stitch the fabric
edges. Find the center of the
chart and the center of the
fabric; begin stitching there.
Use two plies of floss to work
cross-stitches over two threads of
fabric. Work the remaining
stitches as indicated in the key.
 Press the stitchery from the
back. Mat and frame as desired.

continued on page 74

ANCHOR		DMC	
CROSS-STITCH (2X)			
9046	☒	349	Dark coral
011	◪	351	True coral
370	◉	434	Caramel
267	✶	469	Avocado
256	◇	704	Chartreuse
298	‖	725	Topaz
307	▽	783	Christmas gold
148	◆	803	Deep baby blue
142	◎	826	Powder blue
874	+	833	Bronze
1041	■	844	Beaver gray
258	✕	904	Parrot green
339	✳	920	Copper

ANCHOR		DMC	
CROSS-STITCH (2X)			
140	▬	3755	True baby blue
1015	◗	3777	Terra-cotta
279	⌃	3819	Moss green
306	∿	3820	Dark straw
891	▢	3822	Light straw
170	✚	3842	Wedgwood blue
1076	#	3847	Teal green
186	✱	3851	Bright green
1003	≡	3853	Dark autumn gold
313	I	3854	Medium autumn gold
002	·	3865	Winter white
BACKSTITCH			
1041	╱	844	Beaver gray – stems (3X)

ANCHOR		DMC	
BACKSTITCH			
891	╱	3822	Light straw – flower center (2X)
308	╱	3852	Deep straw – stems (3X)
002	╱	3865	Winter white – flowers (2X)
LAZY DAISY STITCH (2X)			
256	╱	704	Chartreuse – leaves
186	╱	3851	Bright green – leaves
308	╱	3852	Deep straw – flowers
FRENCH KNOT (3X wrapped once)			
298	●	725	Topaz – flowers
140	●	3755	True baby blue – dew drops
002	●	3865	Winter white – dew drops
GRADED FRENCH KNOT			
891	●	3822	Light straw – dew drops

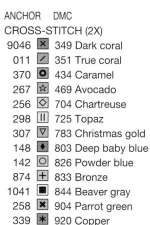

Floral Tote—instructions, chart, and key, pages 76–77

ROSEMALING

FLORAL TOTE

MATERIALS

FABRIC
*7×15-inch piece of 28-count
natural linen*

FLOSS
*Cotton embroidery floss in colors
listed in the key, opposite*

SUPPLIES
*Embroidery hoop; needle
Ruler; scissors
Two 1×11-inch strips of
contrasting fabric
½ yard of print fabric
½ yard lining fabric
Cording for piping
Batting; pins
Matching thread
Press cloth*

INSTRUCTIONS

Tape or zigzag stitch linen edges. Find the center of the banding chart, *opposite,* and the center of the fabric; begin stitching there.

Use two plies of floss to work cross-stitches over two threads of fabric. Work remaining stitches using the plies indicated in the key.

Center the design and cut the stitchery band to 3½×11 inches.

To construct the tote bag, use ¼-inch seam allowances. Wrong sides together, fold each 1×11-inch strip in half lengthwise; press. Align the raw edges of each strip with a top and bottom of the stitched band. Pin, sew, and use a press cloth to press the seam allowance to the backside of the band.

From print fabric cut two 11-inch-square front and back panels, two 10×3-inch side panels, two 2¼×13-inch handles, and one 2×28-inch strip for piping, piecing as needed. From batting cut two 11-inch squares and two 10×3-inch rectangles. Layer the batting on the wrong side of matching size fabric pieces and baste together. Right sides together sew the front and back panels together along one side; press. Topstitch the stitched band on the front of the tote, approximately 1½ inches from the top edge. Sew a side panel to each long side of the front and back, squaring the bottom corners of the tote to fit.

Wrong sides together, fold the handle pieces in half lengthwise and press. Turn the raw edges inside toward the center fold, press, and topstitch. Position the raw edges of the handles along the top edges of the front and back panels, spacing each handle approximately 4½ inches apart; pin in place. Cover cording with piping fabric. Raw edges aligned, baste the piping to the top of the tote, catching the handles edges.

MORE PROJECT IDEAS

• *Stitch the tote bag design on banding to make a tie-style belt.*
• *Stitch either of the stemmed flower designs to make a pretty brooch.*
• *Use waste canvas to stitch the center motif on a pocket of a blouse or jacket.*
• *Use duplicate stitch to stitch the design on a plain sweater.*
• *Alternate the small flowers vertically on a bookmark.*
• *Embellish a hand towel with the scrolled leaf designs.*
• *Stitch one of the small flowers on perforated paper and adhere it to a pencil holder.*
• *Stitch the design on banding to brighten an album or journal cover.*
• *Use waste canvas to add the motifs to curtains, valances, and tiebacks.*
• *Stitch the center motif as is, turn the fabric, and stitch it again to create a lovely pincushion top.*

ROSEMALING

From lining fabric cut two front and back panels and two side panels the same measurements as the print. Right sides together, sew the pieces, leaving a 6-inch opening in one side for turning. Press the seams and place the lining over the right side of the pieced tote matching seams. Sew together along the top, catching the handle and piping in the seam allowance. Turn the lining to the inside of the tote through the opening; stitch the opening closed.

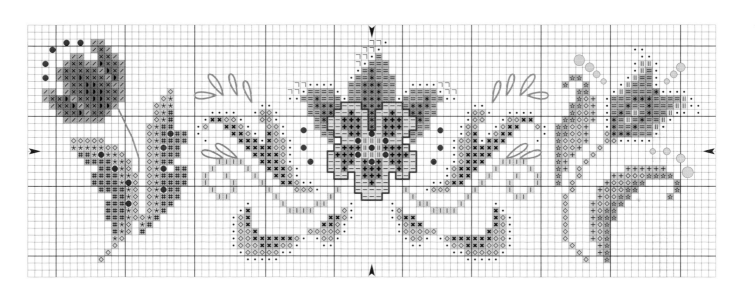

ANCHOR		DMC		ANCHOR		DMC	
CROSS-STITCH (2X)				BACKSTITCH (2X)			
9046	⊠	349	Dark coral	256	╱	704	Chartreuse – stem
011	╱	351	True coral	002	╱	3865	Winter white – flower
267	☆	469	Avocado	LAZY DAISY (2X)			
256	◇	704	Chartreuse	256	⊘	704	Chartreuse – leaves
298	‖	725	Topaz	308	⊘	3854	Medium autumn gold – leaves
874	✛	833	Bronze	FRENCH KNOT (3X wrapped once)			
258	✖	904	Parrot green	002	●	3865	Winter white – dew drops
339	✳	920	Copper	GRADED FRENCH KNOT			
140	−	3755	True baby blue	891	○	3822	Light straw – dew drops
1015	◗	3777	Terra-cotta				
891	⊓	3822	Light straw				
170	✚	3842	Wedgwood blue				
1070	✇	3847	Teal green				
186	★	3851	Bright green				
1003	=	3853	Dark autumn gold				
313	Ⅰ	3854	Medium autumn gold				
002	•	3865	Winter white				

ART OF MEXICO

V isitors to Mexico are intrigued by the vibrant colors and patterns of textiles, pottery, wood carvings, and leather. Art and everyday items showcase intricate patterns and details that inspire people all over the world to collect Mexican objects. The design below, in all its brilliance, is indicative of the lively motifs from south of the border.

Sampler
ART OF MEXICO

SAMPLER

MATERIALS

FABRIC
*14-inch square of 28-count
tan evenweave*

FLOSS
*Cotton embroidery floss in colors
listed in the key, page 82*

SUPPLIES
*Embroidery hoop
Needle
Mats and frame*

INSTRUCTIONS

Tape or zigzag stitch the fabric
edges. Find the center of the
chart and the center of the
fabric; begin stitching there.
Use two plies of floss to work
cross-stitches over two threads of
fabric. Work the remaining
stitches as listed in the key.

Press the stitchery from the
back. Mat and frame as desired.

continued on page 82

ART OF MEXICO

ANCHOR		DMC	
CROSS-STITCH (2X)			
002	•	000	White
403	■	310	Black
218	▲	319	Pistachio
9046	◉	349	Dark coral
011	♡	351	True coral
371	◆	433	Caramel
1038	◇	519	Sky blue
256	+	704	Chartreuse
326	▽	720	Bittersweet
295	–	726	True topaz
307	◯	728	Dark topaz
316	✕	740	Dark tangerine
304	☆	741	Medium tangerine
137	✳	798	Delft blue
257	◩	905	Parrot green
006	⊓	967	Pale melon
433	◺	996	Electric blue
328	Ⅰ	3341	Medium melon
306	◻	3820	Straw

ANCHOR		DMC	
BACKSTITCH (2X)			
218	╱	319	Pistachio – border design
256	╱	704	Chartreuse – cornstalk
326	╱	720	Bittersweet – border design
295	╱	726	True topaz – corn tassle
279	╱	3819	Moss green – top tassle, leaf veins
403	╱	310	Black – all other stitches

ANCHOR		DMC	
FRENCH KNOT			
137	●	798	Delft blue – moon (2X wrapped 3 times)
403	●	310	Black – tendril ends (2X wrapped twice)

MORE PROJECT IDEAS

- Stitch the sun on perforated paper to make a note card that reads, "You really brighten my day!"
- Create a lovely curtain edge by stitching one of the borders along the hem or on tiebacks.
- Make a pendant by stitching the sun or flower motif on white linen.
- Stitch the mask design and mount on the cover of a travel journal.
- Stitch several moon and sun motifs on perforated plastic, trim around designs, and use as holiday ornaments.
- Duplicate-stitch the sun and moon on a black cotton sweater.
- Trim the edge of a pillowcase with the corn border.
- Alternate the flower motifs to trim a towel or bread cloth.
- Stitch the yellow border on narrow premade banding to use as trim for a young girl's dress.
- Embellish a dresser scarf by stitching a colorful border along each short end.
- Use waste canvas to stitch the large floral border around shirt cuffs.

ART OF MEXICO

Tray Scarf and Coasters

ART OF MEXICO

TRAY SCARF AND COASTERS

MATERIALS
FABRIC
8-inch square of 18-count white
Aida for each coaster
14-count white polyester Aida
napkin for tray scarf

FLOSS
Cotton embroidery floss in colors
listed in the keys, opposite

SUPPLIES
Embroidery hoop; needle; scissors

INSTRUCTIONS
For the coaster, tape or zigzag stitch the fabric edges. Find the center of the chart, *opposite top,* and the center of the fabric; begin stitching there. For the napkin, find the center of the chart and the center of one fabric end. Measure 2 inches from the fringe; begin stitching there.

For either project, use two plies of floss to work cross-stitches over one square of fabric. Work the remaining stitches as listed in the key. Press from the back.

For the coaster, center the stitchery on the mounting piece and trim away the edges. Mount the stitchery in the coaster as instructed by the manufacturer.

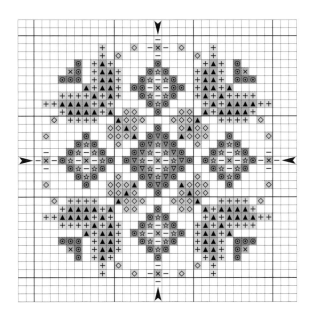

ANCHOR DMC
CROSS-STITCH (2X)

218	▲	319 Pistachio
9046	⊙	349 Dark coral
1038	◇	519 Sky blue
256	+	704 Chartreuse
326	▽	720 Bittersweet
295	−	726 True topaz
316	✕	740 Dark tangerine
304	☆	741 Medium tangerine

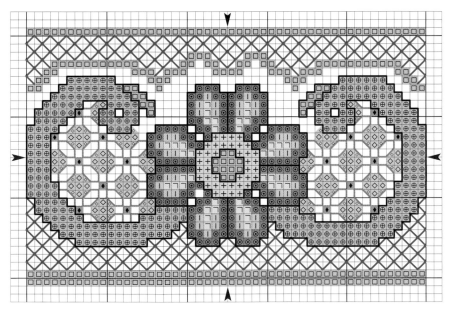

ANCHOR DMC
CROSS-STITCH (2X)

9046	⊙	349 Dark coral
371	◆	433 Caramel
1038	◇	519 Sky blue
256	+	704 Chartreuse
006	⌐	967 Pale melon
328	I	3341 Medium melon
306	☐	3820 Straw
1074	⊕	3848 Teal green

BACKSTITCH (2X)

307	╱	728 Dark topaz – motif detail
137	╱	798 Delft blue – crisscross pattern
403	╱	310 Black – all other stitches

EASTERN EUROPEAN FOLK ART

B old patterns with intricate details, such as those shown on the sampler, are inspired by the motifs of Eastern Europe. Choose designs that are rich with specialty stitch accents or very simple patterns that use few colors. Whichever designs suit your stitching fancy, enjoy re-creating these lovely images.

Sampler

EASTERN EUROPEAN FOLK ART

SAMPLER

MATERIALS
FABRIC
14-inch square of 32-count cream
Belfast linen

FLOSS
Cotton embroidery floss in colors
listed in the key, page 90

SUPPLIES
Embroidery hoop
Needle
Mats and frame

INSTRUCTIONS
Tape or zigzag stitch the fabric edges. Find the center of the chart and the center of the fabric; begin stitching there. Use two plies of floss to work cross-stitches over two threads of fabric. Work the remaining stitches using the plies as indicated in the key.

Press the stitchery from the back. Mat and frame as desired.

continued on page 90

EASTERN EUROPEAN FOLK ART

ANCHOR		DMC	
CROSS-STITCH (2X)			
128	I	157	Light Delft blue
280	◩	166	Moss green
403	■	310	Black
008	⋀	352	Light coral
326	+	720	Bittersweet
307	○	728	Dark topaz
301	−	744	Yellow
137	▲	798	Dark Delft blue
136	✕	799	Medium Delft blue
045	✚	814	Garnet
047	◇	817	Deep coral
888	#	831	Bronze
185	=	964	Aqua
292	☐	3078	Pale topaz
308	★	3852	Straw
1003	╱	3853	Autumn gold
002	·	3865	Winter white
BACKSTITCH (2X)			
326	╱	720	Bittersweet – leaf, stem detail
301	╱	744	Yellow – wing
142	╱	797	Royal blue – stem, "Gzhel"
047	╱	817	Deep coral – berries, "Kaluga," "Estonian"
258	╱	904	Parrot green – stem, "Khokhloma"
185	╱	964	Light aqua – stem
308	╱	3852	Straw – pear, leaves, strawberry stems, raspberry stems
403	╱	310	Black – all other stitches

ANCHOR		DMC	
STRAIGHT STITCH (2X)			
403	╱	310	Black – raspberry and flower detail
307	╱	728	Dark topaz – berry detail
258	╱	904	Parrot green – stem detail
LAZY DAISY STITCH (2X)			
403	⟋	310	Black – berry tops
142	⟋	797	Royal blue – leaves
258	⟋	904	Parrot green – leaves
185	⟋	964	Aqua – leaves
LAZY DAISY with LONG STITCH (2X)			
137 128	⟋	798 157	Dark Delft blue with Light Delft blue – leaves
308 403	⟋	3852 310	Straw with Black – leaves

ANCHOR		DMC	
OVERSTITCH			
047 403	◇ ✕	817 310	Deep coral (2X) and Black (1X)
FRENCH KNOT			
142	●	797	Royal blue – bud (2X wrapped twice)
047	●	817	Deep coral – berry essence (2X wrapped twice)
292	○	3078	Pale topaz – flower tips (1X wrapped twice)
308	●	3852	Straw – flower center, raspberry accents (2X wrapped twice)
GRADED FRENCH KNOT (2X)			
301	●	744	Yellow – pear

MORE PROJECT IDEAS

- Stitch a sprinkling of floral motifs on cross-stitch fabric to make a roll-style pillow.
- Make a beautiful sachet using the blue floral design.
- Stitch the strawberries and raspberries on a jar topper for jelly or jam.
- Repeat the bird motif across a bath towel.
- To make a plain shower curtain fancy, stitch a row of flowers across the hem or along the top.
- Using yarn, duplicate stitch the leaves on a sweater.
- Alternate the berry motifs on banding for kitchen curtain tiebacks.
- Transform the sampler into seat cushions for dining chairs.
- Make a pendant using one of the small floral patterns.
- Stitch the center design and frame it in shades of blue.
- Stitch the bird on a toddler's jeans pocket.
- Create an album cover using the berry motifs.
- Stitch single strawberries in a row to border a towel.
- Make a Thanksgiving card by stitching the fruit on perforated paper.

EASTERN EUROPEAN
FOLK ART

Kaluga

Gzhel

Estonian

Khokhloma

EASTERN EUROPEAN FOLK ART

INSTRUCTIONS

Tape or zigzag stitch the fabric edges. Find the center of the chart and the center of one fabric half; begin stitching there. Use two plies of floss to work cross-stitches over two threads of fabric. Work the remaining stitches using the plies indicated in the key. Press from the back.

With the design at one end, trim the cross-stitch band to $2\frac{5}{8} \times 8\frac{1}{2}$ inches. Cut red fabric $5\frac{1}{4} \times 8\frac{1}{2}$ inches. Sew the bottom of the cross-stitch band to an $8\frac{1}{2}$-inch edge of the red fabric with right sides together. Press open. Line the piece with fleece and quilt as desired. Trim the piece to $7\frac{1}{4} \times 8\frac{1}{2}$ inches. Cut a red lining piece $7\frac{1}{4} \times 8\frac{1}{2}$ inches.

With the design at the top right, stitch piping beginning $\frac{1}{2}$ inch down from the top left corner, rounding the corners as you stitch and sewing to the halfway point of the bottom. Fold the case in half. Stitch along piping across the side and bottom.

Stitch the lining along the same edges, leaving an opening to turn.

Stitch the lining to the case along the top edge; turn through opening; stitch opening closed.

EYEGLASSES CASE

MATERIALS

FABRIC

6×12-inch piece of 32-count cream Belfast linen

FLOSS

Cotton embroidery floss in colors listed in the key, opposite

SUPPLIES

Embroidery hoop
Needle
Scissors; ruler
¼ yard red fabric
Thread
¾ yard red sew-in piping
Fleece
Red quilting thread

EASTERN EUROPEAN FOLK ART

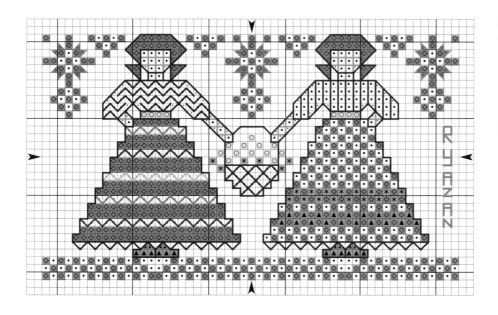

ANCHOR		DMC	
CROSS-STITCH (2X)			
307	○	728	Dark topaz
137	▲	798	Dark Delft blue
047	◇	817	Deep coral
258	✳	904	Parrot green
002	·	3865	Winter white
BACKSTITCH (1X)			
008	╱	352	Light coral – faces, arms
307	╱	728	Dark topaz – dress detail
142	╱	797	Royal blue – dress detail
258	╱	904	Parrot green – dress detail, "Ryazan"
047	╱	817	Deep coral – basket and dress detail (1X); all other stitches (2X)

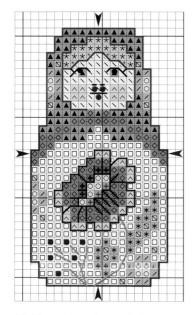

ANCHOR		DMC	
CROSS-STITCH (2X)			
280	◨	166	Moss green
008	⌃	352	Light coral
326	+	720	Bittersweet
307	○	728	Dark topaz
137	▲	798	Dark Delft blue
045	✚	814	Garnet
047	◇	817	Deep coral
258	✳	904	Parrot green
881	◺	945	Blush
292	▢	3078	Pale topaz
308	✳	3852	Straw
1003	╱	3853	Autumn gold

ANCHOR		DMC	
BACKSTITCH (2X)			
403	╱	310	Black – flower detail, nose, eyes
142	╱	797	Royal blue – scarf
047	╱	817	Deep coral – flower, doll (2X); doll base (4X)
258	╱	904	Parrot green – stems
308	╱	3852	Straw – hair
FRENCH KNOT (1X wrapped once)			
403	●	310	Black – eyes
047	●	817	Deep coral – mouth; flowers (2X wrapped three times)

Necklace—instructions and photo, page 94

EASTERN EUROPEAN FOLK ART

NECKLACE

MATERIALS
FABRIC
6×4-inch piece of 28-count khaki evenweave

FLOSS
Cotton embroidery floss in colors listed in the key, page 93

SUPPLIES
Embroidery hoop; needle; scissors
Tracing paper; pencil
2×6-inch piece of fleece
2×3-inch piece of paper-backed fusible web; iron
Mat board
1 yard narrow twisted red cord
Tacky fabric glue
8 gold beads with large hole
1 larger gold bead
Felt in coordinating color

INSTRUCTIONS

Tape or zigzag stitch the evenweave fabric edges. Find the center of the chart and the center of the fabric; begin stitching there. Use two plies of floss to work cross-stitches over two threads of fabric. Work the remaining stitches using the plies indicated in the key. Press the stitchery from the back.

Draw a line around the doll shape several threads past the cross-stitch design. Trace and shape on tracing paper and then onto transweb paper.

Fuse paper-backed fusible web to fleece and cut out. Fuse fleece to wrong side of cross-stitch. Cut mat board slightly smaller than the shape. Glue a layer of fleece to mat board.

Center design over mat board and trim fabric ½ inch beyond edges. Clip into excess fabric and glue shape to back side. Center cord at bottom of cross-stitch and glue around shape. String both ends of cord through large bead and glue to secure. String four beads spaced 1 inch apart to each side of cord. Glue to secure. Tie ends of cord. Glue felt to necklace back.

EASTERN EUROPEAN FOLK ART

BROOCH

MATERIALS

FABRIC

8-inch square of 32-count cream Belfast linen

FLOSS

Cotton embroidery floss in colors listed in the key, below right

SUPPLIES

*Embroidery hoop; needle
2½-inch covered button kit; scissors
⅝ yard of purchased blue cord
(or make cord from twisted
embroidery floss); fleece
Paper-backed fusible web; iron
Tacky fabric glue; pencil
Felt; pin back*

INSTRUCTIONS

Tape or zigzag stitch the fabric edges. Find the center of the chart and the center of the fabric; begin stitching there. Use two plies of floss to work cross-stitches over two threads of fabric. Work the remaining stitches using the plies indicated in the key. Press the stitchery from the back.

Trace around the button shape onto transweb paper. Fuse to fleece. Center, cut out, and fuse

ANCHOR		DMC	
CROSS-STITCH (2X)			
128	I	157	Light Delft blue
137	▲	798	Dark Delft blue
136	✕	799	Medium Delft blue
BACKSTITCH (2X)			
142	╱	797	Royal blue – all stitches
LAZY DAISY with LONG STITCH (2X)			
137	∅	798	Dark Delft blue with
128		157	Light Delft blue – leaves
FRENCH KNOT (2X wrapped twice)			
142	●	797	Royal blue – buds

to wrong side of cross-stitch. Assemble the button according to the manufacturer's instructions.

Glue two rows of cord around the button edge. Glue a felt circle on the back. Attach a pin back.

BIRDS
AND
INSECTS

This chapter pays tribute to the world of birds and insects. Colors that range from bright to muted and textures and patterns from a variety of species provide beautiful inspiration for an array of wonderful projects.

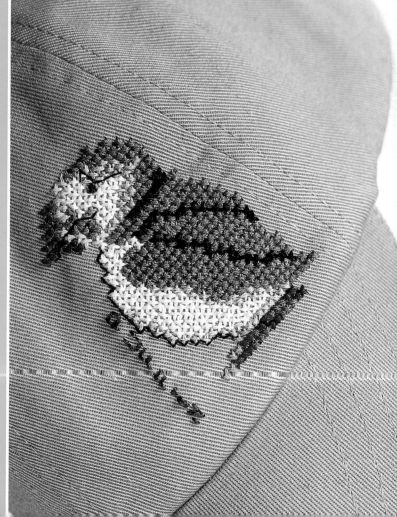

BEAUTIFUL BIRDS

*W*hether you watch them through the cages at the zoo or binoculars in the wild, birds are *fascinating—from colorful feathers to recognizable profiles and familiar calls. If you study a certain species of feathered creatures or feel compelled to identify birds by sight and sound, this interesting collection will inspire you to capture these creatures on fabric in cross-stitches.*

Sampler
BEAUTIFUL BIRDS

SAMPLER

MATERIALS
FABRIC
*14-inch square of 28-count
forget-me-knot blue Jobelan*

FLOSS
*Cotton embroidery floss in colors
listed in the key, page 102*

SUPPLIES
*Embroidery hoop
Needle
Mats and frame
Peacock feather and
crafts glue, optional*

INSTRUCTIONS
Tape or zigzag stitch the fabric
edges. Find the center of the
chart and the center of the
fabric; begin stitching there.
Use two plies of floss to work
cross-stitches over two threads of
fabric. Work the remaining
stitches using the plies indicated
in the key.

Press the stitchery from the
back. Mat and frame as desired.

continued on page 102

BEAUTIFUL BIRDS

ANCHOR		DMC	
CROSS-STITCH (2X)			
375	⊟	167	Yellow-beige
403	■	310	Black
400	⊞	317	True charcoal
011	▣	351	Coral
398	◣	415	Pearl gray
1038	◿	519	Sky blue
210	◈	562	Seafoam
046	◪	666	Red
239	⊙	702	Christmas green
256	△	704	Chartreuse
324	✳	721	Bittersweet
358	⋈	801	Coffee brown
142	✚	826	Powder blue
1035	◉	930	Antique blue
291	▽	973	Lemon
433	◇	996	Electric blue
328	⊟	3341	Melon
118	✚	3746	Dark periwinkle
1049	✕	3826	Dark golden brown
363	▢	3827	Pale golden brown
339	⊕	3830	Medium terra-cotta
170	▲	3842	Wedgwood blue
308	☆	3852	Straw
897	♥	3857	Rosewood
002	·	3865	Winter white

ANCHOR		DMC	
BACKSTITCH			
683	╱	500	Blue-green – leaves (1X); CRANE, OWL (2X)
324	╱	721	Bittersweet – BARN SWALLOW, HERON (2X)
178	╱	791	Cornflower blue – PEACOCK (2X)
152	╱	939	Blue-black – swallow, FLAMINGO (2X)
381	╱	3031	Mocha – branches, cardinal, owl (2X)
1015	╱	3777	Deep terra-cotta – TOUCAN, GOOSE (2X)
236	╱	3799	Dark charcoal – peacock, flowers (1X); goose (2X)
170	╱	3842	Wedgwood blue – CARDINAL (2X)
403	╱	310	Black – all other stitches (1X)

ANCHOR		DMC	
FRENCH KNOT			
403	●	310	Black – eyes of toucan, flamingo, swallow, cardinal, heron (2X wrapped twice); eyes of crane, peacock, owl, goose (1X wrapped twice)
142	●	826	Powder blue – peacock (1X wrapped twice)
1015	●	3777	Deep terra-cotta – berries, flowers (1X wrapped twice)

MORE PROJECT IDEAS

- *Stitch the peacock on one side of a straight-cut sweatshirt, the head near the shoulder. Make a mirror-image color copy of the pattern and stitch it on the opposite side of the sweatshirt, near the lower hem.*
- *For scrapbook embellishments, stitch birds on perforated paper and trim close to stitching.*
- *Stitch a cardinal on perforated paper to make a special Christmas card.*
- *Use banding to make a personalized bird strap for binoculars.*
- *Make holiday ornaments for friends around the world, using bird designs that are significant in their region or yours.*
- *Stitch an owl on the pocket of denim jeans.*
- *Use the sampler design to make a tote bag or pillow.*
- *Stitch a towering crane or heron on a bookmark.*
- *Chart out a circle from the peacock tail to stitch as a design for a pincushion, mirror case, or brooch.*
- *Stitch a row of flamingos on bath towels and on a shower curtain.*

BEAUTIFUL BIRDS

BEAUTIFUL BIRDS

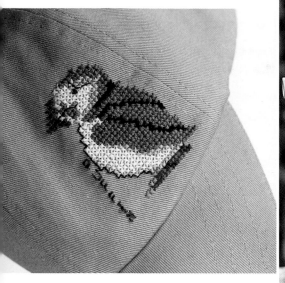

CAP

MATERIALS

FABRIC
*4×6-inch piece of 14-count
waste canvas*

FLOSS
*Cotton embroidery floss in colors
listed in the key, opposite*

SUPPLIES
*Needle
Solid color baseball cap*

INSTRUCTIONS

Baste waste canvas to the cap
where stitchery is desired.
Find the center of the chart
and the center of the waste
canvas; begin stitching there.

Use two plies of floss to work
cross-stitches over each waste
canvas square stitching through
the cap. Work the remaining
stitches using the plies indicated
in the key.

Following the manufacturer's
instructions, carefully remove the
waste canvas.

T-SHIRT

MATERIALS

FABRIC
*6-inch square of 14-count
waste canvas*

FLOSS
*Cotton embroidery floss in colors
listed in the key, opposite*

SUPPLIES
*Needle
Solid color T-shirt*

INSTRUCTIONS

Baste waste canvas to the T-shirt
sleeve where stitchery is desired.
Find the center of the chart
and the center of the waste
canvas; begin stitching there.

Use two plies of floss to work
cross-stitches over each waste
canvas square, stitching through
the T-shirt. Work the remaining
stitches using the plies indicated
in the key.

Following the manufacturer's
instructions, carefully remove the
waste canvas.

BEAUTIFUL BIRDS

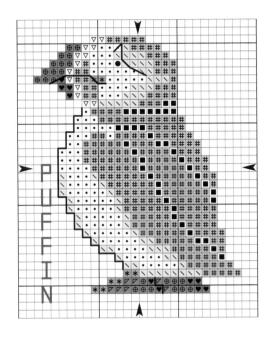

ANCHOR		DMC	
CROSS-STITCH (2X)			
403	■	310	Black
400	#	317	True charcoal
398	\	415	Pearl gray
046	◪	666	Red
324	✳	721	Bittersweet
291	▽	973	Lemon
339	⊕	3830	Medium terra-cotta
897	♥	3857	Rosewood
002	•	3865	Winter white
BACKSTITCH (2X)			
683	╱	500	Blue-green – PUFFIN
403	╱	310	Black – all other stitches
FRENCH KNOT (2X wrapped twice)			
403	●	310	Black – eye

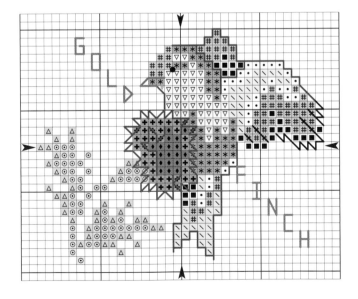

ANCHOR		DMC	
CROSS-STITCH (2X)			
403	■	310	Black
400	#	317	True charcoal
398	\	415	Pearl gray
239	⊙	702	Christmas green
256	△	704	Chartreuse
324	✳	721	Bittersweet
178	◆	791	Cornflower blue
291	▽	973	Lemon
118	✚	3746	Dark periwinkle
002	•	3865	Winter white
BACKSTITCH (2X)			
403	╱	310	Black – wings (1X)
324	╱	721	Bittersweet – beak, GOLD FINCH
178	╱	791	Cornflower blue – flower
236	╱	3799	Dark charcoal – finch
FRENCH KNOT (2X wrapped twice)			
403	●	310	Black – eye

Inspiration
GEMS OF NATURE

*W*herever you look, in the air or on the ground, you will find the magic of Mother Nature at work. This wonderful design collection includes itty-bitty bugs, artful winged beauties, mushrooms, flowers, hummingbirds, and a wheat stalk. Although the motifs are ingeniously integrated to stitch as a sampler plate, you also can stitch designs individually to capture your favorite gem of nature.

GEMS OF NATURE

SAMPLER

MATERIALS
FABRIC
*14-inch square of 28-count Cashel
raw linen*

FLOSS
*Cotton embroidery floss in colors
listed in the key, page 110*

SUPPLIES
*Embroidery hoop
Needle
Mat and frame*

INSTRUCTIONS
Tape or zigzag stitch the fabric
edges. Find the center of the
chart and the center of the
fabric; begin stitching there.
Use two plies of floss to work
cross-stitches over two threads of
fabric. Work the remaining
stitches using the plies indicated
in the key.

Press the stitchery from the
back. Mat and frame as desired.

continued on page 110

ANCHOR		DMC	
CROSS-STITCH (2X)			
002	•	000	White
235	○	169	Pewter
118	◪	340	Periwinkle
333	◪	350	Medium coral
008	∧	352	Light coral
267	◉	469	Dark avocado
281	✚	581	True moss green
874	□	676	Light old gold
885	—	677	Pale old gold
256	✕	704	Chartreuse
295	▽	726	True topaz
307	S	728	Dark topaz
281	◆	732	Olive
275	╎	746	Off-white
136	◇	799	Delft blue
277	▲	830	Dark bronze
907	◩	832	Medium bronze
874	✳	833	Light bronze
340	◕	919	Dark copper
338	✳	921	True copper
274	╲	928	Slate green
055	⊕	962	Pink
397	∿	3072	Beaver gray
382	■	3371	Black-brown
236	⌗	3799	Charcoal
122	⊞	3807	Dark blue-violet
279	△	3819	Light moss green
306	◆	3820	Straw
090	≡	3836	Grape
120	▱	3840	Pale blue-violet

ANCHOR		DMC	
HALF CROSS-STITCH (2X)			
118	╱	340	Periwinkle – mushroom shading
BACKSTITCH (2X)			
002	╱	000	White – moth body butterfly antenna, hummingbird eye detail
256	╱	704	Chartreuse – flower tendril
281	╱	732	Olive – beetle, grasshopper
275	╱	746	Off-white – hummingbird wing detail, grasshopper detail
277	╱	830	Dark bronze – mushroom stems
382	╱	3371	Black-brown – frog, grasshopper's twig, mushrooms
236	╱	3799	Charcoal – all other stitches

ANCHOR		DMC	
BLENDED NEEDLE BACKSTITCH			
235	╱	169	Pewter (1X) and
236		3799	Charcoal (2X) – ladybug's legs
FRENCH KNOT (1X wrapped once)			
002	●	000	White – moth, birds' eyes
382	●	3371	Black-brown – frog's feet, butterfly's eyes, blue bug's eyes, mushroom spots
236	●	3799	Charcoal – ladybug's antennae
LAZY DAISY STITCH (2X)			
1045	◗	436	Caramel – wheat stalks
236	◗	3799	Charcoal – moth and butterfly antennae

MORE PROJECT IDEAS

• *Use the sampler design to cover the front of a scrapbook.*
• *Stitch ladybugs marching across a baby bib.*
• *Stitch the hummingbird and flower for a small decorative pillow top.*
• *Alternate beetles and frogs on pant cuffs for a little boy.*
• *Stitch a frog on the pocket of denim overalls.*
• *Cut a mat from perforated paper and stitch bees buzzing around the edges.*
• *Use waste canvas to stitch a dragonfly to the pocket of a plain T-shirt.*
• *Stitch a row of winged beauties at the top of a tote bag or purse.*
• *On gingham fabric, randomly stitch ladybugs and beetles to make a fun picnic tablecloth.*
• *Stitch butterflies and moths on perforated plastic for colorful refrigerator magnets.*
• *Stitch birds on fabric to cover a book.*
• *Stitch bees along the edge of a bread cloth.*
• *Embellish a sunglasses case with cross-stitched mushrooms.*

GEMS OF NATURE

Moth Sewing Box

GEMS OF NATURE

MOTH SEWING BOX

MATERIALS

FABRIC
14-inch square of 32-count star sapphire linen

FLOSS
Cotton embroidery floss in colors listed in the key, opposite

SUPPLIES
Embroidery hoop; needle
Scissors
6-inch square papier mâché box
¼ yard tan faux suede
Fabric glue
Fleece; 1¼ yard trim
1½-inch purchased stitched adhesive monogram

INSTRUCTIONS

Tape or zigzag stitch the linen edges. Find the center of the chart and the center of the fabric; begin stitching there. Use two plies of floss to work cross-stitches over two threads of fabric. Work remaining stitches using the plies indicated in the key. Press stitchery from the back. Adhere monogram in the center.

Wrap the box bottom with faux suede, trimming to fit; secure with fabric glue.

Cover the lid with fleece. Trim stitchery large enough to cover lid and wrap underneath. Carefully center design on lid; glue edges underneath. Cut a piece of suede to line the lid; glue in place. Glue trim around edge of lid.

GEMS OF NATURE

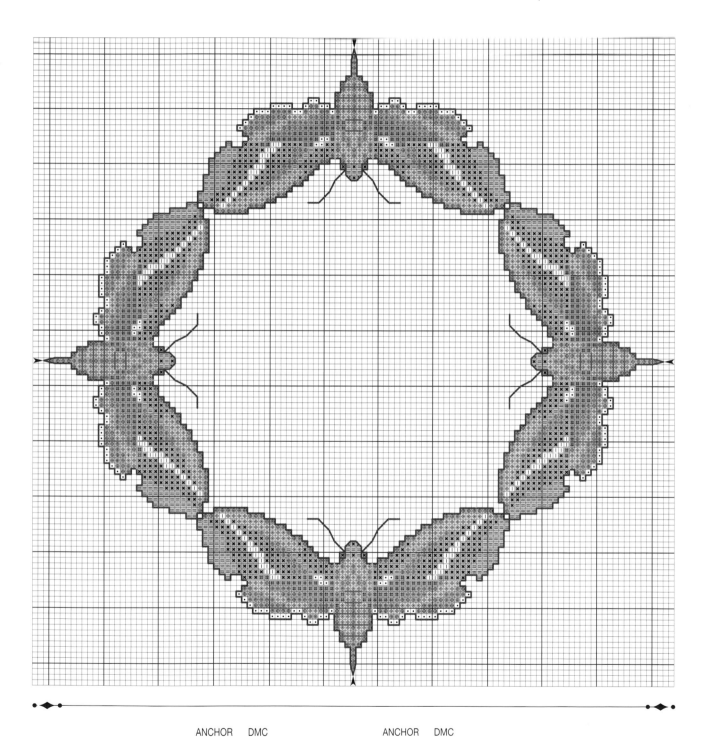

ANCHOR		DMC	
CROSS-STITCH (2X)			
002	•	000	White
370	▣	434	Medium caramel
1045	◈	436	Light caramel
275	I	746	Off-white
055	⊕	962	Pink
236	⊞	3799	Charcoal
090	⊟	3836	Grape

ANCHOR		DMC	
BACKSTITCH (2X)			
277	╱	830	Dark bronze – body detail
275	╱	746	Off-white – wing detail
382	╱	3371	Black-brown – all other stitches

GEMS OF NATURE

BUMBLE BEE SACHET

MATERIALS

FABRIC

*10×13-inch piece of
32-count water lily linen*

FLOSS

*Cotton embroidery floss in colors
listed in the key*

SUPPLIES

*Embroidery hoop; needle; scissors
7×10-inch piece of lining fabric
10 inches of decorative trim*

*Pins; potpourri
12-inch pieces of ⅛-inch-wide ribbon*

INSTRUCTIONS

Tape or zigzag stitch linen edges; measure up 2¼ inches from the bottom; begin stitching in center. Use two plies of floss to work cross-stitches over two threads of fabric. Work remaining stitches using the plies indicated in key.

Trim stitchery to 7×10 inches. Right sides facing, stitch short ends together using ¼-inch seams. Repeat with the lining, leaving an opening to turn. With seam in back of the stitched linen, stitch the bottom seam. Repeat for lining. Pin the trim to the top of the linen bag, raw edges aligned. Place bag in lining; stitch top edge. Turn through the lining opening; stitch opening closed.

Fill the sachet with potpourri. Clip and pull out five rows of horizontal threads 1¾ inches from the top edge. Weave the ribbons through the vertical threads. Tie the ribbons in a bow.

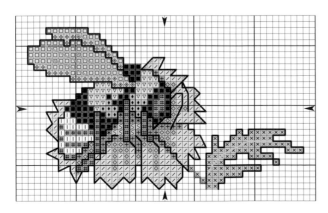

ANCHOR	DMC	
CROSS-STITCH (2X)		
1045	436	Caramel
874	676	Light old gold
256	704	Chartreuse
295	726	True topaz
307	728	Dark topaz
275	746	Off-white
136	799	Delft blue
338	921	True copper
382	3371	Black-brown
236	3799	Charcoal
122	3807	Dark blue-violet
306	3820	Straw
120	3840	Pale blue-violet

ANCHOR	DMC	
BACKSTITCH (2X)		
281	732	Olive – stem
275	746	Off-white – wing detail
277	830	Dark bronze – eye detail
279	3819	Light moss green – leaf veins
236	3799	Charcoal – all other stitches

GEMS OF NATURE

SNAIL PILLOW

MATERIALS

FABRIC

*6×7-inch piece of 28-count
Cashel raw linen*

FLOSS

*Cotton embroidery floss in colors
listed in the key*

SUPPLIES

*Embroidery hoop; needle; thread
¼ yard faux suede; ¼ yard calico
1¼ yards lace; polyfill; cording*

INSTRUCTIONS

Tape or zigzag stitch linen edges. Find the center of chart and of fabric; begin stitching there. Use two plies of floss to work cross–stitches over two threads of fabric. Work remaining stitches using the plies indicated in the key. Press from back.

Using ¼-inch seams, stitch calico triangles (cut to fit stitchery) to sides of stitchery. Stitch suede triangle (cut to fit calico) to calico triangles. Stitch lace at calico edge.

Cover cording with suede. Right sides facing, align raw edges of pillow front and piping; stitch around edge. Cut a calico back piece the size of front; stitch to front leaving an opening; turn. Insert polyfill through opening; stitch opening closed.

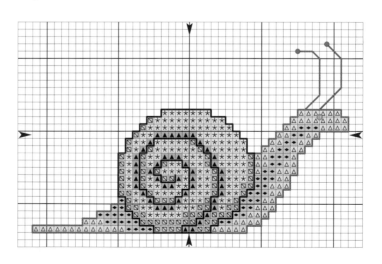

ANCHOR	DMC	
CROSS-STITCH (2X)		
281	◆	732 Olive
277	▲	830 Dark bronze
907	◨	832 Medium bronze
874	✶	833 Light bronze
279	△	3819 Light moss green

ANCHOR	DMC	
BACKSTITCH (2X)		
281	╱	732 Olive – antennae, body
236	╱	3799 Charcoal – shell
FRENCH KNOT		
281	●	732 Olive – antennae
BEAD		
	○	00557 Mill Hill Gold seed bead – eye

COUNTRY FAVORITES

Some people consider it "quaint." Others refer to it as "vintage." However you classify "country," you're sure to find a favorite in this extraordinary collection of more than 30 designs—ranging from stylized roosters to dainty bonneted girls created in the stamped embroidery style of days past.

COUNTRY

hings considered "country" share something comfortably familiar. Woven baskets, quilted patterns, roosters, pineapples, and churches with steeples are some of the classic motifs of this homey style. The cross-stitch plate offers these designs and more—including repetitive floral and heart patterns to embellish stitchery with more country charm.

Sampler
COUNTRY

SAMPLER

MATERIALS

FABRIC
*14-inch square of 28-count
shell linen*

FLOSS
*Cotton embroidery floss in colors
listed in the key, page 122*

SUPPLIES
*Embroidery hoop
Needle
Mats and frame*

INSTRUCTIONS

Tape or zigzag stitch the fabric
edges. Find the center of the
chart and the center of the
fabric; begin stitching there.
Use two plies of floss to work
cross-stitches over two threads of
fabric. Work the remaining
stitches using the plies indicated
in the key.

Press the stitchery from the
back. Mat and frame as desired.

continued on page 122

COUNTRY

ANCHOR		DMC	
CROSS-STITCH (2X)			
403	■	310	Black
371	☆	433	Caramel
879	▲	501	Dark blue-green
212	⊞	561	Dark seafoam
204	⊙	563	True seafoam
302	✳	743	True yellow
307	⊙	783	Christmas gold
148	◆	803	Baby blue
145	⊠	809	Delft blue
1041	✳	844	Beaver gray
22	♥	902	Garnet
381	⊞	3031	Mocha
896	✕	3721	Shell pink
386	⊟	3823	Pale yellow
1049	⊡	3826	Golden brown

ANCHOR		DMC	
BACKSTITCH			
403	╱	310	Black – rooster eye, fence (1X)
683	╱	500	Deep blue-green – rooster (1X)
302	╱	743	True yellow – church (2X)
148	╱	803	Baby blue – windows, door (1X)
22	╱	902	Garnet – steeple (1X)
381	╱	3031	Mocha – basket, key (2X)
896	╱	3721	Shell pink – rooster, steeple (1X)
1049	╱	3826	Golden brown – rooster (2X)

ANCHOR		DMC	
STRAIGHT STITCH (2X)			
204	╱	563	True seafoam – apple leaves
381	╱	3031	Mocha – apple stems
FRENCH KNOT (1X wrapped twice)			
403	●	310	Black – roof fence peaks, steeple
381	●	3031	Mocha – apple stems

MORE PROJECT IDEAS

- *Use waste canvas to stitch the large rooster on a solid-color toaster cover, adding a repetitive floral design across the lower edge.*
- *Stitch the small rooster motif in the corners of napkins.*
- *Stitch the bluebird on small-count cross-stitch fabric for a pillow front.*
- *For a treasured housewarming gift, stitch a row of pineapples, keys, or houses on a bread cloth.*
- *Stitch the church design at the top of a bookmark for a confirmation gift.*
- *Trim the edge of a plain pillowcase with alternating hearts and flowers.*
- *Stitch the basket of apples on a piece of fabric large enough to wrap around a can to make a pencil holder for a favorite teacher.*
- *Embellish a plain picnic tablecloth with watermelon slice motifs spaced randomly across the fabric.*
- *Surprise a special quilting friend by stitching the red basket design for the top of a pincushion.*
- *Stitch a watermelon slice on perforated paper for a summery note card.*

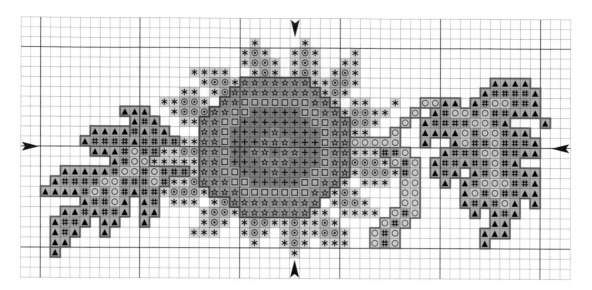

ANCHOR   DMC

CROSS-STITCH (2X)

371	☆	433 Caramel
879	▲	501 Dark blue-green
212	▦	561 Dark seafoam
204	⊙	563 True seafoam
302	✳	743 Yellow
307	⊙	783 Christmas gold
381	✚	3031 Mocha
1049	☐	3826 Golden brown

BACKSTITCH (2X)

| 683 | ╱ | 500 Deep blue-green – leaves |
| 381 | ╱ | 3031 Mocha – flower |

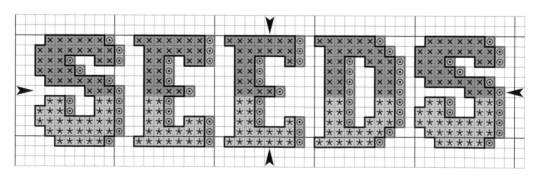

ANCHOR   DMC

CROSS-STITCH (2X)

307	⊙	783 Christmas gold
1041	✴	844 Beaver gray
896	✗	3721 Shell pink

BACKSTITCH (2X)

| 307 | ╱ | 783 Christmas gold – SEEDS |
| 403 | ╱ | 310 Black – all other stitches |

COUNTRY

HAND TOWELS

MATERIALS

FABRIC

*Two white towels with 14-count
Aida stitching band inserts*

FLOSS

*Cotton embroidery floss in colors
listed in the keys, opposite*

SUPPLIES

*Embroidery hoop
Needle*

INSTRUCTIONS

For each towel, find the center
of the chart and the center of the
Aida insert; begin stitching there.
Use two plies of floss to work

cross-stitches over one square
of fabric. Work the backstitches
using the plies indicated in
the key.

STAMPED GOODS

*I*f you love the look of vintage stamped embroidery, you'll enjoy the fresh designs in this section. Stitched with the familiar bright colors and simple motifs of decades ago, these new cross-stitch designs work up quickly with much of the fabric showing through the outlined areas. The endearing images are accented with stem stitches, lazy daisies, and French knots, just like old-fashioned embroidery that your grandmothers mastered.

Sampler
STAMPED GOODS

SAMPLER

MATERIALS
FABRIC
*14-inch square of 28-count
cream linen*

FLOSS
*Cotton embroidery floss in colors
listed in the key, page 130*

SUPPLIES
*Embroidery hoop
Needle
Mats and frame*

INSTRUCTIONS
Tape or zigzag stitch the fabric
edges. Find the center of the
chart and the center of the
fabric; begin stitching there.
Use two plies of floss to work
cross-stitches over two threads of
fabric. Work the remaining
stitches using the plies indicated
in the key.

Press the stitchery from the
back. Mat and frame as desired.

continued on page 130

STAMPED GOODS

ANCHOR		DMC	
CROSS-STITCH (2X)			
1030	☒	155	Light periwinkle
978	◇	322	Baby blue
239	✚	702	Christmas green
256	⊘	704	Chartreuse
324	☆	721	Bittersweet
303	✳	742	Yellow
336	⊟	758	Terra-cotta
309	⊕	781	Christmas gold
358	▲	801	Coffee brown
145	⊡	809	Delft blue
042	⊞	3831	Raspberry
BACKSTITCH (2X)			
218	/	319	Pistachio – stems, leaves
978	/	322	Baby blue – flowers
239	/	702	Chartreuse – stems
324	/	721	Bittersweet – sunflower center
303	/	742	Yellow – butterfly
336	/	758	Terra-cotta – skin
309	/	781	Christmas gold – baskets
358	/	801	Coffee brown – butterflies, stems, umbrella
042	/	3831	Raspberry – roses, bows

ANCHOR		DMC	
LAZY DAISY STITCH (2X)			
978	⟋	322	Baby blue – flower
239	⟋	702	Christmas green – leaves
303	⟋	742	Yellow – sunflower
042	⟋	3831	Raspberry – bows
303	⟋	742	Yellow – flower with
324	/	721	Bittersweet – tacking stitch
026	⟋	899	Rose – flower with
042	/	3831	Raspberry – tacking stitch

ANCHOR		DMC	
FRENCH KNOT (3X wrapped once)			
978	●	322	Baby blue – necklace
119	●	333	Deep periwinkle – flowers
239	●	702	Christmas green – stems
324	●	721	Bittersweet – flower centers, umbrella
303	●	742	Yellow – flower centers
358	●	801	Coffee brown – sunflower center, rose, large basket, butterfly
042	●	3831	Raspberry – flowers, bow ends, sleeve bows

MORE PROJECT IDEAS

- Using waste canvas, trim lace-edged white pillowcases with a row of floral motifs.
- Stitch the bonnet girl on fabric large enough to cover a diary or album.
- Use waste canvas to make delightful place mats by stitching tulips along the bottom edge.
- Cut a square tablecloth from gingham fabric and use the squares for cross-stitch fabric to stitch your favorite country motifs.
- Use waste canvas to embellish a plain white shower curtain with colorful country images.
- Stitch the floral basket on 32-count linen to make a dainty pin.
- Use waste canvas to stitch butterflies on the cuffs of little girls' socks.
- Embellish an eyeglasses case by stitching the tulip at the top.
- Stitch blue lazy-daisy flowers around the neck of a T-shirt or sweatshirt.
- Create personalized shower invitations by stitching the umbrella motif on perforated paper. To carry out the theme at the shower, stitch the same design on the tablecloth, napkins, and napkin rings.
- Make guest towels special by stitching daisies randomly across an Aida insert.
- Make a feminine pillow top by stitching the entire sampler design and finishing the pillow with coordinating calico fabrics.

STAMPED GOODS

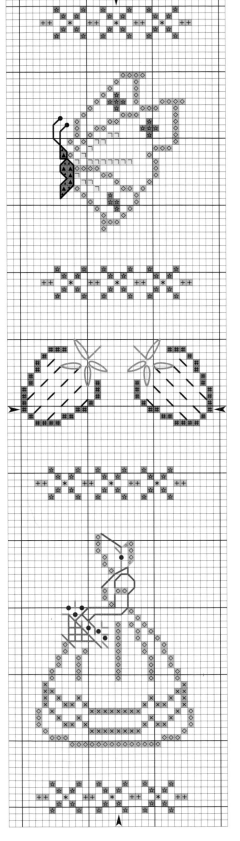

BOOKMARK

MATERIALS

FABRIC

18-count white Aida lace-edge bookmark

FLOSS

Cotton embroidery floss in colors
listed in the key

SUPPLIES

Needle

INSTRUCTIONS

Find center of the chart and of
bookmark; begin stitching there.
Use two plies of floss to work
cross-stitches over one square of
fabric. Work the remaining
stitches using plies indicated in
key. Press stitchery from back.

ANCHOR		DMC	
CROSS-STITCH (2X)			
1030	☒	155	Light periwinkle
978	◇	322	Baby blue
239	+	702	Christmas green
324	☆	721	Bittersweet
303	✳	742	Yellow
358	▲	801	Coffee brown
145	⊐	809	Delft blue
042	▦	3831	Raspberry
BACKSTITCH (2X)			
978	╱	322	Baby blue – hat
239	╱	702	Christmas green – strawberry, hat
309	╱	781	Christmas gold – basket
358	╱	801	Coffee brown – butterfly
RUNNING STITCH (2X)			
358	╱	801	Coffee brown – strawberry
LAZY DAISY STITCH (2X)			
239	◠	702	Christmas green – strawberry
FRENCH KNOT (2X wrapped once)			
358	●	801	Coffee brown – butterfly
042	●	3831	Raspberry – flowers, hat

Table Doily
STAMPED GOODS

TABLE DOILY

MATERIALS

FABRIC
14-count premade crochet-edge white Aida doily

FLOSS
Cotton embroidery floss in colors listed in the key

SUPPLIES
Embroidery hoop; needle

INSTRUCTIONS

Find the center of the chart and the center of one edge of the doily; begin stitching bottom of pansy 12 squares from the edge. Use two plies of floss to work cross-stitches over two threads of fabric. Work the other stitches using the plies indicated in key. Press the stitchery from the back.

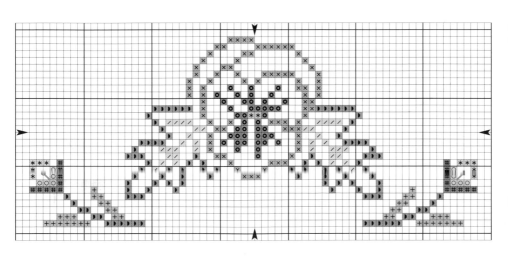

ANCHOR		DMC
CROSS-STITCH (2X)		
1030	✕	155 Light periwinkle
399	▶	318 Light steel
119	⊙	333 Deep periwinkle
239	+	702 Christmas green
256	∕	704 Chartreuse
303	✳	742 Yellow
026	○	899 Rose
042	⊞	3831 Raspberry
BACKSTITCH (2X)		
324	∕	721 Bittersweet
FRENCH KNOT (2X wrapped twice)		
324	●	721 Bittersweet

THE
GREAT
OUTDOORS

There is something energizing about being out in the fresh air, enjoying the things that make you happy. If activities such as fishing, sailing, horseback riding, or walking along the beach make you smile, you'll be downright giddy with these cross-stitch designs that capture what you love most about life outdoors.

135

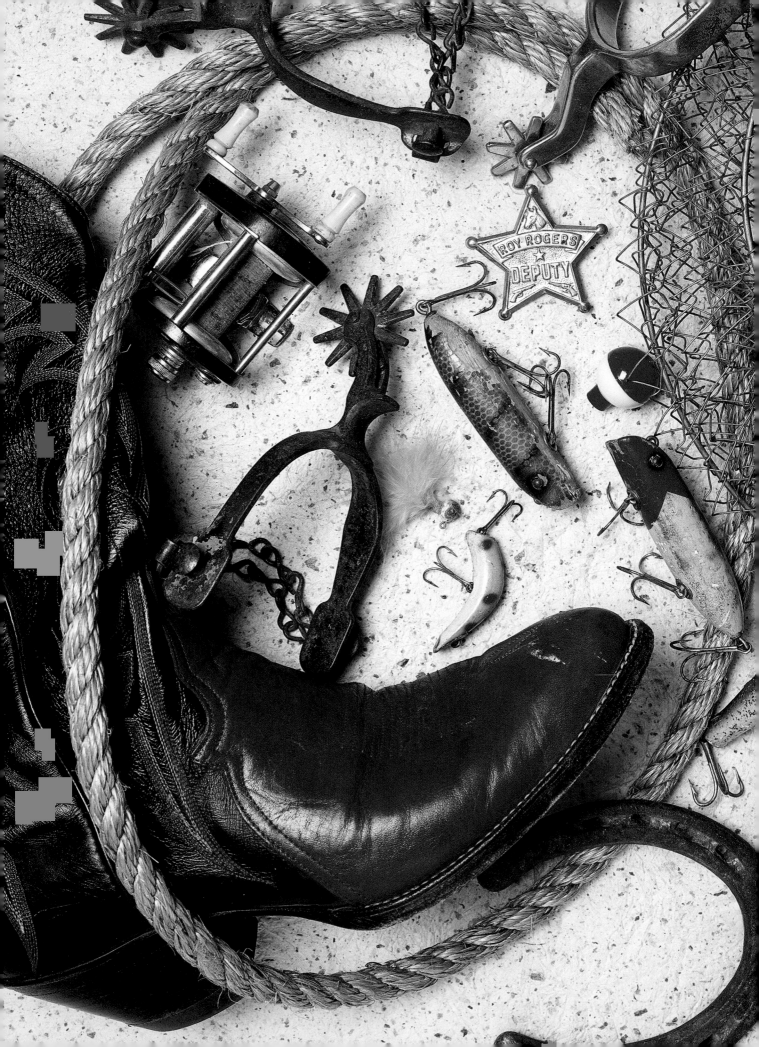

OUTDOORS

Enjoying life in the great outdoors often includes such hobbies as fishing, horseback riding, and sailing—all symbolized by the realistic designs below. This combination of nautical and cowboy motifs is wonderfully handsome and sure to be loved by any outdoorsman. More rugged designs (a horse, fish, and pelican) are on pages 142–145. Grab your needle and floss and get ready to stitch something spectacular!

Sampler
OUTDOORS

SAMPLER

MATERIALS

FABRIC

*14-inch square of 28-count antique
white Cashel linen*

FLOSS

*Cotton embroidery floss in colors
listed in the key, page 140*

SUPPLIES

*Embroidery hoop
Needle
Mat and frame
Rope and glue, optional*

INSTRUCTIONS

Tape or zigzag stitch the fabric
edges. Find the center of the
chart and the center of the
fabric; begin stitching there.
Use three plies of floss to work
cross-stitches over two threads of
fabric. Work the remaining
stitches using the plies indicated
in the key.

Press the stitchery from the
back. Mat and frame as desired.

continued on page 140

OUTDOORS

ANCHOR	DMC	
CROSS-STITCH (2X)		
002	⊡	000 White
1049	⬆	301 Medium mahogany
1025	✕	347 Deep salmon
351	◗	400 Dark mahogany
374	▼	420 Hazel
1045	✶	436 Caramel
890	▽	680 Old gold
590	╱	712 Cream
924	✳	731 Medium olive
280	▯	733 Light olive
302	△	743 True yellow
300	○	745 Light yellow
137	▲	798 Dark Delft blue
136	✚	799 Medium Delft blue
906	▦	829 Bronze
381	◆	938 Coffee brown
187	◈	958 Medium aqua
185	▭	964 Light aqua
1024	◇	3328 Dark salmon
1017	✩	3727 Antique mauve
1050	✖	3781 Dark mocha
899	▢	3782 Light mocha
1086	♡	3790 Beige-gray
305	◿	3821 True straw
308	▤	3852 Deep straw
1003	⊕	3853 Dark autumn gold
313	▯	3854 Medium autumn gold
944	◉	3862 Dark mocha-beige
376	‖	3864 Light mocha-beige

ANCHOR	DMC	
BACKSTITCH (2X)		
1025	╱	347 Deep salmon – lure, flag, fish gill
137	╱	798 Dark Delft blue – lighthouse
381	╱	938 Coffee brown – creel, anchor chain, boat, lure
1050	╱	3781 Dark mocha – boat, fish, rope, bobber
1003	╱	3853 Dark autumn gold – crab legs
382	╱	3371 Black-brown – all other stitches
BLENDED NEEDLE BACKSTITCH		
1086 590	╱	3790 Beige-gray (1X) and 712 Cream (1X) – "DAPHNIA"
RUNNING STITCH (2X)		
381	▬▬	938 Coffee brown – boot
STRAIGHT STITCH (2X)		
890	╱	680 Old gold – lure
302	╱	743 True yellow – fly on creel
137	╱	798 Dark Delft blue – fly on creel
187	╱	958 Medium aqua – lure
185	╱	964 Light aqua – lure

ANCHOR	DMC	
FRENCH KNOT (2X)		
381	●	938 Coffee brown – boot (2X wrapped once)
382	●	3371 Black-brown – badge, eyes, spur (2X wrapped once)
305	●	3821 True straw – fly on creel, boat top (3X wrapped twice)
1003	●	3853 Dark autumn gold – fly on creel (3X wrapped twice)
BLENDED NEEDLE FRENCH KNOT (wrapped once)		
890 305	●	680 Old gold (2X) and 3821 True straw (2X) – badge points

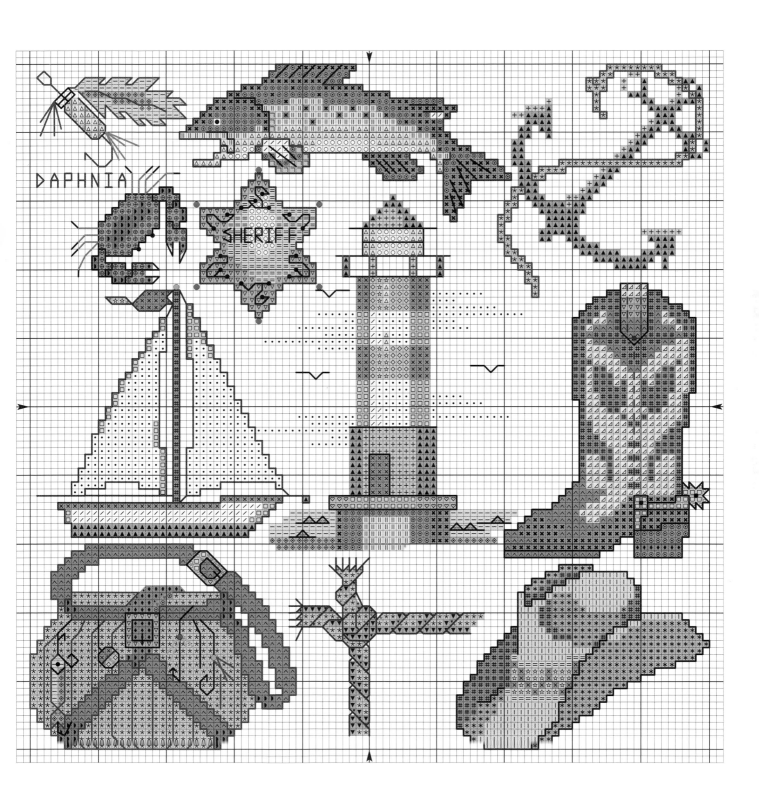

PEN HOLDER

MATERIALS

FABRIC

6×8-inch piece of of 28-count antique white Cashel linen (or size to fit pen holder base)

FLOSS

Cotton embroidery floss in colors listed in the key, opposite

SUPPLIES

Embroidery hoop; needle
Wooden pen holder with base for needlework insertion
Jute twine; thick white crafts glue

INSTRUCTIONS

Tape or zigzag fabric edges. Find the center of the chart and the center of the fabric; begin stitching there. Use two plies of floss to work cross-stitches over two threads of fabric. Work the remaining stitches using the plies indicated in the key. Press the stitchery from the back.

Mount and insert the stitchery as directed by the pen holder manufacturer, trimming stitchery if needed. Braid jute to fit around stitchery; knot ends. Glue braid in place as shown, *above*. Let the glue dry.

OUTDOORS

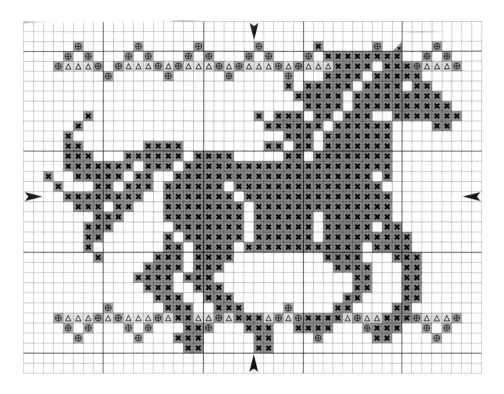

ANCHOR   DMC
CROSS-STITCH (2X)

302	△	743	True yellow
1050	✖	3781	Dark mocha
1003	⊕	3853	Dark autumn gold

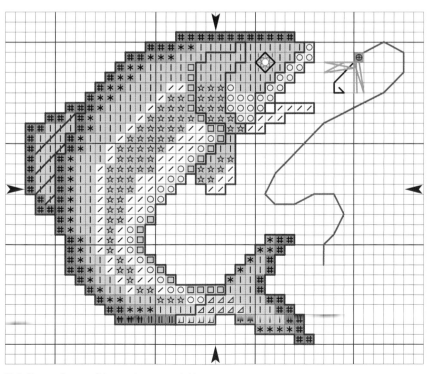

ANCHOR   DMC
CROSS-STITCH (2X)

590	∕	712	Cream
924	✳	731	Medium olive
280	I	733	Light olive
300	○	745	Light yellow
906	#	829	Bronze
1017	☆	3727	Antique mauve
899	□	3782	Light mocha
305	◿	3821	True straw
1003	⊕	3853	Dark autumn gold

BACKSTITCH (2X)

137	∕	798	Dark Delft blue – line
382	∕	3371	Black-brown – eye, hook
1050	∕	3781	Dark mocha – fish

STRAIGHT STITCH (2X)

302	∕	743	True yellow – fly

FRENCH KNOT
(2X wrapped once)

002	○	000	White – eye

Fish Box—photo and instructions, page 144

OUTDOORS

FISH BOX

MATERIALS
FABRIC
*10-inch square of 28-count antique
white Cashel linen*

FLOSS
*Cotton embroidery floss in colors
listed in the key, page 143*

SUPPLIES
*Embroidery hoop; needle
Wooden box with lid for
needlework insertion*

INSTRUCTIONS
Tape or zigzag fabric edges.
Find the center of the chart,
page 143, and the center of the
fabric; begin stitching there.
Use two plies of floss to work
cross-stitches over two threads
of fabric. Work the remaining
stitches using the plies indicated
in the key.

Press the stitchery from
the back.

Insert the stitchery into the lid
as directed by the manufacturer.

Paperweight
OUTDOORS

PAPERWEIGHT

MATERIALS

FABRIC
5×8-inch piece of 28-count antique white Cashel linen

FLOSS
Cotton embroidery floss in colors listed in the key, below

SUPPLIES
*Embroidery hoop; needle
Glass paperweight for needlework insertion*

INSTRUCTIONS

Tape or zigzag fabric edges. Find the center of the chart and of the fabric; begin stitching there. Use two plies of floss to work cross-stitches over two threads of fabric. Work the remaining stitches using the plies indicated in the key. Press stitchery from back.

Mount and insert the stitchery into the paper weight as directed by the manufacturer.

ANCHOR	DMC	
CROSS-STITCH (2X)		
002	·	000 White
374	▼	420 Medium hazel
302	△	743 True yellow
136	＋	799 Medium Delft blue
185	―	964 Light aqua
1050	✖	3781 Dark mocha
899	□	3782 Light mocha
1003	⊕	3853 Dark autumn gold
313	⅂	3854 Medium autumn gold
944	◎	3862 Dark mocha-beige

ANCHOR	DMC	
BACKSTITCH (2X)		
381	╱	938 Coffee brown – pelican
382	╱	3371 Black-brown – post
1050	╱	3781 Dark mocha – post
FRENCH KNOT (2X wrapped once)		
382	●	3371 Black-brown – eye

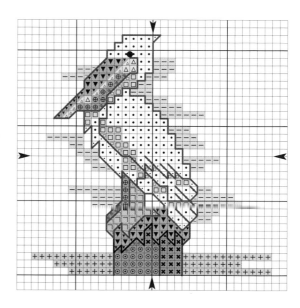

UNDER THE SEA

*L ife by the sea conjures images of vast ocean waters, seashells, fish, crabs, seahorses,
starfish, seaweed, and graceful fairy-tale mermaids—as the sampler, below, depicts.
For even more by-the-sea inspiration, see the dolphin, lobster, and fish designs on page 152.
Any of the detailed motifs can be stitched on a brilliant blue background to enhance the
beauty of these ocean creatures.*

Sampler
UNDER THE SEA

SAMPLER

MATERIALS
FABRIC
*14-inch square of 28-count Nordic
blue Jobelan*

FLOSS
*Cotton embroidery floss in colors
listed in the key, page 150*

SUPPLIES
*Embroidery hoop; needle
Mats and frame
Acrylic paints in medium and
dark green; small flat paintbrush
Starfish, shells, and seahorse, optional
(available in crafts stores); crafts glue*

INSTRUCTIONS
Tape or zigzag stitch the fabric edges. Find the center of the chart and the center of the fabric; begin stitching there. Use two plies of floss to work cross-stitches over two threads of fabric. Work the remaining stitches using the plies indicated in the key. Press the stitchery from the back.

Mat and frame as desired. To embellish the mat, load a paintbrush with both colors and paint simple seaweed; let dry. Glue starfish, shells, and seahorse over seaweed; let dry.

continued on page 150

UNDER THE SEA

ANCHOR	DMC	
CROSS-STITCH (2X)		
002	⊡	000 White
1030	⊟	155 Light periwinkle
9159	◺	162 Sky blue
109	◇	209 Lavender
1049	◆	301 Mahogany
399	◪	318 Steel
041	⫼	335 Medium rose
150	▲	336 Navy
1025	♥	347 Salmon
914	∼	407 Cocoa
371	■	433 Caramel
239	✕	702 Christmas green
256	△	704 Chartreuse
324	✳	721 Medium bittersweet
323	⊕	722 Light bittersweet
295	▽	726 True topaz
307	✶	728 Dark topaz
309	◎	781 Christmas gold
133	◨	796 Royal blue
140	⋀	813 True powder blue
147	⊞	825 Dark powder blue
026	▷	899 True rose
881	⊟	945 Blush
052	▢	957 Geranium
186	⊖	959 Aqua
048	⟋	963 Pink
246	◆	986 Forest green
363	▢	3827 Golden brown
311	⊡	3855 Autumn gold

ANCHOR	DMC	
BACKSTITCH (2X)		
002	╱	000 White – crab detail (1X)
119	╱	333 Deep periwinkle – shells, fish
1025	╱	347 Salmon – coral, mermaid's mouth
371	╱	433 Caramel – mermaid's top, body and tail, starfish (2X); mermaid's eyebrows (1X)
281	╱	581 Moss green – seaweed
256	╱	704 Chartreuse – seaweed
295	╱	726 True topaz – fish eye
147	╱	825 Dark powder blue – fish gills
341	╱	918 Copper – fish fins
246	╱	986 Forest green – fish fins, seahorse
186	╱	3851 Bright green – seahorse
382	╱	3371 Black-brown – all other stitches (1X)

ANCHOR	DMC	
FRENCH KNOT		
002	○	000 White – starfish (1X wrapped twice)
9159	●	162 Sky blue – seahorse (2X wrapped three times)
1025	●	347 Salmon – mermaid's mouth (1X wrapped twice)
147	●	825 Dark powder blue – fish eye (1X wrapped three times)
382	●	3371 Black-brown – crab (1X wrapped three times); mermaid's eyes, seahorse eye, remaining fish eyes (1X wrapped twice)
186	●	3851 Bright green – bracelets (2X wrapped twice)
LAZY DAISY STITCH (2X)		
281	⟊	581 Moss green – seaweed

MORE PROJECT IDEAS

- *Stitch favorite from-the-sea designs on banding to machine-stitch along one edge of a beach towel.*
- *Buy cross-stitch fabric that coordinates with a cloth beach bag. Stitch the mermaid motif on the fabric and sew it on the tote for a pocket.*
- *Embellish a case for sunglasses with fish and shells.*
- *For the sea enthusiast, stitch a set of fish and crab coasters using yarn and half cross-stitches on perforated plastic circles.*
- *Stitch a shell on perforated paper for a lovely note card.*
- *Use waste canvas to stitch a school of fish on a shower curtain.*
- *Stitch a shell border on banding for summery curtain tiebacks.*
- *Use waste canvas to stitch seahorses to a plain swimsuit coverup.*
- *Stitch a starfish on perforated paper for a "you are a star" greeting card.*
- *Add a colorful touch to a plain T-shirt by stitching the mermaid front and center, using waste canvas.*

UNDER THE SEA

ALBUM COVER

MATERIALS

FABRIC
7×12-inch piece 14-count white Aida

FLOSS
*Cotton embroidery floss in colors
listed in the key, opposite*

SUPPLIES
*Embroidery hoop; needle
Small photo album; scissors*

*⅜ yard blue faux suede; 6×11-inch
piece of contrasting faux suede
1¾ yard purchased blue piping
1 yard green cording; pinking shears
3×8-inch piece of matboard
3×8-inch piece of fleece; fabric glue*

INSTRUCTIONS

Tape or zigzag fabric edges. Find center of chart and of fabric; begin stitching there. Use three plies of floss to work cross-stitches over one square of fabric. Work remaining stitches using plies indicated in key. Press from back.

Cover album with ⅜ yard of suede; glue along inside cover. Trim stitchery to 5×10 inches. Glue fleece to mat board. Center cross-stitch on fleece; glue edges to back. Glue to contrasting suede; trim suede with pinking shears. Glue to album front. Glue cording and piping around stitchery and album. Let dry.

UNDER THE SEA

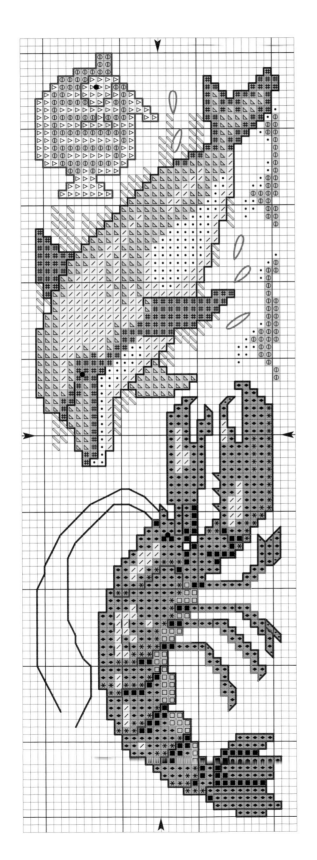

ANCHOR   DMC
CROSS-STITCH (2X)

ANCHOR	DMC	
002	•	000 White
9159	◣	162 Sky blue
1049	◆	301 Mahogany
399	◺	318 Steel
371	◼	433 Caramel
324	✳	721 Medium bittersweet
295	▽	726 True topaz
1034	#	931 Antique blue
186	⊕	959 Aqua
363	▢	3827 Golden brown

ANCHOR   DMC
HALF CROSS-STITCH (2X)

9159   ⟋   162 Sky blue – dolphin shadow

BACKSTITCH (2X)

119	╱	333 Deep periwinkle – dolphin
371	╱	433 Caramel – lobster joints and details
324	╱	721 Medium bittersweet – lobster legs
341	╱	918 Copper – lobster body and antennae
246	╱	986 Forest green – fish

ANCHOR   DMC
FRENCH KNOT

382   ●   3371 Black-brown – fish eye (1X wrapped three times); lobster and dolphin eyes (2X wrapped three times)

LAZY DAISY STITCH (2X)

186   ⬯   3851 Bright green – droplets

UNDER THE SEA

DOLPHIN PENCIL HOLDER

MATERIALS

FABRIC
10×18-inch piece of 28-count white Jobelan

FLOSS
Cotton embroidery floss in colors listed in the key, below

SUPPLIES
Embroidery hoop; needle; scissors
Ceramic pencil or toothbrush holder
6×14-inch piece of gray faux suede
Fabric glue; ¾ yard blue piping

INSTRUCTIONS

Tape or zigzag Jobelan edges. Find the center of the chart and center of the fabric; begin stitching there. Use two plies of floss to work cross–stitches over two threads of fabric. Work the remaining stitches using the plies indicated in the key. Press.

Trim the stitchery to wrap around the holder as shown, *opposite*, allowing for ¼ inch to be pressed under along the long edges and at the back seam.

Stitch the piping to the top edge. Pink one edge of the suede; stitch to bottom of stitched piece. Wrap the stitchery around the holder; glue in place. Let glue dry.

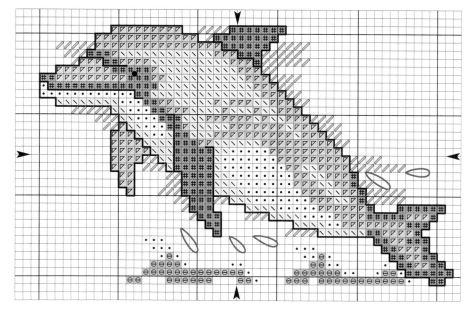

ANCHOR		DMC	
CROSS-STITCH (2X)			
002	•	000	White
9159	◣	162	Sky blue
399	◩	318	Steel
1034	#	931	Antique blue
186	⊖	959	Aqua
HALF CROSS-STITCH (2X)			
9159	╱	162	Sky blue – dolphin shadow
BACKSTITCH (2X)			
119	╱	333	Deep periwinkle – dolphin
FRENCH KNOT (2X wrapped three times)			
382	●	3371	Black-brown – eye
LAZY DAISY STITCH (2X)			
186	◗	3851	Bright green – droplets

Dolphin Pencil Holder
UNDER THE SEA

STAINED GLASS

*A*rtistic stained glass dates to the early 1100s when it was used for cathedral windows. This art form, later incorporated into lamp making, is still appreciated today. The images below represent typical stained glass motifs, with the diamond design and intersecting bars in the background contributing to the look of leading. This lovely design can be stitched on many fabric colors.

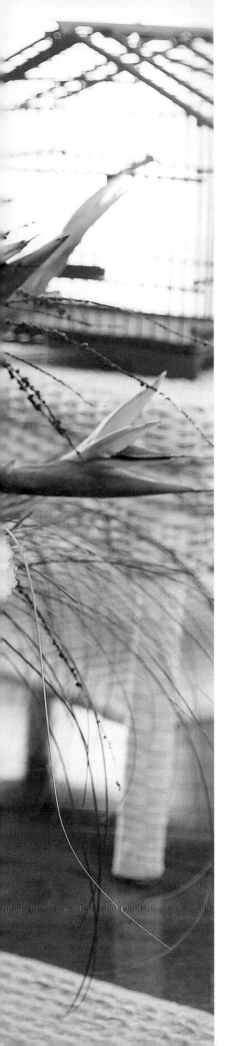

SAMPLER

MATERIALS
FABRIC
*14-inch square of 28-count antique
white Cashel linen*

FLOSS
*Cotton embroidery floss in colors
listed in the key, page 160*

SUPPLIES
*Embroidery hoop
Needle
Mats and frame*

INSTRUCTIONS
Tape or zigzag stitch the fabric
edges. Find the center of the
chart and the center of the
fabric; begin stitching there.
Use two plies of floss to work
cross-stitches over two threads
of fabric. Work the remaining
stitches using the plies indicated
in the key.

Press the stitchery from the
back. Mat and frame as desired.

continued on page 160

STAINED GLASS

ANCHOR	DMC	
		CROSS-STITCH (2X)
059	✶	150 Dusty rose
1030	◇	155 Light periwinkle
128	–	157 Delft blue
280	▧	166 Moss green
109	◣	209 Lavender
119	◪	333 Deep periwinkle
041	▢	335 Medium rose
9046	‖	349 Coral
370	⊞	434 Caramel
890	★	680 Dark old gold
239	✕	702 Christmas green
256	△	704 Chartreuse
326	◉	720 Bittersweet
295	▽	726 Topaz
306	═	729 Medium old gold
304	☆	741 Medium tangerine
147	◆	825 Dark powder blue
142	✾	826 Medium powder blue
256	◉	906 Parrot green
381	✚	938 Coffee brown
186	⋀	959 True aqua
298	✛	972 Light tangerine
246	▶	986 Forest green

ANCHOR	DMC	
		CROSS-STITCH (2X)
433	⬓	996 Electric blue
085	◿	3609 Plum
167	∿	3766 Peacock blue
1015	◈	3777 Terra-cotta
236	■	3799 Charcoal
066	◯	3806 Cyclamen
188	◆	3812 Deep aqua
386	❘	3823 Yellow
308	⊕	3852 Straw
1003	✳	3853 Autumn gold
897	♥	3857 Rosewood
002	⊡	3865 Winter white

ANCHOR	DMC	
		BACKSTITCH (2X)
306	╱	729 Medium old gold – parrot eye
403	╱	310 Black – all other stitches
		FRENCH KNOT
403	●	310 Black – carp nostrils (2X wrapped once); carp eyes (2X wrapped three times)

MORE PROJECT IDEAS

- *Stitch the sampler and finish it as a tote bag.*
- *Create a keepsake card by stitching the dragonfly on perforated paper.*
- *Add a touch of the tropics to a yellow sweatshirt or T-shirt by stitching the parrot on the front of the shirt, using waste canvas.*
- *For a tiny box lid insert, stitch the bee design on black linen.*
- *Embellish the corners of table linens with floral motifs.*
- *Trim the pocket of a white blouse with the lily pad design.*
- *Use waste canvas to stitch the floral designs across a window valance.*
- *Make a cross-stitched photo mat by stitching only the background leading design.*
- *Make a beach tote that features the koi.*
- *Stitch the dragonfly on perforated plastic, trim, and attach it to a narrow dowel for a plant poke.*
- *Make a set of button covers using the bee motif.*
- *Make a photo album or scrapbook cover using the entire sampler design.*
- *Cross-stitch several bee and dragonfly motifs on perforated paper to enhance the album pages.*
- *Stitch the grapes on the corners of a gingham tablecloth.*

STAINED GLASS

STAINED GLASS

BREAD CLOTH

MATERIALS
FABRIC
Prefinished 14-count white
Aida bread cloth

FLOSS
Cotton embroidery floss in colors
listed in the key, opposite

SUPPLIES
Embroidery hoop
Needle
Ruler

INSTRUCTIONS
Allowing 1½ inches unstitched at the fabric edges, begin stitching the butterfly in one corner of the bread cloth. Use two plies of floss to work cross-stitches over one square of fabric. Work the remaining stitches using the plies indicated in the key.

Press the stitchery from the back.

ANCHOR		DMC	
CROSS-STITCH (2X)			
059	★	150	Dusty rose
1030	◇	155	Light periwinkle
109	◣	209	Lavender
890	★	680	Dark old gold
239	✕	702	Christmas green
256	△	704	Chartreuse
326	◉	720	Bittersweet
295	▽	726	Topaz
306	═	729	Medium old gold
304	✪	741	Medium tangerine

ANCHOR		DMC	
CROSS-STITCH (2X)			
381	✚	938	Coffee brown
246	◗	986	Forest green
167	∿	3766	Peacock blue
236	■	3799	Charcoal
066	◯	3806	Cyclamen
386	⊔	3823	Yellow
308	⊕	3852	Straw
1003	✱	3853	Autumn gold
BACKSTITCH (2X)			
403	╱	310	Black – all stitches

HOLIDAYS

From "I love you" to "Merry Christmas," the festive wishes in this collection celebrate the holidays with cross-stitch. The seasonal motifs are quick to stitch, so you'll have plenty of projects to work all year long.

HALLOWEEN & THANKSGIVING

he splendor of autumn also brings holiday celebrations. Below are familiar sights of the season—acorns, pumpkins, and falling leaves—as well as striking Halloween and Thanksgiving motifs. This rich sampler is a tribute to the leaf-falling, trick-or-treating, giving-thanks season treasured by Americans.

Sampler
HALLOWEEN &
THANKSGIVING

SAMPLER

MATERIALS
FABRIC
14-inch square of 32-count cream
Belfast linen

FLOSS
Cotton embroidery floss in colors
listed in the key, page 170

SUPPLIES
Embroidery hoop
Needle
Mats and frame

INSTRUCTIONS
Tape or zigzag stitch the fabric
edges. Find the center of the
chart and the center of the
fabric; begin stitching there.
Use two plies of floss to work
cross-stitches over two threads
of fabric. Work the remaining
stitches using the plies indicated
in the key.

 Press the stitchery from the
back. Mat and frame as desired.

continued on page 170

HALLOWEEN & THANKSGIVING

ANCHOR		DMC	
CROSS-STITCH (2X)			
001	⊡	000	White
072	◆	154	Deep grape
280	△	166	Moss green
352	◪	300	Mahogany
403	■	310	Black
1025	♥	347	Salmon
008	○	352	Coral
1046	⊛	435	True caramel
1045	□	436	Light caramel
266	☒	470	Medium avocado
877	∼	502	Medium blue green
924	◆	731	Olive
303	▽	742	Dark yellow
302	╱	743	True yellow
158	∧	747	Pale peacock blue
308	✳	782	Christmas gold
339	★	920	Medium copper
338	◈	921	True copper
1034	✕	931	Medium antique blue
242	⊿	989	Forest green
263	‖	3051	Dark gray-green
267	⊙	3346	Hunter green
869	◺	3743	Pale antique violet
1036	▲	3750	Deep antique blue
1032	◇	3752	Pale antique blue
167	⊕	3766	Light peacock blue
1050	⋈	3781	Mocha
1068	◉	3808	Turquoise
099	⊖	3835	Medium grape
308	⊟	3852	Straw
1003	✚	3853	Dark autumn gold
313	⊟	3854	Medium autumn gold
944	▦	3862	Mocha-beige
002	⊡	3865	Winter white

ANCHOR		DMC	
HALF CROSS-STITCH (2X)			
1042	╱	504	Pale blue-green – background
1032	╱	3752	Pale antique blue – background
BACKSTITCH (1X)			
072	╱	154	Deep grape – grapes
280	╱	166	Moss green – grape vine (2X)
352	╱	300	Mahogany – leaf
403	╱	310	Black – turkey, witch
1025	╱	347	Salmon – cherries
235	╱	414	Steel – turkey feathers, wing
1045	╱	436	Light caramel – leaf veins
877	╱	502	Medium blue-green – turkey breast
924	╱	731	Olive – acorns
308	╱	782	Christmas gold – leaf
263	╱	3051	Dark gray-green – leaves, Let us give Thanks
1003	╱	3853	Dark autumn gold – orange, leaf
381	╱	938	Coffee brown – all remaining stitches

ANCHOR		DMC	
STRAIGHT STITCH			
403	╱	310	Black – detail on turkey wing (1X)
235	╱	414	Steel – turkey feathers, wing (1X)
266	╱	470	Medium avocado – grass (2X)
FRENCH KNOT			
403	●	310	Black – turkey eye, witch eye (1X wrapped 3 times)
381	●	938	Coffee brown – stem ends (1X wrapped twice)
263	●	3051	Dark gray-green – dot on "i" (1X wrapped twice)
099	●	3835	Medium grape – grapes on arbor (4X wrapped twice)

HALLOWEEN & THANKSGIVING

TREAT TOTE

MATERIALS
FABRIC
Two 8-inch squares of 11-count
white Aida

FLOSS
Cotton embroidery floss in colors
listed in the key, opposite

SUPPLIES
Embroidery hoop; needle
Scissors; ruler
½ yard orange print
½ yard black print
4½-inch square yellow print
4½-inch square green print
Fleece; thread in black and orange
Iron; 1 yard black sew-in piping
Nine large black sew-through buttons

INSTRUCTIONS

Tape or zigzag stitch Aida edges. For each pumpkin, find the center of the chart and the center of the fabric; begin stitching there. Use three plies of floss to work cross-stitches over one square of fabric. Work the remaining stitches using the plies indicated in the key. Press the stitchery from the back.

Center the design and trim each stitched piece to 4½ inches square. From orange print cut the following pieces that include ¼-inch seam allowances: one 12¾-inch square for back, one 2½×37½-inch boxing strip, two 2½×13⅓-inch handle strips, and twelve 1¾×4½-inch sashing strips.

From black print cut two 12¾-inch squares for lining, one 2½×37½-inch boxing strip, and nine 1¾-inch corner squares.

Refer to the photo, *left;* sew sashing strips to join each row of one 4½-inch print square and one cross-stitch square; press. Piece three ¾-inch black squares alternately with two sashing strips to make three 12¾-inch-long strips. Sew long pieced strips to the two pieced rows; press. Join rows together to complete front.

Layer fleece on wrong side of front, back, and boxing strip; quilt

HALLOWEEN & THANKSGIVING

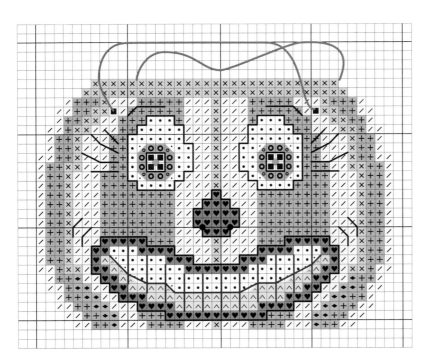

ANCHOR		DMC	
CROSS-STITCH (2X)			
001	·	000	White
403	■	310	Black
1025	♥	347	Salmon
266	✕	470	Medium avocado
924	◆	731	Olive
302	╱	743	True yellow
158	∧	747	Pale peacock blue
1068	⊙	3808	Turquoise
1003	+	3853	Dark autumn gold
BACKSTITCH (2X)			
403	╱	310	Black – jack-o'-lantern detail
1025	╱	347	Salmon – teeth
FRENCH KNOT (2X wrapped three times)			
001	●	000	White – eyes
403	●	310	Black – nostrils
COUCHING			
944	╱	3862	Mocha-beige – jack-o'-lantern handles (arrange thread as desired 4X, then tack with 1X)

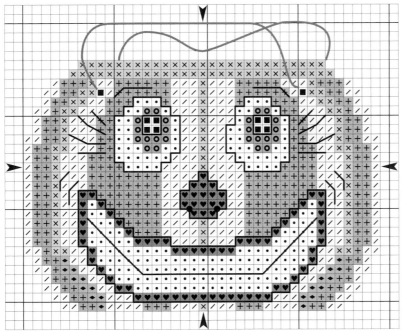

handle strip toward the center. Turn under and press ¼ inch of the opposite long side, then fold it over long raw edge. Topstitch the overlapped folded edge of each handle. Baste handles approximately 4½ inches apart to the right sides of the front and back of the bag.

Fit and sew the lining to the bag along the top edge. Turn lining to inside through opening. Sew opening closed. Sew buttons on black squares.

as desired. Sew the boxing strip to the front and to the back to shape the bag. Sew together the lining pieces, leaving an opening

along one side for turning.

Stitch piping around the top of the bag. Right sides down, turn one long edge of each

HALLOWEEN & THANKSGIVING

TODDLER SHIRT

MATERIALS
FABRIC
6×12-inch piece of 32-count antique white Belfast linen

FLOSS
Cotton embroidery floss in colors listed in the key, opposite

SUPPLIES
Embroidery hoop; needle; scissors
Sweatshirt; ruler
⅛ yard each of 3 coordinating fabrics
1 yard narrow piping
4×14-inch piece of white cotton fabric for lining; seam ripper

INSTRUCTIONS
Tape or zigzag linen edges. Find the center of the chart and the center of the fabric; begin stitching there. Use two plies of floss to work cross-stitches over two threads of fabric. Work remaining stitches using the plies indicated in the key. Press.

Cut two strips each from two coordinating colors of fabric, 1½×3½-inches. Cut two strips of remaining coordinating fabric 4×3½ inches.

Centering cross-stitch, trim to 3¾×7¼ inches. Line with white fabric. Piece strips of fabric to each side of design, as shown in photo, *above*. Cover piping with coordinating fabric. Sew piping to top and bottom of piecing. Open sleeve seams of sweatshirt. Center design on shirt front. Topstitch along piping seam. Resew sleeves, catching panel in the seams. Trim seam allowances.

HALLOWEEN &
THANKSGIVING

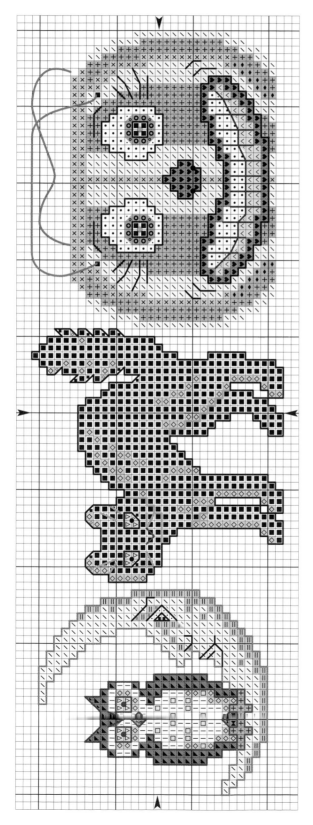

ANCHOR	DMC	
FRENCH KNOT (1X wrapped three times)		
001	◉	000 White – jack-o'-lantern eyes
403	●	310 Black – cat eyes, jack-o'-lantern nostrils
381	●	938 Coffee brown – owl eyes
COUCHING		
944	⟋	3862 Mocha-beige – jack-o'-lantern handles (arrange thread as desired 4X, then tack with 1X)

ANCHOR	DMC	
BACKSTITCH (1X)		
403	⟋	310 Black – cat, faces
1025	⟋	347 Salmon – teeth
308	⟋	782 Christmas gold – moon
381	⟋	938 Coffee brown – owl
1003	⟋	3853 Dark autumn gold – beak, feet, cat's mouth
002	⟋	3865 Winter white – cat detail (2X)

ANCHOR	DMC	
CROSS-STITCH (2X)		
001	⊡	000 White
352	◼	300 Mahogany
403	◼	310 Black
1025	◆	347 Salmon
1045	▢	436 Light caramel
266	✕	470 Medium avocado
924	◆	731 Olive
303	▽	742 Dark yellow
302	⟋	743 True yellow
158	⟨	747 Pale peacock blue
1032	◇	3752 Pale antique blue
1050	◼	3781 Mocha
1068	◉	3808 Turquoise
308	═	3852 Straw
1003	➕	3853 Dark autumn gold
002	⊟	3865 Winter white

CHRISTMAS

*C*hristmas is one of the most celebrated holidays for card giving and decorating. The plate below offers a festive sample of traditional motifs through the years. These designs will bring you hours of stitching pleasure and that when displayed will bring joy to the friends and family who gather in your holiday home.

Sampler
CHRISTMAS

SAMPLER

MATERIALS

FABRIC
*14-inch square of 28-count
ivory linen*

FLOSS
*Cotton embroidery floss, cord, and
braid in colors listed in the key,
page 180*

SUPPLIES
*Embroidery hoop
Needle
Mats and frame*

INSTRUCTIONS

Tape or zigzag stitch the fabric
edges. Find the center of the
chart and the center of the
fabric; begin stitching there.
Use two plies of floss to work
cross-stitches over two threads of
fabric. Work the remaining
stitches using the plies indicated
in the key.

Press the stitchery from the
back. Mat and frame as desired.

continued on page 180

ANCHOR   DMC

CROSS-STITCH (2X)

122	▲	161	Gray-blue
876	◹	163	Celadon green
400	⊞	317	Charcoal
266	✕	470	Medium avocado
265	△	471	Light avocado
879	⊟	501	Blue-green
161	◉	518	Wedgwood blue
062	◯	603	Cranberry
302	⌃	743	Yellow
336	✳	758	Terra-cotta
1022	♡	760	True salmon
1021	╱	761	Light salmon
309	◆	781	Dark Christmas gold
307	▽	783	True Christmas gold
169	✛	806	Peacock blue
340	✴	919	Dark copper
339	◓	920	Medium copper
861	★	935	Dark pine green
268	◆	937	Moss green
881	—	945	Blush
381	⋈	3031	Mocha
382	■	3371	Black-brown
120	◺	3747	Periwinkle
928	◇	3761	Sky blue
897	♥	3857	Rosewood
944	▢	3862	Dark mocha-beige
379	◠	3863	Medium mocha-beige
002	▪	3865	Winter white
	⊕	001C	Kreinik Silver cord
	I	100	Kreinik White #8 braid
	✳	202HL	Kreinik Aztec gold hi-luster #8 braid

ANCHOR   DMC

BACKSTITCH (1X)

265	╱	471	Light avocado – holly (2X); string, flower stem on angel's bag
062	╱	603	Cranberry – string, angel's sandals, horse's bridle
309	╱	781	Dark Christmas gold – ornament
169	╱	806	Peacock blue – ornaments
340	╱	919	Dark copper – "Noel" (3X)
339	╱	920	Medium copper – string, mouths, tie on angel's bag
1034	╱	931	Antique blue – angel, Santa with staff
862	╱	934	Deep pine green – Santa's hat, mittens, bag (2X)
382	╱	3371	Black-brown – "Christmas Cheer" (2X); Santa head and angel faces
897	╱	3857	Rosewood – Santa with staff (2X); leaf veins and berries
	╱	001C	Kreinik Silver cord – ornaments
	╱	100	Kreinik White #8 braid – bells
	╱	202HL	Kreinik Aztec gold hi-luster #8 braid – ribbon on bells, angel's wings and gown, ball ornament
381	╱	3031	Mocha – all other stitches (2X)

ANCHOR   DMC

LAZY DAISY STITCH (2X)

876	⟁	163	Celadon green – bell
309	⟁	781	Dark Christmas gold – bell
169	⟁	806	Peacock blue – bell
	⟁	100	Kreinik White #8 braid – bell

FRENCH KNOT (2X wrapped once)

062	●	603	Cranberry – angel's sandal
340	●	919	Dark copper – letters (1X wrapped three times)
339	●	920	Medium copper – flower on angel's bag, Santa's mouth (1X wrapped once)
1034	●	931	Antique blue – eye
381	●	3031	Mocha – Santa's eyes, horse's eye and nose
382	●	3371	Black-brown – angel's eyes (1X wrapped twice); angel's nostrils (1X wrapped once) Santa head eyes, letters (2X wrapped three times)
	●	100	Kreinik White – ornament, bells (1X wrapped once)
	◌	202HL	Kreinik Aztec gold hi-luster #8 braid – gown detail (1X wrapped once)

BLENDED NEEDLE FRENCH KNOT

| 339 | ● | 920 | Medium copper (1X) and |
| 381 | | 3031 | Mocha (1X) – angel's mouth (wrapped once) |

CHRISTMAS

ORNAMENT

MATERIALS
FABRIC
8×10-inch piece of 32-count antique white Belgium linen

FLOSS
Cotton embroidery floss in colors listed in the key, opposite

SUPPLIES
Embroidery hoop
Needle; thread
Tracing paper; pencil; scissors
4×5-inch piece of backing fabric
3½×4½-inch piece of fusible fleece
Iron; 3½×4½-inch matboard
16×1½-inch bias fabric strip
½ yard of ⅛-inch cord
6-inch piece of ¼-inch-wide ribbon
2 holly-shape buttons; fabric glue

INSTRUCTIONS
Tape or zigzag linen edges. Find center of chart and center of fabric; begin stitching there. Use two plies of floss to work cross-stitches over two threads of fabric. Work remaining stitches using the plies indicated in the key. Press from back. Sew buttons below stitching.

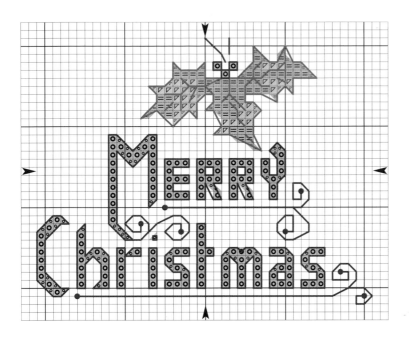

ANCHOR   DMC
CROSS-STITCH (2X)
876 [▨] 163 Celadon green
879 [≡] 501 Blue-green
339 [◉] 920 Medium copper
BACKSTITCH (1X)
862 [╱] 934 Deep pine green –
            leaves
897 [╱] 3857 Rosewood –
            letters, details, berries
944 [╱] 3862 Dark mocha-beige –
            stems
FRENCH KNOT (1X wrapped three times)
897 ●   3857 Rosewood –
            details

Trace oval, *right,* and cut out. Trace around oval on back of stitchery; cut out ¼ inch beyond line. Use oval pattern to cut fleece, matboard, and backing fabric pieces.

Cover cord with bias strip. Sew around ornament.

Fuse the fleece to the matboard. Cover fleece with stitchery, gluing edges to the back of the matboard. Glue the fabric oval to the back. Attach a ribbon hanging loop at the top of the ornament.

Holly Ornament
Pattern

CHRISTMAS

GREETING CARDS

MATERIALS

FABRIC

*5×7-inch piece of 32-count cream
Belgium linen for goose
4×6-inch piece of 11-count white
Aida cloth for elf*

FLOSS

*Cotton embroidery floss, braid, and
cord in colors listed in the keys,
opposite*

SUPPLIES

*Embroidery hoop
Needle; scissors
Solid-color greeting cards with an
area for stitchery
Thick white crafts glue, optional*

INSTRUCTIONS

Tape or zigzag fabric edges. For
each design, find the center of
the chart and the center of the
fabric; begin stitching there.
Use two plies of floss to work

cross-stitches over two threads of
linen fabric or three plies to
work stitches over one square of
the Aida cloth. Work the
remaining stitches using the plies
indicated in the key. Press the
stitchery from the back.

If necessary, trim around
stitchery to fit card sleeve. Insert
stitchery into cards or fringe
edge and glue to the front.

ANCHOR		DMC	
CROSS-STITCH (2X)			
266	✖	470	Medium avocado
265	△	471	Light avocado
161	⊙	518	Wedgwood blue
062	○	603	Cranberry
302	∧	743	Yellow
307	▽	783	True Christmas gold
120	⟍	3747	Periwinkle
	⊕	001C	Kreinik Silver cord
	Ɪ	100	Kreinik White #8 braid (1X)
	✳	202HL	Kreinik Aztec gold hi-luster #8 braid (1X)
BACKSTITCH (1X)			
400	╱	317	Charcoal – "Greetings"
062	╱	603	Cranberry – bird back
340	╱	919	Dark copper – string
	╱	3231	Gemstone Thread Moonstone – ornament hanger
	╱	202HL	Kreinik Aztec gold hi-luster #8 braid – bird
FRENCH KNOT			
400	●	317	Charcoal – dot over "i" (1X wrapped twice)
340	●	919	Dark copper – knot (1X wrapped three times)
382	●	3371	Black-brown – eye (1X wrapped twice)

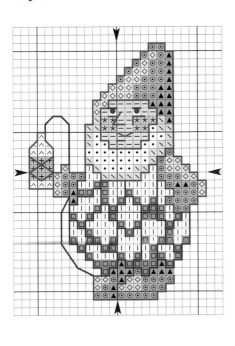

ANCHOR		DMC	
CROSS-STITCH (2X)			
122	▲	161	Gray-blue
161	⊙	518	Wedgwood blue
302	∧	743	Yellow
336	✳	758	Terra-cotta
169	＋	806	Peacock blue
881	─	945	Blush
120	⟍	3747	Periwinkle
928	◇	3761	Sky blue
944	▣	3862	Dark mocha-beige
002	·	3865	Winter white
	Ɪ	100	Kreinik White #8 braid

ANCHOR		DMC	
BACKSTITCH (1X)			
122	╱	161	Gray-blue – clothes, face detail, lantern detail
340	╱	919	Dark copper – mouth
381	╱	3031	Mocha – elf, brows, hanger and cord
FRENCH KNOT (1X wrapped twice)			
169	●	806	Peacock blue – eyes

VALENTINE'S DAY & EASTER

*C*aring cupids and romantic flowers aplenty…jelly beans and delightful bunnies— these symbols of Valentine's Day and Easter make people feel young again. Stitch these endearing, playful designs for all your sweethearts.

Sampler
VALENTINE'S DAY & EASTER

SAMPLER

MATERIALS
FABRIC
*14-inch square of 28-count
white Jobelan*

FLOSS
*Cotton embroidery floss in colors
listed in the key, page 190*

SUPPLIES
*Embroidery hoop
Needle
Mats and frame*

INSTRUCTIONS
Tape or zigzag stitch the fabric
edges. Find the center of the
chart and the center of the
fabric; begin stitching there.
Use two plies of floss to work
cross-stitches over two threads of
fabric. Work the remaining
stitches using the plies indicated
in the key.

Press the stitchery from the
back. Mat and frame as desired.

continued on page 190

VALENTINE'S DAY & EASTER

ANCHOR   DMC

CROSS-STITCH (2X)

375	⊞	167	Yellow-beige
403	■	310	Black
9046	◉	349	Dark coral
008	◯	352	Light coral
1047	⁓	402	Light mahogany
362	⬜	437	Caramel
267	▲	469	Avocado
281	◩	581	Moss green
256	△	704	Chartreuse
590	⬒	712	Cream
295	✕	726	Topaz
361	◺	738	Tan
303	⊕	742	Yellow
1002	☆	977	Light golden brown
397	⬓	3072	Pale beaver-gray
267	‖	3346	Hunter green
035	⊞	3705	Watermelon
1020	◿	3713	Salmon
928	◇	3761	Sky blue
1015	♥	3777	Terra-cotta
1049	◆	3826	Dark golden brown
373	◉	3828	Hazel
100	◆	3834	Dark grape
090	▨	3836	Light grape
1003	✳	3853	Autumn gold
002	◦	3865	Winter white

ANCHOR   DMC

BLENDED NEEDLE CROSS-STITCH

1042	⌃	504	Blue-green (2X) and
103		775	Baby blue (1X)
167	⊟	945	Blush (2X) and
347		3856	Pale mahogany (1X)
167	✖	3766	Light peacock blue (2X) and
168		807	Medium peacock blue (1X)

BACKSTITCH (2X)

8581	╱	646	Medium beaver-gray – sash, egg, bonnet
309	╱	781	Christmas gold – chick
359	╱	898	Coffee brown – wreath, cherub, flowers and ribbon on egg, jelly beans, dog, girl, cherub's wings (1X)
263	╱	3051	Gray-green – veins, leaves (1X)
267	╱	3346	Hunter green – dress detail
897	╱	3857	Rosewood – dog's bow, roses (1X)
002	╱	3865	Winter white – "I Love You"
403	╱	310	Black – cherub's eyes (1X), all other stitches (2X)

ANCHOR   DMC

STRAIGHT STITCH (2X)

9046	╱	349	Dark coral – cherub's mouth
359	╱	898	Coffee brown – dog
1049	╱	3826	Dark golden brown – rabbit head

LAZY DAISY (2X)

256	⟡	704	Chartreuse – leaves on chick's hat
267	⟡	3346	Hunter green – leaves
167	⟡	3766	Light peacock blue – flowers

FRENCH KNOT (1X wrapped twice)

403	●	310	Black – eyes of rabbit, dog, girl (2X wrapped three times); cherub's eyes, letter detail (1X wrapped twice)
295	⬤	726	Topaz – flower centers, chick's hat
002	◦	3865	Winter white – dog's bow

VALENTINE'S DAY & EASTER

SUPPLIES
Embroidery hoop
Needle; scissors
3½-inch bellpull hardware
½ yard of ¼-inch-wide blue
satin ribbon; ruler; thread
Yellow picot ribbon for bow

INSTRUCTIONS

Tape or zigzag stitch the fabric edges. Find the center of the chart and the center of the fabric; begin stitching there. Use three plies of floss to work cross-stitches over two threads of fabric. Work the remaining stitches using the plies indicated in the key. Trim stitchery to measure 9¼ inches wide. Press stitchery from back, turning under 3 inches along each side.

For ribbon weaving, pull out six horizontal threads evenly spaced between designs. Weave ribbon in and out over four threads. Trim fabric 2¾ inches past the design at the top and bottom. Fold and press fabric along vertical pressing.

Hand-tack along back side. Fold under top and bottom edge, allowing 1 inch past design. Insert hardware. Tie a yellow bow at the top.

BELLPULL

MATERIALS
FABRIC
12×15-inch piece of 28-count
overdyed babbling brook Jobelan

FLOSS
Cotton embroidery floss in colors
listed in key, opposite

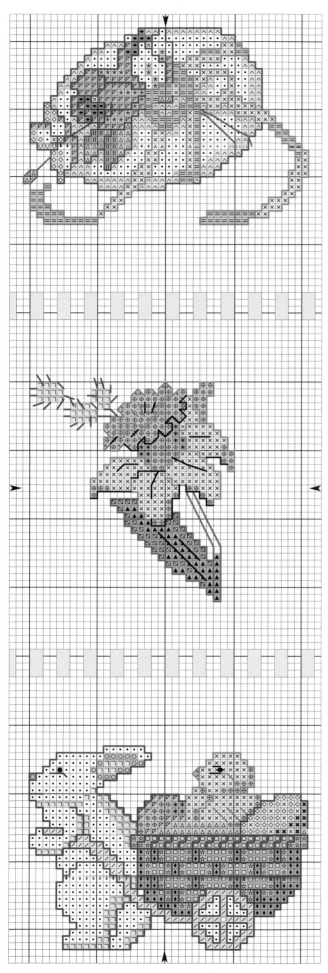

VALENTINE'S DAY & EASTER

ANCHOR		DMC	
CROSS-STITCH (2X)			
008	◯	352	Light coral
362	▢	437	Caramel
267	▲	469	Avocado
281	◩	581	Moss green
256	△	704	Chartreuse
295	✕	726	Topaz
303	⊕	742	Yellow
055	✴	962	Pink
298	⹀	972	Tangerine
1002	✫	977	Light golden brown
397	◻	3072	Pale beaver-gray
267	‖	3346	Hunter green
1020	╱	3713	Salmon
928	◇	3761	Sky blue
1049	◆	3826	Dark golden brown
100	◗	3834	Dark grape
090	▱	3836	Light grape
1003	✳	3853	Autumn gold
002	⊡	3865	Winter white
BLENDED NEEDLE CROSS-STITCH			
1042	∧	504	Blue-green (2X) and
103		775	Baby blue (1X)
167	✖	3766	Light peacock blue (2X) and
168		807	Medium peacock blue (1X)
BACKSTITCH (2X)			
403	╱	310	Black – daffodil, chick's eye
8581	╱	646	Medium beaver-gray – eggs, bunny
309	╱	781	Christmas gold – ribbon, daffodil, chick
359	╱	898	Coffee brown – wagon
263	╱	3051	Gray-green – flower stems on egg (2X); daffodil stem (3X)
STRAIGHT STITCH (2X)			
8581	╱	646	Medium beaver-gray – pussy willows
FRENCH KNOT (1X wrapped twice)			
403	●	310	Black – eyes
295	○	726	Topaz – daffodil
002	○	3865	Winter white – wagon wheel

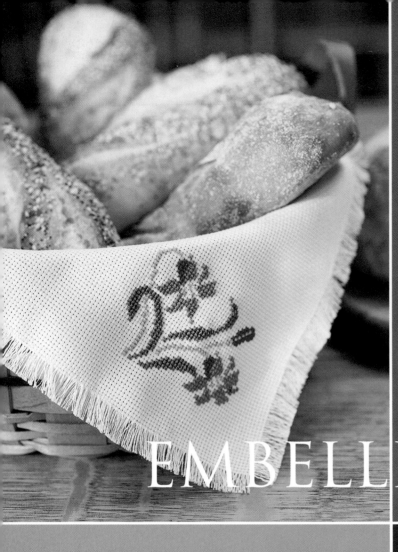

BORDERS
AND
EMBELLISHMENTS

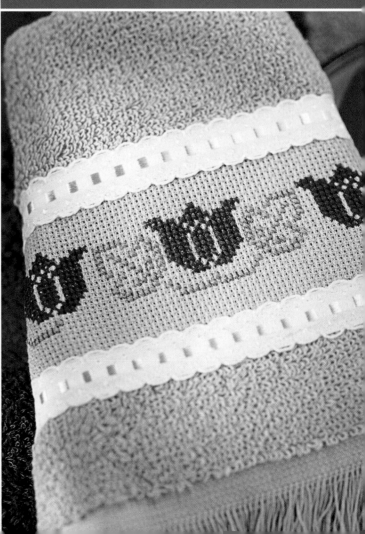

Sometimes all it takes is a little accent, a smidgen of color, or a simple border of design to transform something plain into something spectacular. This chapter offers a wide array of motifs to add design touches to ordinary items or to enhance any of the projects from the previous chapters.

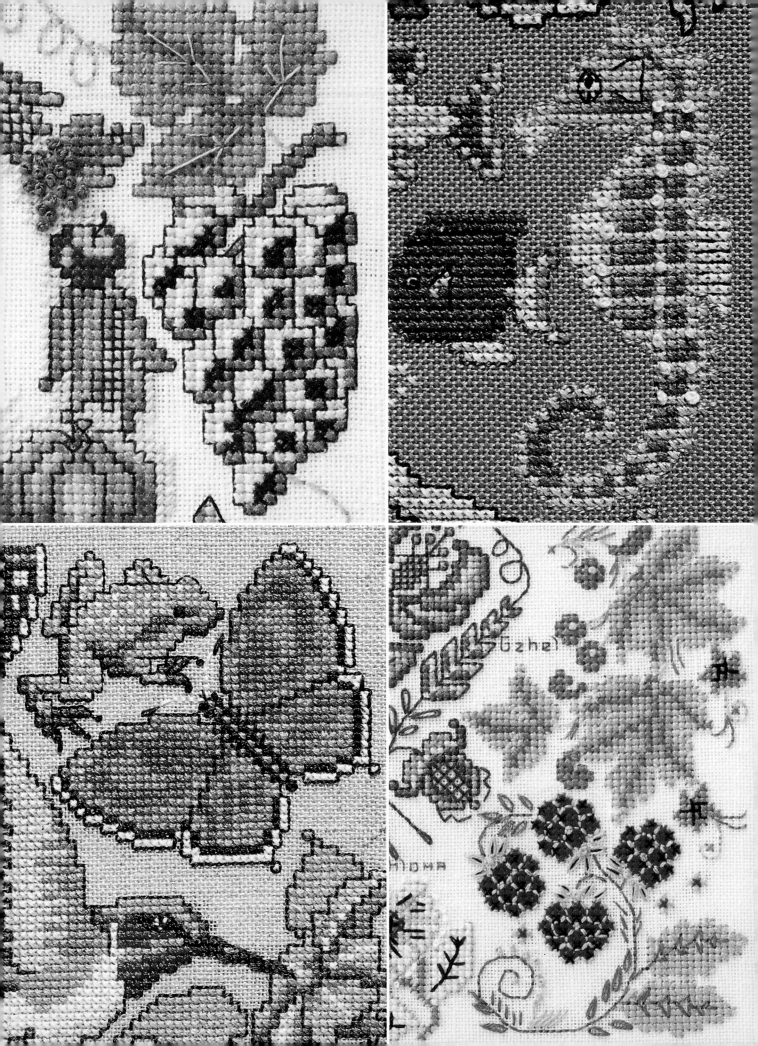

NATURE BORDERS

he treasures in our world that inspired the cross-stitch nature motifs in the previous chapters also inspired the lovely border designs below. Combine the borders with other nature-theme projects sprinkled throughout the book to create cross-stitch pieces that are yours alone.

Sampler

NATURE
BORDERS

SAMPLER

MATERIALS

FABRIC
*14-inch square of 28-count
cream Cashel linen*

FLOSS
*Cotton embroidery floss in colors
listed in the key, page 200*

SUPPLIES
*Embroidery hoop
Needle
Mats and frame*

INSTRUCTIONS

Tape or zigzag stitch the edges
of the fabric to prevent fraying.
Find the center of the chart and
the center of the fabric; begin
stitching there. Use two plies of
floss to work cross–stitches over
two threads of fabric. Work the
remaining stitches as listed
in the key.

Press stitchery from the back.
Mat and frame as desired.

continued on page 200

NATURE BORDERS

ANCHOR   DMC

CROSS-STITCH (2X)

926	⊡	Ecru
123	▲	158 Cornflower blue
280	Ⅱ	166 Moss green
011	⊙	351 Coral
306	⊟	729 Old gold
281	✳	732 Olive
277	⊠	830 Bronze
339	◩	920 Copper
905	◆	3021 Brown-gray
267	⊞	3346 Hunter green
069	◈	3803 Mauve
176	⋀	3839 Blue-violet
1072	▽	3849 Teal green
308	⊞	3852 Straw
1003	⧄	3853 Autumn gold

BACKSTITCH (2X)

926	╱	Ecru – seahorse, fish
280	╱	166 Moss green – leaf veins, stems
905	╱	3021 Brown-gray – butterfly, grape stems
1072	╱	3849 Teal green – butterflies

FRENCH KNOT (2X wrapped three times)

123	●	158 Cornflower blue – fish eyes

MORE PROJECT IDEAS

- Stitch the seahorse motif on a sunglasses case.
- Embellish a beach towel with the fish border.
- Stitch a geometric border around the edges of table linens.
- Alternate the leaf and acorn motifs at the ends of a table runner.
- Stitch the grapes on perforated paper for a Thanksgiving greeting.
- Trim a blouse pocket with the single rose design, using waste canvas.
- Duplicate-stitch the butterflies on the front of a white cotton sweater.
- Stitch a pair of roses on the pocket of a denim jacket, using waste canvas.
- Create a brooch using the single rose motif.
- Stitch the solid geometric design (from the upper right hand corner of the chart) on perforated plastic for a handsome bookmark.
- Stitch the grape border along the hem of a gingham apron.
- Stitch the fish border along the edge of a baby blanket.
- Make a pendant by stitching the seahorse design on blue fabric.
- Cross-stitch the butterflies in a circle and finish to cover a box lid or use to cover a clock face.
- Stitch the acorn border across the front of a sweatshirt, using waste canvas.
- Use waste canvas to add a fish border to a beach tote or cosmetic bag.
- Stitch the leaf border on fabric napkins for autumn get-togethers.
- Embellish a table scarf by stitching the butterflies in one corner.
- Stich a geometric border on a long fabric strip and finish as a belt.
- Choose favorite border designs, stitch in rows, and finish the stitchery as a pillow top.
- Embellish an album cover with the acorn motif.

NATURE BORDERS

Napkin and Place Mat

NATURE BORDERS

NAPKIN AND PLACE MAT

MATERIALS

FABRIC

14-count premade cream Aida napkin and place mat

FLOSS

Cotton embroidery floss in colors listed in the key, opposite

SUPPLIES

Embroidery hoop
Needle

INSTRUCTIONS

Allowing approximately five unstitched squares on napkin edges, begin stitching to position leaf in lower left hand corner.

Use two plies of floss to work cross-stitches over one square of fabric. Work remaining stitches as listed in the key.

Allowing approximately five unstitched squares on place mat edges, begin stitching trio of leaves in lower right hand corner. Press both pieces of stitchery from the back.

202

NATURE BORDERS

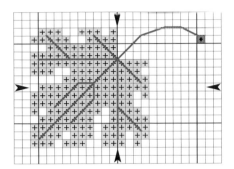

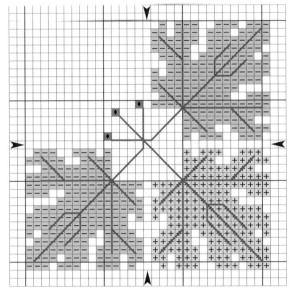

ANCHOR   DMC
CROSS-STITCH (2X)
277 ◆ 830 Bronze
308 ✛ 3852 Straw
BACKSTITCH (2X)
277 ╱ 830 Bronze –
          veins and stems

ANCHOR   DMC
CROSS-STITCH (2X)
306 ▬ 729 Old gold
277 ◆ 830 Bronze
308 ✛ 3852 Straw
BACKSTITCH (2X)
277 ╱ 830 Bronze –
          veins, stems

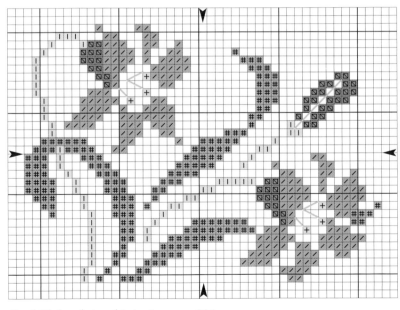

ANCHOR   DMC
CROSS-STITCH (2X)
280   ▯   166 Moss green
339   ◪   920 Copper
267   ▦   3346 Hunter green
308   ✛   3852 Straw
1003 ╱   3853 Autumn gold
BACKSTITCH (2X)
280   ╱   166 Moss green –
           stems

Bread Cloth—photo and instructions, page 204

203

NATURE BORDERS

BREAD CLOTH

MATERIALS
FABRIC
14-count premade cream
Aida bread cloth

FLOSS
Cotton embroidery floss in colors
listed in the key, page 203

SUPPLIES
Embroidery hoop
Needle

INSTRUCTIONS
Allowing approximately
10 unstitched squares on bread
cloth edges, begin stitching to
position flower in lower right
hand corner. Use two plies of
floss to work cross-stitches over
one square of fabric. Work
remaining stitches as listed in the
key. Press stitchery from the back.

NATURE BORDERS

TOWEL

MATERIALS

FABRIC

*Mauve hand towel with 14-count
Aida insert*

FLOSS

*Cotton embroidery floss in colors
listed in the key, below*

SUPPLIES

*Embroidery hoop; needle
24 inches of coordinating
decorative ribbon
Matching thread*

INSTRUCTIONS

Find the center of the design and
the center of the Aida strip; begin
stitching there. Use two plies of
floss to work cross–stitches over
one square of fabric. Repeat
design as shown on chart for a
longer Aida insert.

Machine-stitch ribbon pieces
at edges of stitchery.

ANCHOR   DMC
CROSS-STITCH (2X)
069   ◈   3803 Mauve
1072   ▽   3849 Teal green

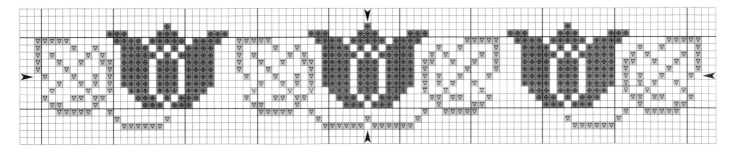

Inspiration
ARTFUL BORDERS

The gracious assortment of designs in this book are inspiration to create the array of borders below. Stitch them to enhance your projects from the other chapters or use your imagination to combine and change the motifs to suit many cross-stitching projects.

Sampler
ARTFUL BORDERS

SAMPLER

MATERIALS

FABRIC
*14-inch square of 14-count
parchment Aida*

FLOSS
*Cotton embroidery floss in colors
listed in the key, page 210*

SUPPLIES
*Embroidery hoop
Needle
Mats and frame*

INSTRUCTIONS

Tape or zigzag stitch the edges
of the fabric to prevent fraying.
Find the center of the chart and
the center of the fabric; begin
stitching there. Use two plies
of floss to work cross-stitches
over one square of fabric. Work
remaining stitches as listed on
the key.

Press stitchery from the back.
Mat and frame as desired.

continued on page 210

ARTFUL BORDERS

ANCHOR   DMC

CROSS-STITCH (2X)

Anchor	Symbol	DMC	Name
002	•	000	White
1030	◉	155	Light periwinkle
119	▦	333	Deep periwinkle
9046	☒	349	Coral
256	+	704	Chartreuse
295	✳	726	True topaz
304	◈	741	Tangerine
137	∧	798	Delft blue
031	▯	894	Carnation
257	◎	905	Parrot green
881	▬	945	Blush
410	‖	995	Electric blue
292	⊘	3078	Pale topaz
1049	▲	3826	Dark golden brown
363	☆	3827	Pale golden brown
433	✶	3846	Bright turquoise
308	▽	3852	Straw

BACKSTITCH (2X)

Anchor	Symbol	DMC	Name
9046	/	349	Coral – sleeves and skirts
256	/	704	Chartreuse – stems
1049	/	3826	Dark golden brown – leaf veins
358	/	801	Coffee brown – all other stitches

FRENCH KNOT (3X wrapped twice)

Anchor	Symbol	DMC	Name
295	●	726	True topaz – flower centers

LAZY DAISY STITCH (2X)

Anchor	Symbol	DMC	Name
256	⟋	704	Chartreuse – leaves
031	⟋	894	Carnation – flower

MORE PROJECT IDEAS

- Stitch a row of trees at the edges of holiday linens.
- Repeat the bird and heart design at the edges of curtains.
- Create hot pad inserts by stitching a single flower.
- Make hand-stitched belts using any of the narrow border designs.
- Use a vertical border to trim a cross-stitch fabric bookmark.
- Stitch a row of flowers along the hem of a gingham apron.
- Using waste canvas, trim the hems of denim capris using any of the horizontal borders.
- Create a Valentine by stitching the heart border, fringe the fabric edges, and apply to a plain card front.
- Stitch the lazy daisy floral design randomly on sheet and pillowcase hems.
- Duplicate-stitch the girl border on a toddler's sweater.
- Trim an autumn table mat with a border of cross-stitched leaves.
- Stitch a wide border across the front of a sweatshirt, using waste canvas.
- Sew a pillow top using a larger motif from this book and add a coordinating border from the designs, opposite.
- Trim a fabric purse flap with a colorful cross-stitch border.
- Stitch button covers using only the flower head motif.
- Create a charming brooch by stitching three girls in a row.
- Stitch three trees to create a handmade holiday card.
- Stitch the heart border on premade banding to wrap a special gift for your sweetheart.
- Use waste canvas to add cross-stitched flowers to a blouse collar.

ANCHOR   DMC
CROSS-STITCH (2X)
002	·	000 White
9046	✕	349 Coral
137	⌃	798 Delft blue
358	■	801 Coffee brown
1049	▲	3826 Dark golden brown
433	✴	3846 Bright turquoise

BACKSTITCH (2X)
358	╱	801 Coffee brown – all stitches

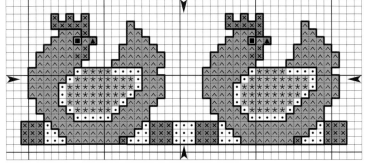

SIPPY CUPS AND BIB

MATERIALS

FABRIC

Sippy cups with plastic canvas inserts
Yellow baby bib with Aida or other
cross-stitch fabric insert

FLOSS

Cotton embroidery floss in colors
listed in the keys, right

SUPPLIES

Needle

INSTRUCTIONS

Find the center of the design and of the sippy cup plastic canvas or bib insert; begin stitching there. Use two plies of floss to work cross-stitches over one square of

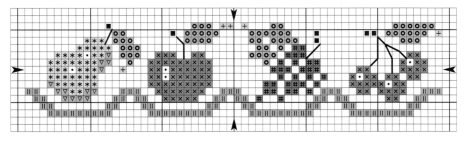

ANCHOR   DMC
CROSS-STITCH (2X)
002	·	000 White
119	▦	333 Deep periwinkle
9046	✕	349 Coral
256	+	704 Chartreuse
295	✳	726 True topaz
358	■	801 Coffee brown
257	◉	905 Parrot green
410	‖	995 Electric blue
308	▽	3852 Straw

BACKSTITCH (2X)
358	╱	801 Coffee brown – all stitches

plastic canvas. Repeat design as shown on chart for a larger insert.

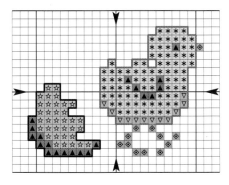

ANCHOR   DMC
CROSS-STITCH (2X)
295	✳	726 True topaz
304	◈	741 Tangerine
1049	▲	3826 Dark golden brown
363	☆	3827 Pale golden brown
308	▽	3852 Straw

BACKSTITCH (2X)
358	╱	801 Coffee brown – eggs
308	╱	3852 Straw – chicks

ARTFUL BORDERS

BIBS FOR BABY

MATERIALS

FABRIC

Baby bibs with Aida or other cross-stitch fabric insert

FLOSS

Cotton embroidery floss in colors listed in the keys, below

SUPPLIES

Embroidery hoop
Needle

INSTRUCTIONS

For each bib, find the center of the design and the center of the Aida strip; begin stitching the bunny there. Use two plies of floss to work cross-stitches over one square of fabric.

Repeat the bunny design as many times as desired spaced equally across the bib insert. Stitch the butterfly over the far right bunny. Press stitchery from the back.

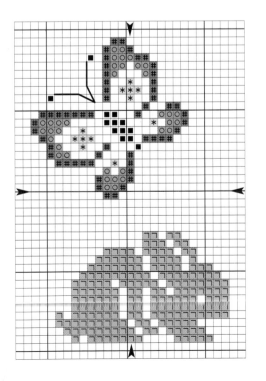

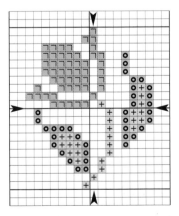

ANCHOR DMC
CROSS-STITCH (2X)
1030	O	155 Light periwinkle
119	#	333 Deep periwinkle
295	*	726 True topaz
358	■	801 Coffee brown
031	⌐	894 Carnation

BACKSTITCH (2X)
358	/	801 Coffee brown – all stitches

ANCHOR DMC
CROSS-STITCH (2X)
256	+	704 Chartreuse
031	⌐	894 Carnation
257	O	905 Parrot green

CROSS-STITCH BASICS

𝒰se the information on the following pages to guide you through each cross-stitch project. Whether you are starting out or have been cross-stitching for years, these tips should make your hobby more enjoyable and successful every stitch of the way.

BASICS

GETTING STARTED

Cut floss into 15- to 18-inch lengths and separate all six plies. Recombine plies as directed in project instructions and thread into a blunt-tip needle. Project instructions indicate where to begin stitching.

BASIC CROSS-STITCH

Make one cross-stitch for each symbol on the chart. For horizontal rows, stitch the first diagonal of each stitch in the row. Work back across the row to complete each stitch. On most linen and even-weave fabrics, stitches usually are worked over two threads, as shown in the diagrams. Each stitch fills one square on Aida cloth.

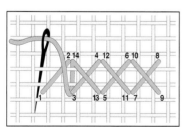

Basic Cross-Stitch in Rows

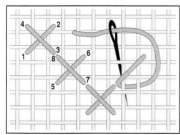

**Basic Cross-Stitch
Worked Individually**

Cross-stitches also can be worked in the reverse direction; remember to stitch uniformly, always working the stitch in the same direction.

HOW TO SECURE THREAD AT BEGINNING

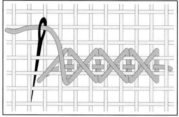

How to Secure Thread at Beginning

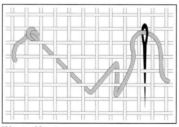

Waste Knot

The most common way to secure the beginning tail of thread is to hold it under the first four or five stitches.

A second method is to use a waste knot. Thread needle and knot end of thread. Insert needle from right side of fabric, away from placement of first stitch. Bring needle up through fabric and work first series of stitches. When stitching is finished, turn piece to right side and clip the knot. Rethread the needle with

the end of the floss and push the needle through the wrong side of the stitchery.

When working with two, four, or six plies of floss, secure threads with a loop knot. Cut half as many plies of thread, and make each one twice as long. Recombine plies, fold the strand in half, and thread the ends into the needle forming a loop. Work the first diagonal of the first stitch, then slip the needle through the loop.

HOW TO SECURE THREAD AT END

To finish stitching, slip the threaded needle under four or five previously stitched threads on the wrong side of the fabric, weaving thread back and forth. Clip the thread.

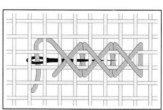

How to Secure Thread at End

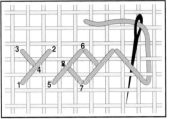
Three-Quarter Cross-Stitch

HALF STITCHES

A half cross-stitch is a single diagonal, or half of a cross-stitch. Half cross-stitches usually are listed under a separate heading in the color key and are indicated on the chart by a diagonal color line in the appropriate direction.

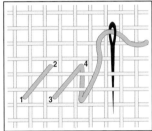
Half Cross-Stitch

QUARTER AND THREE-QUARTER STITCHES

Quarter and three-quarter cross-stitches are used to obtain rounded shapes in a design. On linen and even-weave fabrics, a quarter stitch extends from the corner to the center intersection of threads. To make quarter stitches on Aida cloth, estimate the center of the square. Three-quarter stitches combine

Quarter Cross-Stitch

a quarter stitch with a half cross-stitch. These stitches may slant in any direction.

CROSS-STITCHES WITH BEADS

When beads are attached using a cross-stitch, work half cross-stitches first and attach beads on the return stitch.

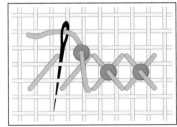
Cross-Stitch with Bead

BACKSTITCHES

Backstitches define and outline the shapes in a design. For most cross-stitch projects, backstitches require only one ply of floss. On the color key, (2X) indicates two plies of floss, (3X) indicates three plies, etc.

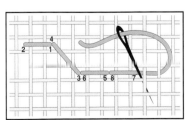
Backstitch

FRENCH KNOTS

Bring threaded needle through front of fabric and wrap floss around needle as illustrated. The color key indicates the number of wraps. Tighten the twists and insert needle back through the same place in the fabric. The floss will slide through the wrapped thread to make the knot.

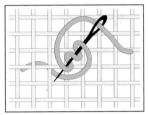
French Knot

WHIPSTITCHES

A whipstitch is an overcast stitch that often is used to finish edges on perforated plastic projects. The stitches are pulled tightly for a neat finished edge. Whipstitches also can be used to join two fabrics.

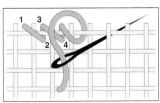
Whipstitch

continued on page 218

FEATHERSTITCHES

This decorative stitch produces a featherlike shape. Bring threaded needle to front at top of feather. Insert needle into fabric approximately four threads away, leaving stitch loose. Bring needle to front again, slightly lower than center of first stitch; catch thread from first stitch. Repeat in an alternating motion until the desired length is achieved. End feather by stitching a diagonal straight-stitched quill.

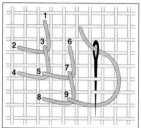

Featherstitch

LAZY DAISY STITCHES

To make this petal-shape stitch, bring the needle through to the front of the fabric. Using a sewing-style stitch, insert the needle through the same hole and out again two or more threads away, catching the loop under the needle. Gently pull to shape the loop. Push the needle

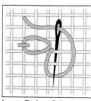

Lazy Daisy Stitch

back through the fabric on the opposite side of the loop to tack the loop in place.

MATERIALS FOR CROSS-STITCH

Cross-stitch is a popular form of stitchery. Many stitchers work cross-stitch designs on a variety of fabrics and use different threads from those specified in the projects. The following sections explain the materials used in projects in this book.

CROSS-STITCH FABRICS

Cross-stitch can be worked on any fabric that enables you to make consistent-size, even stitches.

Aida cloth is the most popular cross-stitch fabric. Threads are woven in groups separated by tiny spaces, which creates a pattern of squares across the surface of the fabric. This fabric enables beginning stitchers to easily identify where cross-stitches should be placed. Aida cloth is measured by squares per inch; 14-count Aida cloth has 14 squares per inch.

Aida cloth comes in many varieties. Aida cloth that is 100-percent cotton is available in thread counts 6, 8, 11, 14, 16, and 18. Fourteen-count cotton Aida

cloth is available in more than 60 colors. For beginners, white Aida cloth is available with a removable grid of prebasted threads.

Linen is the standard of excellence for experienced stitchers. The fibers used to weave linen vary in weight and density, giving the surface a slightly irregular and rich-looking surface. The thread count for linen is measured by threads per inch, and most designs are worked over two threads. Therefore 28-count linen will yield 14 stitches per inch. Linens are woven in counts from 14 (seven stitches per inch) to 40.

The popularity of cross-stitch has created a market for specialty fabrics for counted cross-stitch. They are referred to as evenweave fabrics because they are woven from fibers with a consistent weight, even though some of these fabrics are woven to create a homespun look. Most even-weave fabrics are counted as linen is counted, by threads per inch, and worked over two threads.

Hardanger fabric can be used for very fine counted cross-stitch. The traditional fabric for the Norwegian embroidery of the same name has an over-two, under-two weave that produces 22 small squares per inch.

Waste canvas and needlepoint canvas are frequently used for

FABRIC/NEEDLE/FLOSS

FABRIC	TAPESTRY NEEDLE SIZE	NUMBER OF PLIES
11–count	24	three
14–count	24–26	two or three
18–count	26	two
22–count	26	one

cross-stitching, especially on clothing and other items that are not suitable for cross-stitching alone. Waste canvas is designed to unravel when dampened. It ranges in count from 6½ to 20 stitches per inch. Cross-stitches also can be worked directly on mono-needlepoint canvas, which is available in colors. When the background is left unstitched, it can create an interesting effect.

Designs on sweaters and other knits can be worked in duplicate stitch from cross-stitch charts. Knit stitches are not square; they are wider than they are high. A duplicate-stitched design will appear broader and shorter than the chart.

Gingham or other simple plaid fabrics can be used, although gingham "squares" are not perfectly square. The stitched design will seem slightly taller and narrower than the chart.

Burlap fabric can easily be counted and stitched over as with a traditional counted-thread fabric.

THREADS FOR STITCHING

Most embroidery threads can be used for cross-stitch projects.

Six-ply cotton embroidery floss is available in the widest range of colors, including variegated colors. Six-ply floss is made to be easily separated into single or multiple plies for stitching. Instructions with each project in this book indicate how many plies to use. A greater number of plies will result in an embroidered piece that is rich or heavy; few plies will create a lightweight or fragile texture.

Rayon floss and silk floss are similar in weight to cotton floss, and the threads have more sheen. Either type can be exchanged with cotton floss, one ply for one ply.

Pearl cotton is available in four weights: #3, #5, #8, and #12 (#3 is heavy; #12 is fine). It has an obvious twist and a high sheen.

Flower thread is a 100-percent-cotton matte-finish thread. A single strand of flower thread can be substituted for two plies of cotton floss.

Overdyed threads are popular. Most of them have an irregular variegated, one-of-a-kind appearance. Cotton floss, silk floss, flower thread, and pearl cotton are available as overdyed threads. All of them produce a soft, shaded appearance without having to change thread colors.

Specialty threads add a distinctive look to cross-stitch. They range in size from hair-fine blending filament, usually used with floss, to 1½-inch-wide ribbon. Specialty threads include metallic floss, richly colored and textured threads, and glow-in-the-dark threads.

Wool yarn, usually used for needlepoint or crewel embroidery, also can be used for cross-stitch. Use one or two plies of three-ply Persian yarn and select evenweave fabrics with fewer threads per inch.

Ribbon in silk, rayon, or polyester creates interesting texture for cross-stitching, especially in combination with flower-shape stitches. Look for straight-grain and bias-cut ribbons in solid and variegated colors and in widths from 1/16 to 1½ inches.

continued on page 220

Cross-Stitch
BASICS

TYPES OF NEEDLES

Blunt-tip needles are best for working on most cross-stitch fabrics because they slide through holes and between threads without splitting or snagging the fibers. A large-eye needle accommodates the bulk of embroidery threads. Many companies sell needles labeled cross-stitch that are identical to tapestry, blunt-tip, and large-eye needles. The chart on *page 219* lists the right size needle for the most common fabrics. One exception to the blunt-tip-needle rule is waste canvas; use sharp embroidery needles to pierce through the accompanying fabric.

Working with seed beads requires a very fine needle to slide through the holes. A #8 quilting needle, which is short with a tiny eye, and a long beading needle with a longer eye are readily available. Some shops also carry short beading needles with a long eye.

PREPARING FABRIC

The edges of cross-stitch fabric take abrasion while a project is being stitched. Use one of the following methods to keep fabric from fraying.

The easiest and most widely used method is to bind the edges with masking tape. Because tape leaves a residue that is difficult to remove, trim it away immediately after stitching is complete. All projects in this book that include tape in the instructions were planned with a large margin around the stitched fabric to allow the taped edges to be trimmed away.

When a project does not allow for ample margins, use one of these techniques: If you have a sewing machine, zigzag stitching, serging, and narrow hemming are neat and effective methods. Hand-overcasting also works well, although it is more time-consuming.

Garments, table linens, towels, and other projects that will be washed regularly when they are finished should be washed before stitching to avoid shrinkage later. Wash the fabric in the same manner as the finished project will be washed.

PREPARING FLOSS

Most cotton embroidery floss is colorfast and doesn't fade. A few bright colors, notably reds and greens, contain excess dye that can bleed onto fabrics if they become damp. To remove excess dye before stitching, gently slip off paper bands from the floss and rinse each color in cool water until the water rinses clear. Place the floss on white paper towels to dry. If there is any color on the towels when the floss has dried, repeat the process. When completely dry, slip the paper bands back on the floss.

CENTERING THE DESIGN

Most of the projects in this book indicate that you begin stitching at the center of the chart and fabric. To find the center of the chart, follow the horizontal and vertical arrows on the chart to the point where they intersect.

To find the center of the fabric, fold the fabric in half horizontally and baste along the fold. Then fold the fabric in half vertically and baste along the fold. The point where the basting intersects is the center of the fabric. Some stitchers add lines of basting every 10 or 20 rows as a stitching guide.

CLEANING FINISHED WORK

Because the natural oils from your hands eventually will discolor the stitchery, you may want to wash your needlecraft pieces before mounting and framing them. Wash the stitchery by hand in cool water using mild soap or detergent. Rinse several times until the water is clear.

Do not wring or squeeze the needlecraft piece to remove the water. Hold the piece over the sink until dripping slows, then place it flat on a clean terry-cloth towel and roll tightly. Unroll the stitchery and lay it flat to dry.

PRESSING FINISHED WORK

Using a warm dry iron, carefully press the fabric from the back before framing or finishing it. You may wish to use a pressing cloth for this process. If the piece has many surface texture stitches, place it on a terry-cloth towel or other padded surface to press.

FRAMING THE PIECE

Use determines how cross-stitch pieces should be mounted and framed. Needlework shops, professional framers, and crafts stores offer many options.

For most purposes, omit the glass when framing cross-stitch. Moisture can build up between the glass and the stitchery, and sunlight is intensified by the glass. Both can damage the fabric. If using glass, mat the piece so the stitchery does not touch the glass.

Acorn.........167–171, 197–201
ALBUM COVERS
    Birds.................55–56
    Under the Sea 152–153
Anchor......................137–141
Angel 177–181
ANIMALS
    Bear 39–43
    Bird 39–46, 49–53,
            55–56, 99–111
    Bunny 44–45, 47, 49–53,
            187–193, 213
    Calf...........................49–53
    Cats...39–43, 49–55, 174–175
    Deer 57
    Dog....39–43, 49–53, 187–191
    Goat..............................49–53
    Horse.............49–53, 142–143
    Lamb......................39–43
    Pig 49–53
    Turtle 61–65
Artful Borders
    sampler 207–211
Asian sampler 61–65
Baby Animals sampler.....49–53
Balloon 39–43
Basket...........................119–123
Beautiful Birds
    sampler...................99–103
Bee...........................107–111,
         113–114, 157–161
Beetle........................107–111
Bellpull......................192–193
Bell 177–181
BERRIES
    Blueberry 11–15
    Cherry 11–15
    Raspberry 87–91
    Strawberry 11–15, 87–91
Bib 212–213
BIRDS
    Asian 61–65
    Barn swallow 99–103
    Bluebird 39–43, 119–123
    Borders sampler 207–211
    Cardinal...................99–103
    Chick...49–53, 187–193, 212

Chicken 212
Crane 99–103
Duck.........................49–53
Eastern European 87–91
Flamingo....................99–103
Goldfinch 104–105
Goose.........................99–103
Heron.......................99–103
Hummingbird.........107–111
Owl 99–103, 174–175
Parrot 157–161
Peacock 99–103
Pelican 145
Phoenix.....................61–65
Puffin 104–105
Rooster.........44–46, 61–65,
         119–123
Swan 184–185
Toucan 99–103
Turkey 167–171
Blocks 39–43
BOOKMARKS
    Deer 57
    Stamped Goods..............132
BORDERS
    Artful 207–213
    Asian 66–67
    Floral.........34–35, 133
    Fruit.........................212
    Mexican 79–85
    Nature 197–205
    Scallop 212
    Stained glass............162–163
    Stamped goods..............132
Bowl 16–17
BOXES
    Fish 143–144
    Moth 112–113
BREAD CLOTHS
    Nature 203–204
    Stained glass............162–163
Brooch, Eastern Europe 95
Butterfly 39–43, 61–65,
     107–111, 127–132,
    162–163, 197–201, 213
Card 184–185
Cap 104–105

Casserole cover..............44–45
Christmas sampler 177–181
Church....................119–123
Coasters 84–85
Coral......................147–151
Cornucopia 167–171
Country sampler........119–123
Cowboy boot 137–141
Cowboy hat 137–141
Crab...........137–141, 147–151
Cross-stitch basics 214–221
Cupid.....................187–191
Cute as a Button
    sampler.....................39–43
Doily 133
Dolphin..................152–155
Dragon......................61–65
Dragonfly 107–111, 157–161
Earth's Bounty sampler....11–15
Easter bellpull............192–193
Easter egg.................187–193
Eastern European
    sampler.....................87–91
Eggs.........16–17, 187–193, 212
Elf..............................184–185
Eyeglasses case 92–93
Fan............................61–65
Fish 61–65, 137–141,
     143–144, 147–153,
     157–161, 197–201
Fishing creel 137–141
Fishing lure ...137–141, 143–144
Floral Favorites sampler...29–33
FLOWERS
    Asian 66–69
    Basket....................127–131
    Border....119–123, 197–201,
      205, 207–211, 213
    Decorative 119–123,
     127–131, 133, 187–191,
     197–201, 213
    Eastern European 87–95
    Garden...........11–15, 29–35,
     127–131, 133, 157–163,
     192–193, 213
    Lazy daisy....39–43, 127–131
    Mexican 79–85

Pansy.....................133
Rose 19–27
Rosemaling.............71–77
Sunflowers...........124–125
Waterlily...............157–161
Frog 107–111
FRUIT
   Apple 11–15, 119–123,
            167–171, 212
   Arch 167–171
   Border.......................212
   Cherry...............11–15, 212
   Grape 87–91, 157–161,
       167–171, 197–201, 212
   Pear 87–91, 162–163,
           167–171, 212
   Pineapple...............119–123
   Pumpkin 167–171
   Raspberry 87–91
   Strawberry.............11–15,
          87–91, 132
   Watermelon...........119–123
Garden tools...................11–15
Gems of Nature
   sampler 107–111
Grasshopper.............107–111
Halloween & Thanksgiving
   sampler 167–171
Hand with rose 24–25
Heart.....................119–123,
       187–191, 207–211
Herb 16–17
Holly.....................177–183
Hot pad 44–47
House 119–123
Jack-o'-lantern 167–175
Jar topper 54–55
Jar lid, Asian 68–69
JEWELRY
   Eastern European
      necklace 94
   Floral brooch 95
   Just Roses sampler 19–23
Key 119–123
Ladybug 107–111
Leaf.....................11–17, 87–91,
      167–171, 197–203

Lighthouse 137–141
Lobster 152–153
Mask 79–83
Mermaid 44–45, 147–151
Mexican sampler 79–83
Moon............79–83, 174–175
Moth 107–113
Mushroom 107–111
Napkin, leaf.............202–203
Nature Borders
   sampler 197–201
Necklace, Eastern
   European...................93–94
Ornaments 177–183
Outdoors sampler 137–141
Paperweight 145
Pen and pencil
   holders 142–143, 154–155
PEOPLE
   Cupid 187–191
   Eastern European
      women 92–94
   Girl and boy 39–43
   Girl in bonnet 127–132
   Girl with heart 187–191
   Pincushion 26–27
Pillow, snail 115
Place mat, leaf 202–203
Purse 24–25
Ribbon 19–23
Rooster............44–46, 61–65,
          219–123
Rope 137–141
Rose 18–27
Rosemaling sampler 71–74
Sachet.....................113–114
Sailboat 137–141
Santa Claus................177–181
Scissors case.................26–27
Seahorse........44–45, 147–151,
         197–201
Seashell......................147–151
Sheriff badge 137–141

SHIRTS
   Gold finch T-shirt ...104–105
   Halloween
      sweatshirt............174–175
Shoe.........................49–53
Sippy cup.....................212
Snail............................115
Specialty stitches........216–218
Stained Glass sampler...157–161
Stamped Goods
   sampler 127–131
Starfish 147–151
Sun 79–83
SYMBOLS
   Asian 61–67
Tablerunner, Asian 66–67
TOTE BAGS
   Halloween 172–173
   Rosemaling 75–77
TOWELS
   Floral.........................34–35
   Seeds 124–125
   Sunflower 124–125
   Tulip 205
Tray 16–17
Tray scarf.......................84–85
Turkey.......................167–171
Turtle 61–65
Umbrella 127–131
Under the Sea sampler...147–151
Valentine's Day &
   Easter sampler.........187–191
VEGETABLES
   Carrot 44–45
   Corn 79–83, 167–171
   Eggplant 11–15
   Pea 11–15
   Pepper 11–15
   Tomato 16–17
Watering can..................11–15
Watermelon slice 119–123
Wheat 107–111
Witch..........................167–171
Wording............11–17, 39–43,
      61–69, 87–93, 99–105,
   124–125, 137–141, 167–171,
      177–185, 187–191

FABRICS

ZWEIGART
2 Riverview Drive
Somerset, NJ 08873-1139
908/271-1949

RIBBON

C.M OFFRAY & SON, INC.
Route 24, Box 601
Chester, NJ 07930
908/879-4700

THREADS

ANCHOR
Consumer Service Department
P.O. Box 27-67
Greenville, SC 29616

DMC
Port Kearney Building 10
South Kearney, NJ 07032-0650

FRAMING

WALNUT STREET GALLERY
301 SW Walnut Street
Ankeny, IA 50021
515/964-9434
www.walnutstreetgallery.com

WOOD FINISHING ACCESSORIES

SUDBERRY HOUSE
12 Colton Road
East Lyme, CT 06333
860/739-6951
www.sudberry.com

SPECIAL THANKS TO THESE TALENTED CROSS-STITCH ENTHUSIASTS:

CROSS-STITCH DESIGNER
Barbara Sestock

CHARTING ASSISTANTS
Pat Edwards
Tami Rupiper

FINISHERS
Margaret Sindelar
Lucinda Martin

PHOTOGRAPHERS
Andy Lyons Cameraworks
Meredith Photo Studio

PHOTOSTYLISTS
Donna Chesnut, assistant

STITCHERS
Rusty Banker
Diana Dusing
Pat Edwards
Colleen Johnson
Carla Jutting
Gail Kimel
Tami Rupiper

TECHNICAL ASSISTANT
Judy Bailey

TECHNICAL ILLUSTRATORS
Chris Neubauer Graphics, Inc.